THE NEW INTUITIONISM

Also available from Continuum

Relativism in Contemporary American Philosophy Timothy Mosteller
Free Will Kevin Timpe
Intuitionism David Kaspar

THE NEW INTUITIONISM

EDITED BY JILL GRAPER HERNANDEZ
WITH AN INTRODUCTION BY ROBERT AUDI

continuum

Continuum International Publishing Group
The Tower Building   80 Maiden Lane
11 York Road   Suite 704
London SE1 7NX   New York NY 10038

www.continuumbooks.com

British Library Cataloguing-in-Publication Data
A catalogue record for this book is available from the British Library.

ISBN: 9781441170828 (hardcover)
9781441152480 (paperback)

Library of Congress Cataloging-in-Publication Data
The new intuitionism / edited by Jill Graper Hernandez ; with an introduction by Robert Audi.
  p. cm.
Includes bibliographical references and index.
ISBN 978-1-4411-7082-8 -- ISBN 978-1-4411-5248-0 1. Ethical intuitionism. I. Graper Hernandez, Jill.
BJ1472.N49 2011
171'.2--dc22

2011016509

Typeset by Fakenham Prepress Solutions, Fakenham, Norfolk NR21 8NN
Printed and bound in India

TABLE OF CONTENTS

TABLE OF CONTENTS

BIOGRAPHICAL NOTES

Robert Audi, John A. O'Brien Professor of Philosophy, University of Notre Dame. Professor Audi has made internationally influential contributions in ethics, political philosophy, epistemology, religious epistemology, philosophy of mind and philosophy of action. He has two monographs forthcoming with Oxford, *Democratic Authority and the Separation of Church and State,* and *Rationality and Religious Commitment.* His most recent seminal works include *Practical Reasoning and Ethical Decision* (Routledge 2006), *The Good in the Right* (Princeton 2004), and *Religious Commitment and Secular Reason* (Cambridge 2000). He is a past president of the American Philosophical Association and Editor-in-Chief of *The Cambridge Dictionary of Philosophy* (1995, 1999, 3rd ed. in preparation).

Carla Bagnoli, Professor of Theoretical Philosophy, University of Modena and Reggio Emilia, after being tenured Full Professor at the University of Wisconsin. Bagnoli is the author of numerous articles on objectivity and agency in ethics, as well as *The Authority of Morality* (Feltrinelli 2007) and the forthcoming edited book *Morality and the Emotions* (Oxford). She served as the editor-in-chief of *European Journal of Analytic Philosophy* until 2009.

Roger Crisp, Uehiro Fellow and Tutor in Philosophy, St Anne's College, Oxford and Professor of Moral Philosophy at the University of Oxford. Professor Crisp works especially in the areas of ethics, political philosophy, and ancient philosophy. In 2010–11, he was Findlay Visiting Professor at the Dept. of Philosophy, Boston University. He is the author of *Reasons and the Good* (2006) and *Mill on Utilitarianism* (1997), and has translated Aristotle's *Nicomachean Ethics* for Cambridge University Press. He is Philosophy Delegate to Oxford University Press, an Associate Editor of *Ethics*, and a member of the *Analysis* Committee.

Peter Graham, Professor of Philosophy, University of California, Riverside. He is the author of numerous articles and book chapters on skepticism, the epistemology of perception, the epistemology of testimony, philosophy of language, and philosophy of psychology. Currently, Professor Graham is editing a volume on the philosophical problems of entitlement.

Ralph Kennedy, Professor and department chair, Wake Forest University. He has written on induction, the philosophy of perception, philosophical logic, identity, and the self. His current research focuses on intuitive justification and dogmatism regarding perceptual belief.

Christopher B. Kulp, Associate Professor, Santa Clara University. His research interests are meta-ethics and epistemology, in particular moral epistemology and questions surrounding moral realism. He is the author of *The End of Epistemology* (Greenwood Press 1992) and editor of *Realism/Antirealism* (Roman & Littlefield 1997).

Clayton Littlejohn, Lecturer, King's College London. Professor Littlejohn publishes on topics in epistemology, metaethics, moral psychology, and philosophy of mind. He has a forthcoming edited book, *Epistemic Norms: New Essays on Action, Assertion, and Belief* (Oxford), and a forthcoming monograph, *The Nature of Belief's Justification* (Cambridge).

Hugh J. McCann, Professor of Philosophy, Texas A&M University. Professor McCann is the author of numerous articles and book chapters in action theory, metaphysics, philosophy of religion, and ethics. In addition, he has published *The Works of Agency* (Cornell 1998), and *Creation and the Sovereignty of God* (Indiana 2011).

Walter Sinnott-Armstrong, Chauncey Stillman Professor in Practical Ethics in the Department of Philosophy and the Kenan Institute for Ethics at Duke University. His most significant philosophical work has been done in ethics, philosophy of law, epistemology, philosophy of religion, and informal logic. He is the author of *Morality Without God?* (Oxford 2009) and *Moral Skepticisms* (Oxford 2006), and editor of *Moral Psychology*, volumes I–III (MIT Press 2007–2008).

(editor) Jill Graper Hernandez, Assistant Professor of Philosophy, University of Texas at San Antonio. Her articles and book chapters cover topics in normative and applied ethics, as well as early modern philosophy. She is the author of *Gabriel Marcel's Ethics of Hope*, forthcoming with Continuum.

EDITOR'S PREFACE TO *THE NEW INTUITIONISM*

Ethical intuitionism has emerged as a major alternative in ethics, and its core elements play a prominent role in epistemology as well. One indication of the contemporary importance of the view is Philip Stratton-Lake's *Intuitionism: Re-evaluations* (Oxford University Press 2002), in which internationally distinguished moral philosophers appreciatively assess and in some cases defend the position. Two years later, Robert Audi's *The Good in the Right* (Princeton University Press 2004) set out a nuanced intuitionism that has been increasingly discussed in the literature. We now hear this kind of view referred to as 'the new intuitionism.' Defenses and critiques have become more and more frequent in conferences, and university courses are more often including intuitionism as a major topic in undergraduate and graduate courses in ethics and epistemology.

But how is the nuanced version of intuitionism *new*, and are the differences enough to signal the need for another volume on intuitionism? The new intuitionism debated in this book preserves traditional intuitionism's commitment to justified non-inferential beliefs, while concurrently echoing traditional intuitionism's concreteness, pluralism, and common-sense character. Developments in moral psychology, metaethics, epistemology, and even experimental philosophy have necessitated further explanation by the new intuitionism, and this book helps meet that need. Broadly speaking, the contributions in this book expand on the success of the new intuitionism's view that some moral beliefs can be rationally held independent of an agent's having evidence for them in the form of premises that ground an inference. More specifically, authors in *The New Intuitionism* push forward dialogue about moral disagreement, intuitionism and skepticism, the epistemic priority of moral intuitions, conation and intuitionism, the internalist conception of the mental, moral perception and the non-inferential character of belief, the objectivity of intuitions, and empirical criticisms of a new intuitionism.

If any single philosopher is central in the development of intuitionism since the turn of the century, it is Robert Audi. The four essays Audi provided in *Rationality and the Good* (edited by Timmons, Greco and Mele 2007), along with the thirteen papers in it to which he responded, opened a door to expansive and important applications of his already prominent intuitionism in ethics, moral epistemology, and moral psychology. Audi's focus on the range of internally grounded, rational, justified attitudes as well as on the nuances of empirical intuitions and 'quasi-perceptual intuitive moral judgments,' guaranteed both that more work needs to be done in these areas and that Audi is the pre-eminent guide philosophy needs to direct the movement of dialogue in these fields. This book advances that dialogue towards a new intuitionism.

In *The New Intuitionism*, two new essays by Robert Audi answer the call for fleshing out the implications of this increasingly influential moral intuitionism by making at least five new advances to intuitionism. First, the new intuitionism relies upon a more common use of perception (as a causal response to an object, which enables intuitive moral knowledge to be grounded in the natural world) than that of Rossian intuitionism, and Audi demonstrates how this proper basis of moral claims avoids epistemic error that haunts traditional intuitionism. The new intuitionism also develops a rich notion of agential autonomy, which allows Audi and others to show that actions can be responses to moral judgments. In addition, the new intuitionism expands the metaphysics of traditional intuitionism, since Audi's version of intuitionism given here does not require that the properties of intuitive prima facie (necessary and a priori) principles be non-natural. The normative content of intuitionism is expanded to include not only agential autonomy but also particular moral perceptions and Audi's experientialist theory of value. Finally, whereas in other works Audi has famously integrated intuitionism with a version of the Kantian Humanity Formula of the categorical imperative, in this volume Audi supplements the Kantian/intuitionism integration with a focus on the evidenceability, supportability, and deontological nature of Rossian and Kantian principles.

Joined by leading scholars in ethics and epistemology, Audi's new work provides a point of departure for philosophical progress about intuition and perception, value, pluralism and objectivity, moral knowledge, justification, and the epistemic accessibility of standards for moral judgment. Audi aims to clarify the possibility for moral knowledge in perceptual moral agents, as well as the possibility for rational moral disagreement. The result is, from Audi, an intuitionism that avoids the pitfalls of other forms of intuitionism in the theory of value and, from the other authors, reflection that yields progressively wider responses which will reverberate immediately within the philosophical community.

The text features new work by a number of prominent, internationally-renowned philosophers, all of whom engage with the most recent arguments concerning intuitionism—some of which have only been publicly shared at philosophy conferences within the very recent past. Each essay is also an independent contribution to the growing philosophical literature on intuitions, intuitionism, and the specific problem—whether ethical or epistemological—that is under analysis. There is diversity among the scholarship, certainly, but even amidst the diversity, there is unity as well. The authors in this collection are all committed to pushing the implications of a new intuitionism forward, and to fleshing out nuances of intuitionistic themes—though some invariably support and others reject intuitionism's soundness or efficacy to have a lasting philosophical impact. Contributing to their success is that each writes within one of three sub-fields in ethics: metaethics, moral psychology, and epistemology—especially moral epistemology. Additionally, each piece takes up the issue of the role moral perceptions and emotions play within a naturalized ground of intuitive moral knowledge.

Following the original scholarship of the contributing authors is a further stand-alone article by Audi, in which he reconstructs ethical and epistemic dimensions for intuitionism in the twenty-first century and establishes the parameters for continued debate, especially in tandem with the new arguments put forward in *The New Intuitionism*. Audi investigates, for instance, whether his view of reliabilism (one that is reliabilist for moral knowledge—but not for justification) can be adequately worked out in moral cases. If it can be, then the issue remains as to why there are so many moral disagreements. (Audi also addresses this concern in light of new work by Roger Crisp.)

STRUCTURE OF THE BOOK

Robert Audi's new articles serve as bookends of the volume; one ("Reason and Experience, Obligation and Value: An Introduction to the New Intuitionism") initializes movement for the new intuitionism, and the other ("Intuitions, Intuitionism, and Moral Judgment") examines issues which will be imperative for future scholars to take up. Encased between these pieces are contributions, organized by their emphasis on moral and epistemic intuitionism. The book is naturally divided, then, between articles which present a metaethical or moral-psychological challenge to the new intuitionism's moral theory, and those articles which offer epistemic obstacles to the new intuitionism.

Part I: 'The New Intuitionism, Moral Psychology, and Metaethical Concerns' opens with *Walter Sinnott-Armstrong*'s paper, "An Empirical Challenge to Moral Intuitionism," which distinguishes between weak and strong ways of being non-inferentially justified on the basis of whether a believer is justified regardless of the believer's commitment to a justificatory inferential structure. Sinnott-Armstrong denies that any belief can be strongly non-inferentially justified, and so he dismisses strong intuitionism (like that of Audi). In 'Conative Intuitionism,' *Hugh J. McCann* further develops an argument first offered in *Rationality and the Good* that conative intuitionism (i.e. the view that felt obligations can serve as a proper source of value judgments) functions better than traditional and Audian intuitionisms to defend value realism and the objectivity of value judgments. Their objectivity is defended in a different way by *Christopher B. Kulp*. Moral noncognitivism, in Kulp's view in "Moral Facts and the Centrality of Intuitions," is revealed by moral intuitions to be unconvincing, and Kulp argues it should be replaced by a cognitivist, realist metaethics that is rooted in the epistemic centrality of intuitive moral knowledge.

In Part II: 'The New Intuitionism and Advances in Moral Epistemology,' each paper offers potential epistemic worries for new intuitionism, along with opportunities for development, that are grounded in the role moral perceptions and emotions play in grounding epistemic judgments. *Ralph Kennedy*, in "Intuitionism and Perceptual Representation," refocuses the attack on the possibility of non-inferential knowledge towards perceptual, rather than moral, knowledge. *Carla Bagnoli* examines the integration of Kantian models of perception with intuitionism in 'Moral Perception and Knowledge by Principles.' She agrees with Audi that moral principles should be accorded a crucial epistemic role, but believes this agreement reveals a disagreement between the Kantian and Audian views about the function of practical reason. *Clayton Littlejohn*, in 'Ethical Intuitionism and Moral Skepticism,' seeks to defend intuitionism from the skeptical worries about disagreement. Moral intuitions justify moral judgments if we understand justification as that which is rationally or reasonably permitted, rather than that which is rationally required. *Peter Graham* rejects an evenly bifurcating epistemic status between 'internalism' and 'externalism', and observes that if we can understand the psychological states that correspond to the emerging plurality of epistemic stages, we are closer to understanding perceptual warrant. In "Psychological Capacity and Positive Epistemic Status," Graham argues for 'proper function reliabilism,' a view of perceptual warrant which functions independent of intuitions about whether beliefs are warranted, and which consists of reliably getting things right in normal conditions. *Roger Crisp*, in "Reasonable Disagreement: Sidgwick's Principle and Audi's Intuitionism," uses Henry Sidgwick's neutrality principle to argue that disagreement about whether traditional and new intuitionist duties are self-evident should lead philosophers to suspend judgment on whether they are indeed self-evident, just as disagreement about the duties themselves should lead us to conclude that the principles are unknowable. Crisp suggests that the philosopher can also use Sidgwick's principle as a way to build consensus over years of philosophical debate.

The volume's bookend chapter by Robert Audi, "Intuitions, Intuitionism, and Moral Judgment," positions intuitionism not merely as a historically important normative theory, but one which has moved into the twenty-first century aimed to have crucial contemporary significance as well. This essay clarifies what intuitions are, whether they require non-inferential evidential support, and how they accommodate perceptual seemings. It also makes analogous Audi's view of the grounding of moral knowledge with the grounding of perceptual knowledge and knowledge of the *a priori*. Finally, it simplifies and expounds upon the relationship between self-evidence, non-inferential knowledge, and the arbitration of moral principles in the face of competing obligations. The result of Audi's effort is a paper that engages his interlocutors, makes essential strides in answering long-standing questions about the nature of intuitions, and solidifies a system of justification for moral judgments.

The New Intuitionism is the next evolutionary step in epistemic and ethical intuitionism. It drives forward the central philosophical issues surrounding intuitionism to date, and complements recent work on intuitionism generally and Audi's scholarship particularly. *The New Intuitionism* tackles some of the lingering questions posed by previous scholarship, raises new challenges facing intuitionism, and guides the dialogue over ethical and epistemic intuitionism to fresh directions.

ACKNOWLEDGEMENTS

The editor expresses her sincere thanks to those who participated in making this book a success. Robert Audi was an invaluable resource, motivator, and commentator for each of the individual pieces of this volume. Thank you, Robert, for continuing to make each one of us better philosophers and, dare I say ... better people.

An idea for a book on the new intuitionism was first conceived during preparations for the 2009 Brackenridge Philosophy Symposium honoring the contributions of Robert Audi, held at the University of Texas at San Antonio. I want to recognize Michael Almeida and Terri Gerondale for their help in making that Symposium a reality, as well as the Brackenridge participants who also continued to work to contribute to this volume: Carla Bagnoli, Roger Crisp, Peter Graham, Ralph Kennedy, Christopher Kulp, and Hugh McCann. Of course, this book has transcended the symposium tribute originally conceived for Audi at the Brackenridge, and I want to especially and warmly thank Walter Sinnott-Armstrong and Clayton Littlejohn for their excellent, diligent work in a constrained period of time. I am indebted to you.

I am grateful for the help my research assistant, Thomas P. Newman, gave during the initial development of the book. My thanks also goes to Mark Timmons, who offered editorial and publishing advice along the way, and who continues to encourage me towards excellence. And, as always, I want to fully acknowledge my wonderful family and their gifts to me during this book's coming-to-be. Thank you, Gustavo, Allie, and Sofie.

REASON AND EXPERIENCE, OBLIGATION AND VALUE: AN INTRODUCTION TO THE NEW INTUITIONISM

Robert Audi, University of Notre Dame

Intuitions are perhaps the most basic kind of evidence philosophers depend on, and intuitionism is now held (even if not avowedly) by a growing number of writers in ethics, epistemology, and other areas. Major elements in ethical intuitionism are presupposed in common-sense moral thinking and, if less obviously, in both everyday and philosophical thought about non-moral normative questions: questions about (for instance) evidence, justification, rationality, and value. There is, however, too little understanding of ethical intuitionism even among many whose professional work is in ethics, and there remain many moral philosophers who do not realize what resources the position has gained in recent years. This essay and the much more detailed paper that concludes this volume are intended to enhance understanding of intuitionist resources in ethics and other branches of philosophy.

1. THE DEPARTURE FROM SIDGWICK, MOORE, AND ROSS

Sidgwick, Moore, and Ross did much to develop intuitionism, but they also burdened the position with epistemological, ontic, and valuational assumptions that are not essential to it. Twentieth-century ethics after Ross's *The Right and the Good* (1930) contains many debates in which intuitionists have defended one or another element in their view, but until the 1990s the position lacked a proponent who could develop and defend intuitionism from the vantage point of a full-scale epistemology, a comprehensive theory of value, and a sense of the elements of Kantianism, consequentialism, and indeed virtue ethics, that a moderate intuitionism can accommodate.

To be that proponent of intuitionism has been among the major aims of my work for the past two decades (though the term 'the new intuitionism' is not one I coined—it appeared some time ago in the ethical literature). The philosophers in this volume, as well as those contributing to *Rationality and the Good*,[1] have helped me enormously by forcing me to refine and extend my intuitionist position in both ethics and epistemology. My task in this perspectival essay is simply to indicate, in general terms, what is new in my intuitionism and, so far as I have been persuasive in presenting my view, reflected in recent versions of the view in writings by other moral philosophers. My comprehensive paper in this book will present clarifications and extensions of my view and will respond to various criticisms (including some by contributors to this volume, though not all responded to will be specifically cited). My main concern here will be to sketch only enough of my intuitionist ethics to show how the view may be seen as taking intuitionism beyond Sidgwick, Moore, Ross, and others.

To begin with those three philosophers, my view is not consequentialist, as are Sidgwick's and Moore's (though not Ross's).[2] My view is also epistemologically non-skeptical in a way the other three positions are not,[3] and it responds to the problem of rational disagreement that led Sidgwick to think that peer disagreement must in general force suspended judgment.[4] Moreover, where Moore was at great pains to show that normative properties are non-natural, I have framed intuitionism is such a way that, even if this view is ontologically most congenial to the position, it is not presupposed. The epistemic status I have claimed for intuitive *prima facie* duty principles—being necessary and *a priori*—does not require that the properties figuring in those principles be non-natural.[5] Nor is that entailed by my metaphysics of ethical terms, in particular by moral properties being consequential on natural ones, as Moore and Ross would also take them to be. This neutrality toward naturalism is an advantage in making a version of intuitionism eligible for endorsement by many contemporary moderate naturalists.

2. THE TRADITIONAL INTUITIONIST CONCEPT OF SELF-EVIDENCE

It is Ross who, in my judgment, has provided the best overall version of intuitionism of the leading intuitionists of the past, and, at least in normative ethics, his view has been more influential than that of Sidgwick or Moore. But Ross's view suffers, as did that of virtually all his predecessors, from an epistemological mistake. This is the error taking the self-evident to be unprovable and, as that suggests, such that one must "just see" its truth, as with an intuitive rule of inference.[6] This conception of the self-evident both narrows the resources of intuitionism for integration with other ethical views and creates the impression that the self-evident cannot be argued for but must simply be asserted. Ross also said too little about self-evidence, about intuitions, and about how we should proceed from intuitive judgments of *prima facie* obligation.

My response to the main problems besetting Ross's view has been increasingly comprehensive. Let me cite two major elements. One is an account of the self-evident applicable in both ethics and epistemology. Another element is a theory of intuition that can do justice both to the reflective character of some intuitions and to the evidential role of intuition. Reflection on an action, event, state of affairs, or proposition, I have shown, can lead to a conclusion (as a concluding element in deliberation) by a non-inferential route. Whether a belief or a judgment is inferential is a matter of whether it is premise-based; it is only contingently related to how much, or even how labored, scrutiny or reflection is needed to reach the belief or judgment. Granted, inference may occur in the context in which intuition arises; but inference is not a ladder by which intuition is reached. It may be a contextual requirement for comprehension of the intuited proposition, but it is not a necessary route from a premise for that proposition to the intuition thereof. Thus, doxastic intuitions—those constituted by a kind of belief—may be non-inferentially well-grounded and may serve as (defeasible) foundations. Where intuitions are non-doxastic, for instance seemings, the same holds.[7]

Ross rightly said that seeing the truth of the moral principles he considered self-evident required 'mental maturity', but he obscured the force of this point by comparing the self-evidence of the principles to that of mathematical axioms. He also left some readers wondering whether intuition yields knowledge *only* of the self-evident—something he did not explicitly hold and would likely have rejected—or could yield wider knowledge, or at least justified belief, of singular moral judgments (say, that I must keep my burdensome promise to Jan), which Ross rightly saw can be intuitively held and reasonable. I have clarified intuition (in ways evident in my paper at the end of this volume) in a way that makes it clear that its objects may be either self-evident and *a priori* or singular and empirical (even in some cases false).

The importance of reflection in ethics is not easily exaggerated. My conception of the self-evident makes clear that reflection may be required for knowledge even of what is both self-evident and— once understood—seems obvious, such as the proposition that the mother-in-law of the spouse of a person's youngest female sibling is that person's own mother. (Most people must think this through before seeing its truth.) My conception of intuition indicates ways in which intuitions can be non-inferential even if they are formed only after one thinks about a case, real or hypothetical, in detail. They share a basis in understanding their propositional objects whether or not those propositions are self-evident.

3. A WIDER AND MORE PLAUSIBLE CONCEPTION OF SELF-EVIDENCE

My own account of the self-evident treats self-evident propositions as truths such that (a) in virtue of adequately understanding them one is justified in believing them (which does not entail that all who adequately understand them *do* believe them), and (b) believing them on the basis of adequately understanding them entails knowing them.[8] To put it briefly though not quite equivalently, they are truths such that adequately understanding them suffices for justification, and belief on the basis of it suffices for knowledge. This conception does not imply, and I reject, the unprovability condition on the self-evident affirmed by Pritchard, Moore, Ross, and others. My account—which explains how the self-evident can be proved or evidenced—makes possible a *Kantian intuitionism*, an integration of Rossian principles with a version of Kant's Humanity Formula (Chapter 3 of *The Good in the Right* develops this integration). The account also opens the way for other theorists to seek an integration of intuitionism with, say, consequentialism or virtue ethics. Kantian intuitionism is extended in my paper at the end of the book, but three points about it should be made here.

First, neither the Humanity Formula, nor any other theoretical principle that may support or imply the Rossian intuitive principles need have the status of self-evidence or perhaps even *apriority*. Foundational materials come in many kinds, and they can give support even to superstructures stronger than they are and having other foundations as well. A theory of light and vision might support my perceptual belief that the sky looks blue to me even if I have better ground to trust my visual perception than to believe the theory. The self-evident is parallel to the perceptually evident here. Once it is seen why the self-evident—without *needing* premises—can be provable from them, it can also be seen to be *evidenceable* without proof by that set. Whether, if the self-evident must be *a priori*, as in my view, it can be supported by something empirical is another matter. The best candidates to support Rossian intuitive moral principles are not plausibly considered self-evident, but in any case I have not foreclosed this possibility.

Second, supportability by other propositions does not make intuitive common-sense moral principles (like Rossian ones) less important in themselves or less pervasive in ordinary moral thinking. If they are not basic in the sense Ross and others may have had in mind—being unprovable, or perhaps even unevidenceable, by anything else—they may still be self-evident and both knowable without dependence on independent premises and a crucial guide in moral thinking.

Third, even if Rossian common-sense moral principles receive support from non-deontological principles—say on the consequentialist ground that our internalizing them contributes greatly, and perhaps optimally, to non-moral goodness—it does not follow that they are not themselves deontological.[9] Rightness need not be taken to be a *kind* of goodness simply because internalizing principles of rightness *enhances* goodness. A major demand of morality is that we contribute to goodness in the lives of others; and its major prohibition may well be that we not cause others pain or suffering (intrinsically bad elements in life). Given how large these standards loom in any plausible deontology, it should be expected that internalizing a deontological ethic like that of Kantian intuitionism would tend to contribute to optimizing goodness. My theory of value and my related theory of the basis of reasons for action are designed to show how this is so and why intuitionism is nonetheless not a consequentialist ethic.[10]

4. INTUITION, PERCEPTION, AND SINGULAR MORAL JUDGMENT

In recent work, I have constructed an account of moral perception which enables us to see intuitive moral knowledge as grounded in the natural world.[11] The basis of moral perception is an appropriate response to a subset of the natural properties on which the perceived moral property is consequential. The response may embody moral emotion, but whether it does or not, it reflects the properties of an act (or other object of moral evaluation) that ground the moral truth in question. Ross could have granted this, but did not provide an account of moral perception of this (everyday) kind, as opposed to the Aristotelian intellectual kind of perception of which Ross said that a decision as to which of two conflicting *prima facie* duties prevails "rests with perception."[12] Such intellectual, or in any case non-sensory, perception might best be considered a kind of intuition and is certainly an intuitive kind of cognition.

I recognize the "perception" Ross described; but, in the kinds of cases of conflicting obligation he apparently had in mind, I prefer to speak of a singular, often intuitive, moral judgment. Moral perception as I explicate it is perception of a more ordinary kind. It is a genuinely causal response to its object, has a sensory element, and has a phenomenal aspect suitable to capture the representationality so important for understanding sensory perception. Perceiving a wrong (as such) may be a comprehending visual perception of an observable wrongful deed such as a stabbing. It may immediately yield moral judgment and indeed moral knowledge. Rossian moral perception, by contrast, requires the kind of insight that goes with perceiving—discerning, we might say—that one's promissory obligation is stronger than a conflicting obligation of self-improvement.

In my view, moral knowledge may also arise in part from emotions, whose evidential status is another element which earlier intuitionists have not accounted for. Emotions can produce intuitions that represent moral knowledge or justified moral beliefs; intuitions can also occur as a result of moral perception and can either reinforce a perceptual moral judgment or facilitate making a moral judgment where a moral perception, like the sight of a painting one does not understand, would not otherwise have led to any evaluative cognition.

More broadly, I have sought to advance intuitionism by providing a conception of moral experience, which commonly has perceptual, emotional, and valuational aspects, as with indignation or, on the approbative side, the sense of satisfaction in making a just distribution. With all these elements in view, I have developed an experientialist theory of value that enables us, on the one hand, to see how the common-sense moral principles intuitionism affirms are related to human flourishing but, on the other hand, does not require us to take obligation or rightness to be forms of goodness or to adopt a maximizing consequentialism.

This framework enables me to refine and extend Ross's normative principles—adding (in Chapter 5 of *The Good in the Right*) two to his list (obligations of respectfulness and of liberty) and revising some of his formulations—and it provides resources for further normative, epistemological, and metaethical advances. My theory of value is more pluralistic than Ross's, and it also differs from his in distinguishing two importantly different kinds of non-instrumental value: the intrinsically valuable, which is experiential, and the inherently valuable: the kind which, like fine paintings, is such that an appropriate experience of it has intrinsic value, as does aesthetic pleasure.

***

The new intuitionism, then, retains the common-sense character and the concreteness of the theory articulated by Ross and others but differs in at least four ways. It corrects the epistemology of traditional intuitionism; it extends its metaphysics; it adds to its normative content; and it integrates it with a version of Kantian ethics. The result is a moral philosophy that is epistemologically moderate, psychologically realistic, and unified by integration with Kantian elements on one side and axiological elements on the other. It also accommodates a qualified naturalistic conception of moral properties as at least conceptually and epistemically anchored in the world of everyday experience. The theory makes clear how moral knowledge, whether general or singular, is possible, sometimes perceptual in nature, and often virtually universal; but it also accounts for both the rationality and the pervasiveness of certain moral disagreements. It recognizes pluralism in the theory of obligation and in the categories of value and acknowledges the defeasibility of intuitive justification, but it nonetheless provides interpersonally accessible objective standards of moral judgment.

PART I: THE NEW INTUITIONISM, MORAL PSYCHOLOGY, AND METAETHICAL CONCERNS

CHAPTER ONE

AN EMPIRICAL CHALLENGE TO MORAL INTUITIONISM

Walter Sinnott-Armstrong, Duke University

Some practitioners of experimental or naturalistic moral philosophy believe that available empirical evidence conclusively refutes moral intuitionism and even shows that no moral belief is justified or true. I do not agree with any of those strong claims. Some crude versions of moral intuitionism might leave themselves open to easy refutation by empirical evidence. Even then, however, the needed premises are never purely empirical. The argument always applies some epistemic or moral norm, so it does not (or need not) commit any naturalistic fallacy. Moreover, the assumed norms are never beyond question, so no argument on this controversial topic will be conclusive. In addition, any argument that is applicable to sophisticated versions of moral intuitionism will have to be complex, so it will involve several steps that could be questioned. There is no simple way to settle this basic issue in moral epistemology.

Nonetheless, I still think that much recent empirical evidence about moral beliefs poses a serious challenge to even the most sophisticated versions of moral intuitionism. I also believe that this challenge has not yet been met. Perhaps the challenge was misunderstood because it was not articulated properly. I gave versions of this challenge in a series of articles, but all of my presentations had flaws.[1] Here I will try to do better.

The first step is to define my target: moral intuitionism. The second step is to survey some empirical evidence against the reliability of moral beliefs. The third step uses an analogy to support two epistemic principles. The fourth step is to bring it all together into an argument. The fifth step is to respond to a few common objections. The overall result will not be a proof, but I hope that it will make the challenge clearer, so that intuitionists can try to respond.

1. WHAT IS MORAL INTUITIONISM?

Crude moral intuitionists claim to have direct insight that makes their moral beliefs indefeasibly justified, certain, or infallible. In contrast, sophisticated moral intuitionists usually disavow direct insight, indefeasibility, certainty, and infallibility.[2] Some opponents see these modifications of the crude view as concessions that make moral intuitionism too weak to be interesting. Defenders of moral intuitionism see these changes as improvements that isolate the important claim and make moral intuitionism more plausible than ever before. I agree with defenders of moral intuitionism that the sophisticated version is interesting and initially plausible.

The defining claim of moral intuitionism is that some moral beliefs are justified non-inferentially. A *moral* belief is any explicit belief that something (such as an act, character trait, person, or institution—whether particular or a general kind) is or is not overall or partly morally right or wrong, good or bad, and so on. An *inference* is any transition from other beliefs resulting at least in part from a sense that those other beliefs support the inferred belief in some way (which could be either deductive or inductive). When a moral belief is not actually based on any such inference (even if it could be based on some inference), it is called *immediate* and (at least when it seems plausible to the believer) a moral *intuition*.[3]

Moral intuitionists do not claim only that moral intuitions exist. Everyone should accept that descriptive claim—even moral skeptics. Moreover, the central claim of moral intuitionism is not simply that some moral intuitions are justified. Coherentists and naturalists in moral epistemology can accept that claim. Instead, the defining claim of moral intuitionism is about *how* moral intuitions among other moral beliefs are justified. Moral intuitionists claim that some moral beliefs (which might be moral intuitions) are justified in a particular way: non-inferentially.

The issue of whether a moral belief is justified non-inferentially is not about the content of the belief—that is, the proposition that is believed. What is at stake is, instead, personal justifiedness—that is, whether the person who believes that proposition is justified in being in the mental state of believing it. Thus, it might be less misleading to define moral intuitionism as the claim that some people are non-inferentially justified in believing some moral propositions. I will often talk about how moral beliefs are justified, but this will just be a simpler way to talk about how moral believers are justified.[4]

What matters most here is to clarify the non-inferential way of being justified that moral intuitionists claim and their opponents deny. A believer is justified *non-inferentially* when and only when the believer is justified independent of inference. However, independence of inference can be either weak or strong. A believer is justified non-inferentially in a *weak* way when the believer is justified regardless of whether the believer actually goes through any inference. In contrast, a believer is justified non-inferentially in a *strong* way only when the believer is justified regardless of whether the believer is committed to any justificatory inferential structure.[5] A *justificatory inferential structure* is a set of propositions where some propositions provide epistemic support for others. To be *committed* to such a structure is to accept or have a disposition to accept the supporting propositions in that structure or other propositions that entail or support the supporting propositions in that structure. One can be committed to a structure by having a disposition to accept or believe what would amount to evidence for the supporting propositions in that structure, even if one never explicitly thought about the specific propositions in that structure. For a believer to be non-inferentially justified in a strong way then, requires that the believer would still be justified even if the believer did not have as much as a disposition to accept any propositions that are, entail, or support any propositions that provide epistemic support for what is believed.

The weak way of being non-inferentially justified is not enough to stop the skeptical regress, opposition to which motivates many moral intuitionists. Suppose that a believer is justified non-inferentially in the weak way but not in the strong way. Then the believer's being justified in this belief does not depend on any actual inference but still does depend on the believer being committed to a justificatory inferential structure. The believer would not be justified without a disposition to accept the supporting propositions that would be or support the propositions in that justificatory inferential structure. However, a disposition to accept these supporting propositions cannot make the believer justified unless the believer is or would be justified in believing those supporting propositions. Unsupported support falls flat. This requirement that the believer be justified in accepting the supporting propositions is what leads to a skeptical regress, because skeptics can always ask what makes the believer justified in accepting those supporting propositions, and any response must invoke other supporting propositions that will be subject to the same challenge all over again. In order to escape this skeptical regress, it is not enough for beliefs to be justified non-inferentially in a weak way. For that purpose, moral intuitionists need the strong kind of non-inferential justifiedness.

This strong way of being non-inferentially justified does not require the believer to believe the supporting propositions in the justificatory inferential structure. The believer might not have ever thought of those supporting propositions and might not even understand them. All that is required is a disposition to accept some propositions that would entail or support those supporting propositions. Some psychological connection between the believer and the propositions in the justificatory inferential structure is needed, but that connection need not be actual belief.

Some self-styled moral intuitionists do not deny that this loose connection to a justificatory inferential structure is needed in order for moral beliefs to be justified. They claim only that moral beliefs can be justified non-inferentially in the weak way. But then they cannot really escape the skeptical regress, as I argued. In any case, Audi does seem to claim that some moral beliefs are justified non-inferentially in the strong way that I explained. He claims that some moral belief contents are self-evident so that adequately understanding them is sufficient for being justified in believing them.[6] Still, if adequate understanding required something that ensured a disposition to accept propositions that would support them in an inferential structure, then a belief in a self-evident proposition could not be justified without commitment to a justificatory inferential structure. However, Audi seems to think that a believer can adequately understand a self-evident belief content without such dispositions or commitment. If so, people who understand self-evident propositions can be justified non-inferentially in the strong way that I defined. Thus, my strong definition of moral intuitionism picks out a view that at least some prominent and careful moral intuitionists hold.

I will argue that moral intuitionism of this strong sort is false. I do not deny that moral intuitions exist, that some moral intuitions are justified, or even that some moral intuitions are justified non-inferentially in a weak way. All I deny is that any moral belief is justified non-inferentially in the strong way that Audi claims and that moral intuitionists need to claim in order to escape the skeptical regress.

Does this denial lead to skepticism? No—or at least not directly or completely. Even if moral intuitionism fails, there still might be some other way to escape skeptical regresses. Indeed, I have argued elsewhere that coherentism provides a partial way out of skeptical regresses for some (though not all) contrast classes.[7] If coherentism works, then we can give up moral intuitionism without landing in complete moral skepticism. In any case, the issue here is only about how—not whether—moral beliefs are justified, so everything I say here is compatible with rejecting moral skepticism.

2. EMPIRICAL PREMISES

The basic problem for moral intuitionism starts with scientific evidence that many moral beliefs are not true.[8] Of course, science by itself cannot tell us which moral beliefs *are* true. That requires moral reflection. Nonetheless, science can provide part of the argument for the negative claim that many moral beliefs are *not* true. To do so, science simply shows that moral beliefs exemplify certain patterns—causal or correlational. For some of these patterns, moral theories then agree that beliefs in those patterns cannot all be true, because moral truth cannot depend on the factors reflected in those patterns. I have discussed some of these patterns in previous work, so here I will just list them quickly and add a few new findings.

Disagreement among moral beliefs is widespread. For example, some people believe that early abortions (as well as euthanasia, preventive war, eating meat, affirmative action, genetic enhancement, pornography, polygamy, and so on) are immoral, whereas others deny these beliefs. When two people disagree in this way on such an issue, at least one of their moral beliefs is not true.[9]

Partiality often leads people to hold contrary moral beliefs about favored or disfavored agents.[10] Many people, for example, would endorse more punishment when a stranger kills their child than when their child kills a stranger. However, the stranger's parents would deny these moral beliefs about deserved punishment. They cannot both be right.

Emotions often affect moral beliefs. Many people are less likely to judge an act morally wrong when they are not feeling disgust than when they are caused to feel disgust by something that is independent of the judged act, such as hypnosis[11] or nasty smells and surroundings.[12] Whether the act is morally wrong cannot vary with whether the believer happens to feel disgust, because there are too many believers who vary in disgust levels, so the moral belief must be untrue either when the believer does feel disgust or when the believer does not feel disgust.[13]

Order affects moral beliefs. Some people make contrary moral judgments about scenario *B* when three scenarios are presented in the order A–B–C than when the same scenarios are presented in order C–B–A. Order of presentation cannot affect the truth of moral beliefs, so at least one of these contrary moral beliefs is not true.[14]

Wording can affect moral beliefs even when it does not affect the truth of those beliefs. People sometimes reach different moral judgments when the agent is said to have 'saved 2 of the 5' than when the agent in the same scenario is said to have 'not saved 3 of the 5.' Since these descriptions are equivalent, at least one of these moral beliefs is not true.

Grammatical person also affects some moral beliefs. People are more likely to believe a first person moral judgment (such as "It would be morally wrong for me to do this act in these circum-stances") than an otherwise identical second or third person moral judgment (such as "It would be morally wrong for you or him to do this same act").[15] Assuming that what would be wrong for me would also be wrong for you in the same circumstances, the first and third person moral judgments cannot both be true.

Priming affects some moral beliefs. For example, people who are primed with words reflecting social power tend to endorse different moral beliefs than do people who are primed with words reflecting lack of social power.[16] Again, some of these contrary beliefs must fail to be true.

Sleep affects some moral beliefs. Some people endorse different moral judgments when they have been deprived of sleep that when they are well-rested.[17] If one holds contrary beliefs when one is tired than when one is not tired, then we might not know which belief is true, but we do know that at least one of them is not true.

These studies together provide ample evidence that a large percentage of moral beliefs is not true, according to standards that almost all moral intuitionists (and other moral theorists) do or should grant. Of course, some of these studies have serious imperfections, but there are plenty more good studies where these came from, and the trend is clear. I still cannot specify a precise percentage of moral beliefs that are not true; and the numbers do matter to my argument, since I do not assume that a very small chance of error is enough to create a serious epistemic problem. Nonetheless, the range and number of empirical studies along with the effect sizes in these studies support the conclusion that the error rate among moral beliefs is large enough to create a big problem at the heart of moral intuitionism.

3. EPISTEMIC PRINCIPLES

Of course, existing empirical studies do not cover all moral beliefs or even all kinds of moral belief. However, an argument against moral intuitionism needs to show that no moral belief is justified non-inferentially. How can an argument get from premises about some moral beliefs to a conclusion about all moral beliefs? The answer is that a high error rate in moral beliefs in general creates a presumption that needs to be rebutted in every particular case. To see how this works, consider a non-moral analogue.

Imagine you know 60 per cent of the red wine sold in California was made in California, and the rest comes from elsewhere. You buy a glass of red wine in California, and you know nothing else about the wine you bought: You have not tasted it yet, and you do not know its name, grape varietal, or vendor. What is the probability that this particular wine was made in California? It is reasonable for you to assign a probability of 0.6, because this wine is random in the sense that you have no reason at all to suspect any special property that might suggest deviation from the general probability. This point is about subjective rather than objective probability. It is reasonable to have a proportionate level of confidence in this belief, to report this probability to friends, and to make a proportionate bet on this belief (if you have enough money, trust the person you bet against, and so on). Of course, we rarely have in mind precise probabilities, but we can still make rough comparisons: it would be reasonable accept a bet at even money but refuse to give 5 to 1 or even 2 to 1 odds. You should not be as confident that the wine was made in California as you are that it is red, since you can see its color but not its origin (and you have no inkling of any coloring agent).

Now imagine that you discover some new information about the wine in your glass: It was bought at Tony's Wines in Santa Barbara, and 99 per cent of the wine from that shop was made in Italy. Knowing this, it would become reasonable for you to ascribe a probability much lower than 0.6 to the claim that the wine was made in California. Of course, the opposite can also occur: if you learn that the wine was bought in a California winery that sells only its own wines, then it would become reasonable for you to ascribe a much higher probability to the claim that the wine was made in California.

But what if you do not have any access to any such new information? The wine was in fact bought at Tony's, and 99 per cent of Tony's wine was in fact made in Italy, but you have no access to these facts. More generally, you have no access to any information at all that would justify you in believing that the wine was bought at a store with an unusual percentage of California wines. In this situation, it still seems reasonable for you to ascribe a probability of 0.6 to the claim that the wine was made in California. You need to base your probability assignments on the information that you have or have access to, even if there is contrary information that you do not have access to.

This trivial instance illustrates an important general epistemic principle:

> It is reasonable to assign a probability that a case has a property based on knowledge that the case falls in a first class and that a percentage of cases in that first class has that property until one gains access to new information that the case in question falls within a second class that differs from the first class in the percentage of cases in that second class that has that property.

In our example, the first class was red wines bought in California, and the second class was red wines bought at Tony's (or at the California vineyard). This principle applies to probability assignments about everything from the weather to voting and investments.

The crucial application here is to probabilities that beliefs are correct or incorrect. So imagine that you taste the wine, and the taste makes you believe that it was made in California. You have no idea how or why the wine gives you this impression, but it does. Your belief is immediate in the sense that it is not based on any inference.

How should you assign probabilities after tasting it? That depends. If you are an expert wine taster with years of experience of wines from California and elsewhere, then it might be reasonable for you to assign a high probability that this wine is from California. Your past experience gives you reason to trust your palate on this issue of origin, even if you cannot specify what it is in the taste that gives you the impression that it was made in California and even if you do not form any explicit meta-belief about your reliability in detecting wine origins by taste. In contrast, suppose that you have never tasted any wine before, and you have no reason at all to think that you are able to distinguish wines made in California from wines made elsewhere. Then, despite your impression, it is reasonable for you to continue to ascribe a probability of only 0.6 to the claim that the wine was made in California. Indeed, it seems unreasonable for you to ascribe a much higher probability that the wine was made in California.[18] For all you know, your untutored impressions on wine origins might be wrong much more often than they are right.

This point applies even if your impression that the wine was made in California is in fact both accurate and a reliable indicator of its origin. Suppose that a certain chemical from California soil is what causes your impression, but you have no idea at all that anything like that is going on. Without any access to any relevant information about the source or reliability of your impression, it seems reasonable for you to stick with your original probability based on general statistics about wines in California. Indeed, it seems unreasonable for you to ascribe a much higher probability, to become confident that the wine was made in California, or to give 3 to 1 odds in a bet that the wine was made in California. You would win your bet, since your belief is in fact true, but that does not show it was epistemically reasonable to bet on it.

Admittedly, externalists (including reliabilists) will disagree. The question is whether this response is only a desperate attempt to save their theory. Of course, an ability to detect wine origins on the basis of sensory impressions can be a valuable epistemic virtue even if the believer has no information about how or whether those impressions are reliable. Nonetheless, I doubt that even externalists would advise their friends to form beliefs on the basis of such impressions in the absence of any information that would give them any reason to trust those impressions. I assume that we want a theory of reasonableness to be relevant to advice about how to form moral beliefs. Externalism might serve a different purpose or capture a different notion, but it fails to capture the kind of reasonableness at stake here.[19]

These points so far concern reasonable beliefs about probabilities, but they have implications for justified belief. These implications are specified by a second epistemic principle:

> If it is reasonable for a person to assign a large probability that a certain belief is false, then that person is not epistemically justified in holding that belief.[20]

This standard is vague, but its point should be clear in examples. Suppose that a neophyte believes that the wine in her glass was made in California, but she reasonably ascribes a probability of only 0.6 that she is right, so it is reasonable for her to assign a large probability (0.4) that her belief is false. Then this epistemic principle implies that the neophyte is not epistemically justified in believing that the wine was made in California. She should suspend belief on that issue. Of course, she can still be instrumentally justified in betting that it was made in California if someone offers her even money, she has enough extra cash, and she has no reason to fear any trick. She might even be epistemically justified in *guessing* that the wine was made in California. However, it takes more than this for real belief to be justified.

What counts as real belief? Suppose the neophyte bets even money that the wine was made in California, but she would never take this belief for granted in future reasoning or tell a friend that the wine was made in California. Then she does not really believe that she will win her bet. She just guesses and hopes. Belief of the kind that matters here (that is, for morality) is meant for use in future reasoning, decision-making, and interpersonal communication. That is the kind of belief that this epistemic principle is about. After all, moral intuitionists do not claim only that they are justified in guessing or in betting.

How much does it take for such belief to be justified? It is impossible to be precise, but we can get a vague picture of the range by noticing that the standards seem to vary with costs of errors. This variation can be seen by contrasting wine with science. Scientists do not call a result statistically significant unless the probability that it is due to chance is less than 0.05, so they seem to prescribe suspending belief until the evidence warrants a probability assignment over 0.95.

The reason for this rigor is in part that that scientists rely on each other's results, so they would waste too much time and resources if scientists believed and reported results with probabilities below 0.95. The same standard seems too high for a belief that a wine was made in California, where it normally does not matter if it is false. The probability of error that counts as too large for belief to be justified thus varies with the importance of being correct. That point is all I need for my argument here, because it is clearly important to get moral beliefs right. Morality does not concern trivial matters like wine origins. It is unwise or even unreasonable to take big chances with moral beliefs. If someone replies that a 60 per cent chance of getting their moral beliefs right is good enough for them, then we would and should wonder whether they take morality seriously enough.

4. THE ARGUMENT

The epistemic principles and empirical premises from preceding sections combine to form an argument against moral intuitionism. The trick is to get from scientific evidence about moral judgments as a class to a conclusion about how any particular moral judgment needs to be justified.

The path runs like this: empirical studies give informed moral believers reason to ascribe a large probability of error to moral beliefs in general. It is then reasonable for a moral believer to apply that probability to every particular moral belief unless the believer has some special evidence that that particular moral intuition is in a different class with a smaller probability of error. If the believer does *not* have any such evidence, then it is reasonable for the believer to ascribe a chance of error that is too large for that belief to be justified. And if the believer *does* have such evidence, then that believer is committed to a justificatory inferential structure as defined in Section 1. Either way, the believer is not justified in the strong non-inferential way that moral intuitionists claim and must claim in order to escape the skeptical regress argument.

Of course, moral intuitionists will respond that some (of their) moral beliefs are not distorted by partiality, emotion, context, wording, grammatical person, priming, or lack of sleep. Then isn't it reasonable for these believers to assign a low probability of error to their beliefs? That depends on whether they have a reason to believe that a certain moral belief is not distorted by any such factors, so it has a lower than normal risk of error. Call this a *counter-vailing* reason. If believers have no countervailing reason, then it is reasonable for them to apply the chance of error in the general class of moral beliefs. Like the wine neophyte, it is reasonable for this moral believer to ascribe a high chance of error to her own moral belief, even if she has the impression that her belief is true.

In contrast, suppose a moral believer has a countervailing reason. Then, like the experienced wine taster, it can be reasonable for this moral believer to ascribe a low probability of error to this particular moral belief. Such moral believers can be justified. However, the information that a moral belief is not distorted by any factor like those mentioned above provides support for the proposition that the moral belief has a low probability of error, and that proposition can serve as a premise in an inferential structure whose conclusion is the moral belief. Thus, moral believers who have a countervailing reason are committed to a justificatory inferential structure as defined in Section 1.

These cases together show that commitment to a justificatory inferential structure is necessary for it not to be reasonable for a moral believer to ascribe a large chance of error to a moral belief; and that is necessary for the moral believer to be justified in holding that moral belief, according to the second epistemic principle in Section 3. But then the moral belief is not justified independently of commitment to an inferential structure, so it is not justified non-inferentially in the strong way that defines moral intuitionism in Section 1. The moral belief might be justified, but it is not justified in the way that moral intuitionists need to claim in order to escape the skeptical regress.

It might be useful to restate this argument more formally. The argument starts with simple premises:

(1) Informed adults are justified in believing that their own moral beliefs are in the class of moral beliefs.

(2) Informed adults are justified in believing that a large percentage of moral beliefs are not true.

What justifies premise 2 is the empirical evidence cited in Section 2 above. Premise 2 is about moral beliefs in general rather than any particular moral belief, so it does not require that anyone knows which particular moral beliefs are subject to the distortions listed in Section 2. Nonetheless, we need to restrict premises 1 and 2 to informed adults because children, medieval peasants, and others might not have access to that information. The argument will still apply to all moral intuitionists and to all readers of this essay, so this concession is minor.

Premises 1 and 2 then instantiate the antecedent of a slight variation on the first epistemic principle in Section 3:

(3)   For any subject S, particular belief B, and class of beliefs C, if S is justified in believing that B is in C and is also justified in believing that a large percentage of beliefs in C are not true, but S is not justified in believing that B falls into any class of beliefs C* of which a smaller percentage is not true, then S is justified in believing that B has a large probability of being untrue.

This principle can be supported by generalizing from cases like the example of wine in California. The relevant notion of being justified in believing does not, of course, imply that the person forms any explicit belief or justification. Instead, it amounts to what was previously described by saying that it would be reasonable for the believer to form the belief, even if the believer does not actually bother explicitly to form that belief, much less any argument to justify that belief.

Premises 1–3 together entail our first sub-conclusion:

(4)   Therefore, if an informed adult is not justified in believing that a certain moral belief falls into any class of beliefs of which a smaller percentage is not true, then that adult is justified in believing that this particular moral belief has a large probability of being untrue.

This conclusion does not require that the particular belief be untrue or even objectively unlikely. The point is only that it is reasonable to ascribe a probability to a particular member of a class on the basis of percentages within the whole class when the ascriber has no relevant information other than that this case is a member of that class. That claim holds for the probability that the wine is from California, so it should also hold for the probability that a moral belief is mistaken.

Now we can add a variation on the second principle from Section 3 that linked reasonable belief about probability of error to justified belief:

(5)   A moral believer cannot be justified in holding a particular moral belief when that believer is justified in believing that the moral belief has a large probability of being untrue.

As throughout, this principle is about being justified epistemically, not practically or instrumentally. Premises 4–5 then form a generalized hypothetical syllogism with this sub-conclusion:

(6)   Therefore, if an informed adult is not justified in believing that a certain moral belief falls into any class of beliefs of which a smaller percentage is not true, then that adult is not justified in holding that moral belief.

Now we just need to apply our account in Section 1 of commitment to a justificatory inferential structure:

(7)   If someone is justified in believing that a belief falls into a class of beliefs of which a smaller percentage is not true, then that person is committed to a justificatory inferential structure with that belief as a conclusion.

This premise should be plausible because the antecedent ensures that the believer has information that supports the claim that this belief is more likely than usual to be true. That is the kind of information that can serve as premises in an inferential structure that supports the moral belief as its conclusion. Premises 6–7 then entail this sub-conclusion:

(8)   Therefore, an informed adult is not justified in holding a moral belief unless that adult is committed to a justificatory inferential structure with that belief as a conclusion.

Now we just restate the definition in Section 1 of when a belief is justified non-inferentially in the strong way:

(9)   If a believer is not justified in holding a belief unless the believer is committed to a justificatory inferential structure,

then the believer is not justified non-inferentially in holding the belief.

Premises 8–9 then entail another sub-conclusion:

(10) Therefore, no informed adult is non-inferentially justified in holding any moral belief.

Assuming that moral intuitionism does not apply only to children and uninformed people, the definition of moral intuitionism in Section 1 implies this:

(11) Moral intuitionism claims that some informed adults are non-inferentially justified in holding some moral beliefs.

Now we can draw our overall conclusion from 10–11:

(12) Therefore, moral intuitionism is false.

That is what I said I was going to show.

5. A FEW OBJECTIONS

In response, opponents often present counter-examples of moral beliefs that are so obvious that it seems implausible to deny that they are justified. However, these obvious cases still fall into the same dilemma. Consider an example cited by a moral intuitionist in favor of his theory: "the deliberate humiliation, rape, and torture of a child, for no purpose other than the pleasure of the one inflicting such treatment, is immoral."[21] Let's assume that a person believes this and does not actually base his belief on any inference. I grant that this moral belief is justified. However, the question is not whether but how it is justified and, in particular, whether it is justified in the strong non-inferential way defined above. The dilemma starts from the obvious fact that this belief is a moral belief. The empirical studies then show that a large percentage of moral beliefs are not true. The first epistemic principle in Section 3 then implies that it is reasonable to ascribe a large probability that this belief is not true unless the believer has access to information that this belief falls inside another class that has a smaller percentage of errors. Of course, the believer does have such information in the example we are discussing. The believer presumably feels very confident and is justified in believing that almost nobody would disagree, that the belief will remain stable across emotions and contexts, that partiality is unlikely to distort his belief (at least when he does not know the child's identity), and so on. It is not enough that the belief in fact has these properties. The believer needs some access to this information in order for it to be reasonable for the believer to ascribe a lower than usual chance of error. However, because this special information reveals that the risk of error in this case is low, it also supports premises in a justificatory inferential structure that supports this belief as its conclusion. If an unusual believer did not have any commitment to any such structure, then it would be reasonable for this unusual believer to ascribe a large probability that even this belief is not true; and then that unusual believer (unlike normal people) would not be justified. In order to be justified, a believer does not have to consciously think about any of the relevant features of the belief, but any believer at least needs to be disposed to accept that the belief is not distorted by partiality, emotion, context, and so on. Hence, even though this belief in normal believers is justified, they are still not justified independently of commitment to an inferential structure. So they are not justified non-inferentially in the way that moral intuitionists claim and need to claim in order to escape the skeptical regress. Moral intuitionism, thus, fails in the very cases that moral intuitionists cite to support their theory.

Another kind of purported counter-example cites moral principles. Even if moral beliefs about particular cases are not justified non-inferentially, aren't we justified in believing that it is wrong to break promises or to kill at least *prima facie* or defeasibly (in the absence of any justification or excuse)? Yes, we are justified, but we are still not justified non-inferentially. After all, people often formulate principles inaccurately and are surprised by counter-examples to principles, even to *prima facie* principles. In the absence of any countervailing reason, it is reasonable to ascribe a high probability that any given principle is inaccurate in some way or subject to some counter-example. Moreover, beliefs in such principles are often based on 'intuitive induction' from particular cases.[22] If beliefs about those particular grounding cases are distorted by partiality, emotion, context, and so on, then the resulting principles will also be distorted. Hence, it is reasonable to ascribe a high risk of error to beliefs in the principles in the absence of any countervailing reason. Of course, we do have countervailing reasons in some cases of beliefs in standard principles about central *prima facie* duties. If we are justified in believing that there is no disagreement about a certain general principle and that our belief in that principle is not distorted by partiality, emotion, or other factors (perhaps because we have reflected on a variety of cases in a variety of circumstances), then we can be justified in believing that the principle holds. However, having this information will also make us committed to a justificatory inferential structure, so we still will not be justified non-inferentially. Again, we are justified but not in the special way that defines moral intuitionism.

A second kind of objection refers to the process behind some moral beliefs. The cited experiments show high error rates, but the beliefs that they study are usually not based on lengthy, careful, and serious reflection. Such reflection seems to reduce the effects of partiality, emotion, context, and so on. So it might not be reasonable to ascribe a large probability of error to moral beliefs that are based on reflection. One problem here is that reflection can be either adequate or inadequate. If the reflection is inadequate, then surely it cannot make the believer justified. But if it is adequate, then it would seem to involve a lot of information that could fit into a justificatory inferential structure that supports the moral belief. Moreover, if the believer does not have any disposition to believe or accept that he has reflected adequately, then it is again hard to see how the reflection could make the believer justified. But if the believer does have a disposition to accept that he has reflected adequately, then that proposition again could fit into a justificatory inferential structure that supports the moral belief.[23] And if commitment to such an inferential structure is needed, then the belief is not justified non-inferentially in the strong way that moral intuitionists claim.

A third common objection is that my argument demands too much. One version of this objection claims that young children have justified moral beliefs but fail the demands imposed by my epistemic principles. However, very young children are like neophytes with no experience of wine. Children who are so young that they have not received feedback on their moral beliefs and choices might have no reason to trust their impressions about what is morally wrong. Indeed, it is not even clear that very young children make judgments that are properly characterized as moral judgments, since the basis for their judgments is often no more than self-interest, including fear of punishment. Their judgments might be about issues that we consider as moral issues, but their judgments are not based on the features that make them moral issues. Still, by the age when their judgments are clearly moral in nature—at least 4 years—children become less like wine neophytes and more like wine experts, because they have received feedback on their judgments and decisions from their parents or caregivers, and they have matured conceptually. At that later age, it can be reasonable for them to think that a certain moral judgment is less likely than average to be mistaken, so they can become justified in their moral beliefs. This process is gradual, but it can begin fairly early.

Another respect in which opponents claim that my argument demands too much is that it might seem self-refuting. According to these critics, if the requirements in my epistemic principles were imposed consistently on all beliefs, then nobody could be justified in believing anything. In particular, these objectors claim that my principles would imply that nobody is justified in believing in those principles themselves. None of this follows, however, and the reason is simple. My conclusion is not that moral beliefs are not justified. My conclusion is only that moral beliefs are not justified non-inferentially in a strong way. Hence, I am happy to grant that my epistemic principles and many other common beliefs have the same status as moral beliefs: They can be justified (and true) even if they are not justified non-inferentially in the strong way that intuitionists claim. And if my principles *are* justified, regardless of *how* they are justified, then there is nothing wrong with using these principles in my argument.

There are other objections to which I need to reply. The conversation does not end here, if ever. However, I hope that my reformulation of my argument in this paper at least shows why the basic problem cannot be escaped as easily as many moral intuitionists have assumed.[24]

CHAPTER TWO

CONATIVE INTUITIONISM

Hugh J. McCann, Texas A&M University

This paper defends the view that conation—that is, experiences like desire and felt obligation—can fairly be taken as sources of information about value. Using desire as the main example, it is argued that objects of desire are apprehended as good, and that it would be irrational to desire something understood to have no value. Treating desire as a source of evaluative knowledge helps to shed light on the relationship between value and the descriptive features of the world, and makes it possible to understand decision making as a rational process. Finally, when it comes to defending value realism and the objectivity of value judgments conative intuitionism is in a stronger position than its more familiar cognitive counterpart.

By 'conative intuitionism' I understand the claim that our primary awareness of value and rightness, and of their opposites, comes by way of conation—that is, by way of experiences such as desire and felt obligation, of enjoyment and moral satisfaction.[1] To desire something, I claim, is not just to feel drawn toward the thing, but to be drawn toward it as something worthy, as a fitting object of pursuit. Similarly, to feel obligated to do something is not just to experience a sense of urgency about the action; it is to apprehend the action as objectively demanded, as incumbent upon one regardless of one's own, subjective preferences. In short, experiences of conation come to us as intuitions about objective value—intuitions that in our practical lives are taken very seriously. Conative intuitionism is simply the claim that they should be taken seriously philosophically as well, that such experiences deserve to be viewed as legitimate sources of information.

The possibility that conation can serve as a source of knowledge about value is worth investigating for at least two reasons. First, it offers a way—the only way I know, in fact—to make sense of ourselves as rational decision makers. Second, it provides for an approach to the problems of moral epistemology that although hardly new is seldom explored, and that I think holds promise. But conative intuitionism also promises to be controversial. We are not used to thinking of states such as desire and felt obligation as even purporting to be informative about matters of objective value. Just the opposite: most of us have been taught that as far as anything valuational is concerned conative states are strictly subjective in their import. Accordingly, it may be wondered whether any view that takes the opposite tack gets the content of conative states right. And even if the content is correctly understood, there remains the question whether the purported informativeness is to be taken seriously—that is, whether the insight into matters of value offered by conative states tracks anything real.

In this paper I want to provide a brief defense of conative intuitionism, concentrating mainly on the experience of desire or wanting, although I shall occasionally speak about felt obligation as well. I shall argue first that states of desire are, implicitly, objectively evaluative in their content. Second, I shall sketch out what I think are some useful consequences of this claim for theories of value and practical reasoning. Finally, I shall defend the conative intuitionist view of desire against objections. The first is that it gets the content of the experience of desire wrong, that conation is strictly emotive and therefore not implicitly evaluative in any sense that can rightly be deemed objectively significant. The second objection is that conative intuitionism falls prey to moral skepticism: that any purported insight into an objective realm of value offered by these states must be rejected, either on epistemological or on metaphysical grounds.

1. THE CONTENT OF CONATIVE STATES

Conative states come in quite a variety. Some are strictly dispositional: a person who is sound asleep, for example, may be said to intend to visit Italy next month, or to enjoy ice cream. The states that concern us here are not dispositional but conscious or occurrent, and these too come in a variety. In some, the object of awareness is already present: someone may right now be enjoying a dish of ice cream; or, he might experience satisfaction at the honest behavior of another, or be repelled by someone's dishonesty. In other cases, however, the object of conation is entertained, as it were, only in prospect. Thus I might desire some exercise, or experience a felt obligation to keep a promise. Desire and felt obligation have opposites in aversion and the sense that something is forbidden. It will simplify the discussion, however, to concentrate on positive states—especially states of desire. And my thesis, to repeat, is simply that these states of awareness may properly be taken as sources of knowledge about matters of value. Desire and aversion convey information to us of what is good and bad. Experiences of felt obligation and forbiddenness—that is, the sense that an action must be performed, or in the case of forbiddenness avoided, regardless of what our personal wishes happen to be—tell us about what is right and wrong.[2] I would want to say the same about states whose object is present, like enjoyment and revulsion—but what I would have to say about them would mostly complicate things rather than adding anything important.

It is worth mentioning that there is nothing really new about this claim. The idea that desire involves an apprehension of the good was familiar in mediaeval philosophy as the view that we always desire things *sub specie boni*, or under the aspect of good. Thus when I experience the desire for some exercise, getting some exercise presents itself to me not just as desired but as desir*able*—that is, as in some way valuable or worthy of being desired. Notice that this is not to say to experience a desire is to *judge* that the thing desired is good, or to give some sort of cognitive assent to the idea. It might be thought that this must be the case, that if conation is to be a source of information then I must in the very experience of desiring something form a cognitive judgment that it is valuable. And of course if that were so then the position I am defending would boil down to a version of cognitive intuitionism, rather than something having uniquely to do with the will. It is, however, a mistake to confuse conation with cognitive judgment. In most cases such a judgment will be a reasonable next step. But just as when I look out of my window I need not judge that the tree is green in order to perceive or apprehend it as green, so I need not judge getting some exercise to be good in order to apprehend it as good. A fortiori, it should not be supposed that to have conative apprehension of something as good is to be finally committed either to the veridicality of the experience, or to the idea that the thing desired would count as good overall or in the last analysis. It is always possible to question and to revise our apprehensions of value, no matter how they arise.

The initial persuasiveness of conative intuitionism depends on how plausible we think it is to assert that when we experience desire, what is desired presents itself to us as good. The truth of this assertion seems to me to be self-evident—as is only to be expected if the claim is true at all, since it is a claim about phenomenal experience. And I think most people would find the assertion pretty obvious, provided nothing more controversial is intended—e.g. as to how the appearance of value arises, or whether it is objectively informative. If, however, we are inclined to doubt that desire has this phenomenal feature, I think there are considerations that can help persuade us that it is so. One consideration has to do simply with how our idea of good arises. Obviously, it has to come from some sort of intuition, and I think it is plausible that ideas of value should originate in conation—so that our first awareness of goodness comes in the enjoyment of things, either as actually present or as anticipated in our desires. Indeed if, with most philosophers these days, we think that the value properties of things do not reduce to descriptive or strictly naturalistic ones, and if we believe also that our *cognitive* faculties of perception are attuned only to what *is*, naturalistically considered, then there seems to be no route to value awareness other than by way of the will.[3] The idea of a thing being for us a fitting object for appreciation and pursuit could only arise through our feeling the tug of it, through our being drawn toward it. If so, then it must be by way of conation that we are drawn toward a thing, not just in its naturalistic guise but *qua good*. To desire something just *is* to have it presented to us in valuational terms. And by my account it is, in the end, only in light of this and related experiences that we are able to understand what it would mean to judge something to be good, to comprehend what the term 'good' signifies. There just is no other way.

A second persuasive consideration has to do with how we would react to someone who claimed to desire something, yet appeared to find nothing of value in it, nothing desir*able* in the evaluative sense. Someone tells you, let's say, that he wants to spend the holidays in Switzerland. But, he insists, there is nothing about Switzerland that is good—not the scenery, not the weather, not the people or the culture, not the skiing, the hiking or the climbing. Nor, he says, can anything be done in Switzerland that is conducive to or instrumental toward anything else he thinks is good. And finally he doesn't think being in Switzerland would be good in itself, just simpliciter, as it were. Such a person, it seems to me, would be viewed by almost anyone as suffering from some sort of deficit of rationality—not because it would be a waste of effort, in the circumstances, for him to actually go to Switzerland (perhaps he doesn't intend to go)—but simply because it makes no sense to desire something and yet to find nothing of value in it. The case has a pathological ring, like compulsive hand washing, or a kleptomaniac amassing things for which he has no use. We would not, I submit, be able to make sense of such a person. We would suspect either that he did not want to go to Switzerland at all, or more likely that some kind of subconscious valuation was actually going on, but was being repressed in the person's self-awareness.

A related point pertains to one's own case. What would it be like to experience a desire for something *without* the thing appearing to us as good in any way? It is of course possible to desire something that we believe or know to be bad all things considered, as when the alcoholic desires drink, or when someone with duties to perform wants to watch TV instead. Even so, I submit, the thing desired is, insofar as it is desired, taken as good. The alcoholic in desiring to drink sees the state of intoxication as desirable; the TV watcher sees the enjoyable aspects of the show he wishes to watch as good. Furthermore, it is only because what we desire is presented to us under the aspect of good, that action undertaken out of desire can hope to count as objectively rational; so, only because in desiring exercise I apprehend exercise as good that the desire justifies my exercising. Suppose, on the other hand, that one were to find oneself with a kind of yen for doing something, a tug in the direction of the thing—to have some ice cream, for example—but saw nothing whatever of value in it. For my part, such a desire, if it deserved the name at all, would be to me an utterly alien thing, a blind impulse inimical to any sort of real rationality. Undoubtedly there are compulsions we do not understand—and the phenomenon of felt obligation, which I would claim is quite a bit different from desire, can offer us a reason for doing something to which our desires are opposed, and that they alone could never induce us to do. But a desire unaccompanied by the apprehension of the thing desired as good could be a ground only for behavior that had no semblance of rationality to it.

2. CONATION AND THE THEORY OF VALUE

There are, then, very good reasons for thinking that we desire things under the aspect of good: that when we want something, there is some feature of the thing wanted that presents itself to us as worthy of being wanted, as deserving of our appreciation. The central claim of conative intuitionism about desire is simply that this feature of it is legitimately informative. To say that something is good is, after all, just to say that it is a fit object of desire, that it is appropriate for us to desire it and, other things equal, to pursue it. What conative intuitionism says is simply that one fundamental way of finding out that a thing *is* a fit object of desire—that it is desir*able*—is simply by desiring it. How might one argue for this thesis? Well, for one thing it is hard to imagine how anything else could be so if goodness and desirability are one and the same.[4] Beyond this, the simplest and most basic argument has to be just this: that when, in our direct experience, something seems to us to be so, we have every right to take it as being so, absent evidence to the contrary. So just as when in sensory awareness I apprehend the tree outside my window as green, I have reason to judge that indeed it is green, so also when in desiring some exercise I apprehend exercise as good, I have reason to judge that yes, a bit of exercise would be good. And of course that is precisely what I am likely to do. I might even use a statement to the effect that some exercise would be good to express my desire.

This is not to say, of course, that my judgment that some exercise would be good should be viewed as final. Neither it nor my judgment that the tree is green need be treated as anything but *prima facie*, although admittedly we might feel that our judgments of value, especially if they are grounded in our desires, are in general far less to be trusted than our judgments as to the colors of trees.[5] Just the same, the fact is that we do trust and act upon our wants and desires, seeking out those things that, in our conative experience, are presented to us as good. Furthermore, we rely on appeals to conation in our efforts to persuade others to act. If I were trying to persuade you to visit the Grand Canyon, my efforts would not involve a lecture on aesthetics or value theory. I would simply describe the Canyon for you, and if I had them handy show you some pictures. That is, I would rely on a direct appeal to your desires. Similarly, if I wanted you to contribute to the relief of world hunger I would not engage in discourse about theoretical or even applied ethics. I would show you some pictures of hungry children and rely on the sentiments they would arouse to get you to act in the right way. It is a perfectly good reason to feed the hungry that we should feel sorry for them. And the reason why it is a good reason is not that our personal sympathies have some special claim to being assuaged (a fatuous thing to say, in this context), but simply that, other things being equal, our sympathies can be a very good guide to what is valuable.

There is more than one lesson to be drawn from this kind of practice, but the most important one for the present is that, despite all we tend to hear about the diversity of people's desires and their unreliability as guideposts to value, guideposts are exactly what we treat them as being in many if not most practical situations. And this is to say simply that we treat our desires just as conative intuitionism suggests we should. It is worth considering, therefore, what value theory might look like if it were developed on a conative intuitionist basis. On the whole, I think it would look pretty familiar. Conative intuitionism is, after all, a form of intuitionism. It does not, as does non-cognitivism, mistake value judgments for emotive outpourings. It treats claims like 'exercise is good' as what they plainly are: propositions. The difference is only that it sees these propositions as formed and assented to on the basis of conative states such as the felt desire for exercise. In its fundamental features, therefore, a conative intuitionist approach to value theory will look much like the cognitive variety. Initial value judgments are to be treated as *prima facie*, and subject to correction by further experience, the experiences of others, and perhaps at times on theoretical grounds. It is, however, the experience of conation that is fundamental to our knowledge concerning matters of value. Its relation to theory is essentially the same as that of ordinary sense experience to scientific theory. That is, just as scientific theory does not seek to dictate to us the nature of the world *a priori*, the point of value theory is not to dictate our values. Its purpose is not to provide foundations divorced from experience, but to explain and codify the judgments we are apt to make based on conative experience, and perhaps at times to assist us in re-examining those experiences and judgments that theory finds problematic.[6]

It should be stated too that a conatively based theory of value would have to face many of the same objections that confront cognitive intuitionism. Of these, perhaps the first that springs to mind is that given the amount of diversity and disagreement we find among the things people desire, our desires seem to offer at best a very weak basis for reliable judgments of value. I have addressed this objection elsewhere[7] and I shall have a little more to say about it at the end of this paper. But for the moment I want to set it aside, because it seems to me that neither form of intuitionism is at any special advantage or disadvantage when it comes to this objection. Both need to consider just how much variation there actually is in the things people desire, how it arises, and how, where necessary, it might be resolved. And the resources of the two views for carrying out these tasks seem to me about equal. But the same does not hold when it comes to other objections. There are at least three areas of difficulty where I think conative intuitionism fares better than its cognitive counterpart.

The first of these has to do with the way in which values come to be known. According to cognitive intuitionism this occurs through direct cognitive awareness, not greatly different from the sensory awareness by which we are apprised of the descriptive nature of things. It is common for this account to be criticized as amounting to a kind of moral sense theory: that is, it seems to posit a special intellective faculty for the apprehension of good and evil, right and wrong—features of the world that more mundane cognitive awareness is unable to detect. And of course the objection is that this is much too convenient. A moral skeptic would have us wonder whether there are any objective values at all, not to mention whether we are able to detect them. But just at the point where doubt arises, the cognitive intuitionist posits a faculty ideally ordained to meet the threat: we simply observe that some things are good and others bad, and that is that. To those who find the problems of moral epistemology troubling, this will seem too arbitrary a move—one which, furthermore, brings with it the additional danger that individual judgments of value will be deemed in principle incorrigible, since they are purely a matter of direct intuition. Thus cognitive intuitionism threatens to invest the whole fabric of our values with an air of arbitrariness, of bald assertion in the face of doubt.

A second and related objection has to do with value supervenience. It is widely agreed that the value properties of things supervene upon their natural or non-value properties, so that the value properties will not vary unless the corresponding natural ones do as well. The relationship is, however, somewhat difficult to fathom. It cannot be a matter of simple covariance; values must somehow arise out of the descriptive features of things. But the question is, exactly how? And the problem with cognitive intuitionism is that it sheds no light on this issue. It speaks of our perceiving the value properties of things along with the non-value properties, but it says nothing about how the first are related to the second—and thereby threatens to reduce value supervenience to an occult relationship, concerning whose nature we destined forever to be in the dark.

By contrast, conative intuitionism sheds light on both these issues. Far from postulating what threatens to be a spurious faculty of observation, it lodges our awareness of values in the familiar faculty of desire, and other conative states. That in such states things present themselves to us as valuable is, I have argued, a plausible, even a self-evident claim. But in any case it is a claim subject to assessment by familiar means, as is the further thesis that these deliverances are to be taken seriously. Thus conative intuitionism involves little if any of the arbitrariness that seems to afflict its cognitive counterpart. Conative intuitionism also sheds light on the relation of value supervenience. It holds, in effect, that things are good insofar as they constitute appropriate objects of desire and enjoyment, and similarly for other value properties and conative faculties. This does not *reduce* value properties to natural ones—as most would agree it should not. But it does enable us to see how in light of their descriptive features things can be valuable. They are so precisely in that the descriptive features in question are of a kind that should appeal to us. Why they should so appeal is, of course, a further question, one that we may well need a theory of value to help us answer. But the mechanism through which they appeal is no longer left in the dark, and that helps us to see what, provided conative intuitionism is correct, the supervenience of value on the descriptive nature of things consists in.

Finally, there is a matter concerning which I shall have to make a long story short. It is a mistake to think that a mere judgment as to the value of some course of action—a judgment that it would be good for it to get done, or that it ought to be done, even that it would be best for it to be done—is enough to *get* it done.[8] Even when we judge that some action would be best, which is a rare phenomenon in any case, the problem of weakness of will is enough to show that action need not follow. All the judging in the world that it is best, even that it is morally required, that I get some exercise right now won't get me to exercising if I'm too lazy. The reason for this is that judgments, even about matters of value, are cognitive acts, and cognitive acts need have no influence on the will. In order to perform an action I need to have a motive. In the case of getting some exercise the usual motive is a desire—a thought with a content something like "Would that I get some exercise right now." The difference between this and a cognitive judgment is that the first only *says* that getting some exercise would be good, the second actually *presents* the act to me in its goodness, in its desirability. That is what it takes to get me moving—not a mere affirmed proposition, and not a blind impulse driven by the affirmation either, but a mental experience that *does* prompt action and portrays my exercise project as worthy of my pursuit. And if I do act out of my desire, we can begin to make sense of me as a rational agent, one who acts not just in the presence of reasons, but *for* them.[9]

Suppose, however, that I came to see my desire for exercise as strictly subjective in import, so that no matter how much it might present getting some exercise to me as valuable, the value is strictly a subjective excrescence—a manifestation of my own inclinations, yes, but of nothing real in the world beyond my thoughts. Then, I submit, my action can be rational only in the sense that my beliefs could still be rational if they all derived from the machinations of a Cartesian demon. Like a demonically created delusion, my desire for exercise might make perfect internal sense; it might cohere beautifully with the rest of my thinking. But it would be utterly empty in the sense of having any objective belonging, utterly bereft of sense anywhere but in the playpen world of my self-centered delights. On the other hand, suppose that conative intuitionism is correct in its claim about my experience of desire. Suppose, that is, that in this experience I do exactly what its content purports: I lay hold of an objective realm of values, apprehend them, and am thereby empowered to act according to them. Then I can begin to exhibit something that counts truly as *practical* rationality. I become a truly rational agent, one who escapes the Cartesian demon not just in what he believes and knows but also in what he intends and does.

3. CONATIVE CONTENT AND COGNITIVE IMPORT

Let me now take up objections to conative intuitionism. There are, I think, two major lines of objection to contend with, one of which I shall address in this section and the other in the next. The first has to do with a suspicion one might have that, as an account of value awareness, conative intuitionism postulates an illicit mix of the conative with the cognitive. It combines the two—claiming that in desire some sort of informational content is made available to us, content that, although it cannot be grasped by cognition alone, can be gotten at via conation. That has a strange ring to it. It amounts to saying we first grasp a thing as worthy of our desire (goodness, as I have said, being no more than desirability in the normative sense—i.e. worthiness of being desired) in the very desiring of it, and not by an independent cognitive judgment. And it may be questioned whether this is a licit move. Do we actually *learn* by desiring something that it is good? That seems impossible without our judging it to be so. But surely a judgment of value—i.e. the actual judgment that something is good—should not be regarded as intrinsic to the experience of desire. Why not, then, simply extract the judgment? Make it a proper function of intellectual understanding, as it should be, and leave conation entirely to its commonly understood role: that of providing motivation for the behavior cognition understands as conducive to the (intellectually grasped) good?[10]

I think, however, that this objection misunderstands things. In the first place, conative intuitionism as I have described it does not make the actual judgment that something is good a part of desire. So if we were to understand learning that something is so as requiring an actual propositional judgment that it is so, then we would have to conclude that we do not, in the experience of desire taken by itself, learn that anything is good. This of course is partly a verbal matter, but I am not sure we should understand 'learning' in this way—that is, as invariably including an explicit act of cognitive assent. When through sensation I experience the tree as green I do not judge it to be so. But it seems to me that I do learn in the sense of becoming aware of the tree as green, and that I therefore come to be in a position to judge that it is so, even though I do not do so simply in the act of perception. Similarly it is only the awareness of something *as* desirable that conative intuitionism postulates as intrinsic to desire. The judgment can come later, just as in the case of sensory awareness.

But is it fair even to include this much of the cognitive in the experience of desire? Well, there certainly can be no objection in principle to the idea that conative states include cognitive content. All mental states include some kind of representation of what they are about, and that representation is cognitive in nature. So if I judge that the tree is green then my thought has to include some sort of representation that has the tree being green.[11] Otherwise there is nothing for my judgment to be about, nothing for me to assent to as true in making the judgment. And of course the representation has to count as cognitive—i.e. as something that is comprehended or understood. Similarly, when I decide to perform some action, there has to be a cognitive representation of the action that enters into my decision as content; if it doesn't there can be no decision, for there is nothing present in my mind to decide upon. And we can expect that the same will be true of occurrent or experienced desire, that it must include cognitive representation, lest there be nothing to serve as the content of the experience, nothing to be desired. But there is more. The content of mental states and events, the content of our thoughts, is not neutral as to the modality of the thought— that is, as to the *kind* of thinking that goes on. To judge a tree to be green is, as it were, to think to oneself: the tree is green. That is, it is to think the very assertion that is brought into being by the act of intellectual assent. In that assertion my assent to truth does not stand off to the side, it pervades the thought. Similarly, if I decide to get some exercise the content of my thought is not: I decide to get some exercise. It is: I shall get some exercise—so that the thought is pervaded with the resolution that is characteristic of deciding.

With this in mind, consider again the case of desire. The content of occurrent desire may perhaps be represented in more than one way, but I think it can be seen that the best representation is certainly *not* something like: I desire that I get some exercise. This is not a conation but a second-order judgment, the kind of thing that might occur on the basis of reflective awareness of my conative state. A better representation of the conation itself is more like: Would that I get some exercise. Here the modality of desire—we might call it optativeness or, perhaps better, desideration—again pervades the thought. We have seen reason for thinking, however, that when desideration occurs, the thing desired is presented as desir*able*— that is, as objectively valuable or good. And if this is correct, then although it would be wrong to think that when I desire to get some exercise I *judge* that it would be good to get exercise, the mental content of desire *does* include a representation of getting exercise as good or objectively valuable. As in the case where I judge the tree to be green based on sensory awareness, therefore, I am in a position to judge, based on reflective awareness of what I experience in the occurrent desire, that it would be (*prima facie*) good to get some exercise. The mixture of conative and cognitive I am alleging for occurrent desire arises, then, from a combination of cognitive representation and modality of thought not different in principle from what may be found in any sort of thinking, cognitive or conative. What is peculiar, perhaps, is just this: that desire and other conative experiences *purport* to be informative about objective value. But that is a matter of the *kind* of content that pertains to the modality of thought they involve. One may certainly question whether this sort of content tracks anything real. But that is a problem about veridicality, not about whether conative states have any cognitive content at all, or about the peculiar sort of content they involve.

4. CONATION AND MORAL SKEPTICISM

The second line of objection to conative intuitionism—the one, I think, that we would most expect to hear—arises out of moral skepticism. Moral skepticism is, of course, a threat to any objectivist theory of value, and so must be faced by cognitive and conative intuitionists alike. Here again, however, it seems to me that conative intuitionism turns out to have the stronger footing. As against conative intuitionism, we may phrase the skeptic's objection as follows: that although the experience of desire may purport to be informative as to matters of value, it simply is not; any valuational dimension it has is strictly subjective, and points to nothing of objective worth, nothing that has significance beyond the arena of the individual's personal preferences. And we may expect the same objection to be raised about other conative states and experiences. Desire, enjoyment, felt obligation and similar experiences, the skeptic will argue, can at best inform us about how we would like the world to be; they tell us nothing about any objective preference, any preference lying, as it were, in the world itself.

There are different ways to interpret the claim that the valuational aspect of an experience of desire is strictly 'subjective' in import. For example, we might take the claim to mean that in the experience of desire, there occurs a voluntary bestowal of value by the person who experiences the desire on the thing desired—so, that when I experience the desire for some exercise I willingly invest the notion of exercise with value, by my own volition as it were. I think, however, that this would be a bad interpretation. Desire is simply not a voluntary thing, if by that is meant something that would constitute an active exercise of will on the part of the subject. We can contrive to control our desires indirectly—for example, by controlling the stimuli to which we are exposed. And once a desire is on hand we can indulge it voluntarily, by focusing our attention on the thing desired, and delighting in the contemplation of it. Or, we may try to dismiss it, by concentrating on something else. But the onset of desire is always passive: something that is not directly brought about by the subject, and for which he can be responsible, if at all, only indirectly, by using or misusing mechanisms of mental self control. Yet even at its onset desire purports to be informative. What is desired is in the state of desire itself, apprehended from the beginning as in some way desirable or valuable.

A second interpretation of the claim that desire is strictly subjective in its valuational dimension might be that the evaluative component, while legitimately present, is entirely self-referential. That is, it might be held that the valuational seeming that comes to me with desire is not a presentation of the thing desired as objectively valuable, but rather a presentation of myself as valuing it. But this too seems wrong. To desire something and to be aware of ourselves as desiring it are not the same thing. The former is a conative state and the latter a cognitive one, which need not occur for desire itself to take place. And as far as the phenomenology of desire goes, we do not usually in desiring something dwell on ourselves as desiring it, or reach any judgment that this is what we are doing. Indeed, it is possible for me to desire something without having myself in mind at all, especially when the thing desired is not for me but for someone else, such as a child or a friend. By contrast, it does not seem possible to desire something without taking that thing as worthwhile, as deserving of the time and attention spent in desiring it. Phenomenologically speaking, then, desire is not about us but about the world: we desire things by virtue of their own nature, not ours, and we need not think of ourselves at all in the experience.[12] A fortiori, the value presented to us as belonging to the object of our desire is not to be confused with the altogether different state of affairs of our holding a subjective belief that the thing is valuable.

How then shall we understand the claim that the valuational component of desire has only subjective import? It must, I think, be taken to mean that although the valuation that occurs in desire may not be a matter of our voluntarily conferring value on the thing desired, it is nevertheless entirely a manifestation of our own nature, and not of the nature of anything in the world. That is, the skeptic may grant that in the experience of desire things appear to us as objectively valuable, and that this occurs through no voluntary doing on our part. But he will insist that the phenomenon is indicative only of our own psychological nature—of our own need, perhaps, to see our objectives as having significance beyond ourselves, but of no more than this. It has no worth as an indicator of what we might suppose to be some objective realm of value. And it is important to realize that this is not just an epistemological objection. That is, the skeptic's argument is not that, although there may perhaps be objective values in the world, we could never be sure that any experience of ours conveyed information to us as to what they were. If that is all that is being claimed then the skeptic's objection reduces to nothing but a Cartesian demon argument: that no matter how things look, we could always turn out to be wrong about everything. Any such argument has to be rejected, if only because there could never conceivably be any evidence either in its favor or against it.

Rather, if the skeptic's argument is to have any hope of success its thrust must be understood as metaphysical. The skeptic has to be maintaining that any supposed intuition of objective value, whether by cognition or conation, *must* be spurious, simply because there neither is nor could be any such thing as objective value. But how would one argue for such a claim? One argument might be that it is unscientific to think of the world as containing objective values, unscientific to accord reality to anything but strictly descriptive facts. Taken by itself, however, this is not a very persuasive consideration. It is true that scientists are not in their professional endeavors much on the lookout for objective values. But that doesn't show that such values aren't there, and still less does it show that they could not be. Perhaps some branch of science should be on the lookout for objective value. Or, maybe there should be some other investigative endeavor that aims at such discernment, an endeavor we might not choose to call 'science,' but that we still would take to be addressing something real.

Another argument that could be given for rejecting the idea of objective value is that if we accept that values are matters of objective reality, we will ultimately be forced to postulate some sort of mind or intelligence—perhaps even a God—who frames or entertains these values, so that they will have a place to reside. This, it might be claimed, is a consequence some will be unwilling to accept. I suppose that in strict logic, the proper reply here is that if the evidence indicates something is true we have no choice but to accept it, willing or not. In fact, however, I think the fear expressed in this objection may be overblown. That matters of value should constitute a dimension of objective reality might strengthen theistic arguments somewhat, but it is hardly decisive. No one doubts, after all, that the world is able to be apprehended in its descriptive dimensions by our own intellect. But we do not on that account insist that there must be a divine intellect to apprehend the world as well, or to serve as a repository for the facts we claim to 'discover' when we learn how the world operates. Why then suppose that if there is a dimension of real value to be grasped by way of the human will, there must also be a divine will to grasp it?

Perhaps it will be responded that there is a difference between the two cases, that the descriptive dimension of the world has a foundational metaphysical legitimacy that the valuational dimension posited by conative intuitionism lacks. This brings us to a third argument, that I think gets us to the heart of the matter. That values constitute an objective dimension of reality is a familiar thesis, a tenet not just of conative intuitionism but of the cognitive brand as well, and for that matter, any version of moral realism. And what bothers the moral skeptic is not just the question whether the thesis is true or false, but whether it even makes sense, whether it is plausible to think values even *could* be anything real. There is something profoundly mysterious about the idea of objective value. To say that when I desire exercise I apprehend what is desir*able* is to say that even if I had not actually desired it, the world itself is biased in favor of my getting some exercise; that it comes with a built-in preference for individuals in my sort of circumstances engaging in some physical activity, even if the state of affairs of my actually doing so never obtains, never comes to pass. Now we do not mind thinking of the world as biased in the sense that some things are determined to occur. We may all hope that the world is biased in favor of the sun's rising tomorrow. But if it is, it is so only in the sense that this outcome is already built into the world as it is. If the sun is to rise tomorrow it is because conditions right now are sufficient to make the event occur when the time comes. To speak of this as a bias or preference is perhaps a bit picturesque, but it is not metaphysically offensive. Value realism, on the other hand, implies a bias in favor of what need not be built in, and in fact may never be there, as my getting some exercise will not be if my ultimate choice is not to do so. That is, value realism posits a kind of teleology innate in the world—almost as though what does not exist can influence things. And it may be thought that this *is* metaphysically offensive.[13]

I cannot see, however, that it is, in any truly damaging sense. Moral realism does not require anything to be caused by what does not exist. Values operate through our own intellects and wills, in terms of the motives they engender in us, and as far as anything brought to pass in reality is concerned, it is the motives that do the influencing, not the non-existent. Nor is it the non-existent that engenders motives. We develop our desires and aversions, according to conative intuitionism, either through actual enjoyment or dislike of the things we experience, or by being able to imagine well enough what an object or state of affairs would be like that the content of imagination is itself sufficient to engender in us the relevant conative experience. The metaphysical objection does, however, have a point to make. It is true that, in eschewing the strict naturalism of the moral skeptic, moral realism makes the world out to be irreducibly teleological. If any version of it is correct, then it is a matter of objective reality that some things are, considered only in prospect, to be preferred and sought after, and others to be disdained and avoided. We must remember, however, that all such claims are in the end contingent. The thesis that values are a matter of objective reality is neither necessary nor self-contradictory. It is hard to see therefore that any *a priori* argument, whether for or against the thesis, could succeed. What could there be, about our own nature or that of the world, that *entails* that the world is not teleological? Nothing, as far as I can see.

This brings us back to the matter of experience, and here everything is on the side of the moral realist—most especially if he endorses conative intuitionism. A plausible argument against moral realism must in the end be founded in the idea that actual experience does not in fact offer us any awareness of values that purport to be objective, or that if it does we can be sure such experience constitutes a wholesale deception. As for the first of these alternatives, I have been urging throughout this paper that the precise opposite is the case: rightly or wrongly we do in conative experience apprehend things as having objective value and disvalue. This leaves just one path to the skeptic: that of arguing that conative experience is a wholesale deception. Here I see two tactics that might be employed. The first is the Cartesian demon argument: that is, to maintain that since we cannot be sure our conative apprehensions lay hold of anything real in the world their apparent objectivity must be ignored, and their deliverances treated as mere subjective preferences.

I have already urged that such arguments are not to be taken seriously. We have, in the end, no way to discern the nature of the world except through our experience. Conative experience seems to be oriented toward discerning value in the world. If this is a wholesale illusion, will any independent experience inform us of that fact? I don't see how an appeal to cognitive experience would work unless it could be shown that cognitive experience is better suited than the conative to discerning matters of value if they were there. But I know of no plausible argument of this kind, and I think there is very good reason to think otherwise. Some may find it implausible to think of the world as a teleological place, but it is unquestionable that there are teleological beings in it, namely ourselves. We operate teleologically in a great deal of our conscious behavior, and the same may no doubt be said for animals of many other species. How plausible is it that there should be such beings in the world, that they should ever have evolved, if they were in their teleological dispositions marooned in the universe, if every goal they might select or pursue was only 'subjective'? To me, this is not plausible at all. How plausible, moreover, is it to suppose that whereas our cognitive faculties are attuned to something real in the world in their capacity for belief formation, our conative faculties are, in their capacity for framing objectives, attuned to nothing whatever? Again, to me this is not plausible at all—the more so inasmuch as the phenomenology of these faculties indicates precisely the opposite.

The other tactic the skeptic might employ to argue that conative intuition is of no objective value is to try to turn the faculty against itself, by pointing to the fact that we frequently disagree about values. It might be claimed that such disagreement is wholesale, that there is virtually nothing in the realm of value upon which all are agreed, and that this by itself is sufficient to undo the claims of any version of moral realism, intuitionist or not. Space does not permit complete treatment of this objection, so I shall have to content myself with three observations. First, if the acceptance of an objective reality required that we all agree on it, virtually none of our beliefs about the world, valuational or otherwise, would survive. The standard this argument sets is therefore far too high. A more reasonable standard would be that values, to be acceptable, should be substantially agreed upon by responsible people in a position to discern them. Second, we must remember that values supervene on the descriptive features of things. This means that to get our values right, we have to first get our facts straight. If we don't, factual disagreements are liable to masquerade as disputes about value. If I believe a particular exotic plant has wonderful curative properties, whereas you believe it to be poisonous, our evaluations of the plant may be expected to differ. But of course this disagreement does not tell against value realism, because it is at bottom a dispute about the descriptive features of the world, not its value features. If realism is to be opposed on the ground that people disagree about values, therefore, it must first be ascertained that the parties in question are in agreement about the relevant facts. Once this is done, I think the value realist has every reason to be optimistic about his position. For—and this is my final observation—how many subjects are there in a normal university curriculum that can usefully be taught by beginning with what the Greeks thought? Not very many. But ethics is one of them, which should not be so if the realm of values is located just this side of the border that separates us from chaos.

I would suggest, therefore, that a careful examination of the phenomenon of moral disagreement might well disclose that instead of there being very little agreement about values there is actually quite a preponderance of it—enough, in fact, to justify us in thinking of conative experience as a means of discerning value in everyday life, and therefore as an appropriate basis for developing a theory of value in ethics and related fields.[14]

CHAPTER THREE

MORAL FACTS AND THE CENTRALITY OF INTUITIONS

Christopher B. Kulp, Santa Clara University

1. THE GROUNDING OF METAETHICAL CLAIMS BY FIRST-ORDER MORAL TRUTHS

Walter Sinnott-Armstrong[1] tells us that, "Everyone who relies on moral intuitions—which is everyone—should welcome Robert Audi's masterpiece, *The Good in the Right.*" I concur fully with Sinnott-Armstrong, in particular with his point that *everyone relies on moral intuitions.* In fact it is this last point that I want to emphasize in my remarks here. Let me begin by making several claims. Specifically, I want to claim that I *know* the following:

P1 It is morally wrong for anyone to shoot me to death as I sit here writing this paper.

P2 Slavery, such as that practiced by the Confederate States prior to the American Civil War, is at least *prima facie* morally wrong.

P3 It is false that it is always morally impermissible to use physical force in defense against a violent attacker.

P4 A normative ethical theory is defective if, absent relevant differences, it sanctions inequivalent punishment of persons for equivalent moral offenses.

P5 Morality is such that there are normative moral truths.

What I am claiming knowledge of, then, is a range of moral truths. Regarding P1, I am claiming knowledge of a *first-order* moral truth about a moral prohibition having to do with a present situation, namely, the wrongness of shooting me to death as I write this paper. Regarding P2, I am claiming knowledge of a first-order moral truth about the *prima facie* wrongness of a social practice; regarding P3, knowledge of a first-order moral truth about the falsehood of a moral generalization; and regarding P4, knowledge of a first-order moral truth about the defensibility of a normative ethical theory relative to a specific entailment. In the case of P5, however, I am claiming knowledge of a *second-order* moral truth about the nature of morality: I am claiming to have knowledge of a *metaethical* truth.

The truth of these claims about first-order moral truths is parasitic on the truth of my second-order moral claim: if morality were such that there weren't any non-metaethical moral truths, there couldn't be any first-order moral truths to be known. My purpose now is to draw attention to what *grounds* my metaethical claim.

The ground of my metaethical claim is in fact my knowledge of first-order moral truths such as those just enumerated. But why think I know them? Well, I certainly believe them. Indeed, in the spirit of C. S. Peirce, I consider doubting many moral claims—such as it's wrong for anyone to shoot me dead right here and now as I write this paper!—to be mere 'paper doubt.'[2] And I mean this with the full pejorative connotations Peirce attributed to such doubting. In fact, I think that if anybody were to walk into my office and shoot me as I sit here writing, and that after the shooting someone (else) were to say, *seriously*, that he or she doubted that killing me was genuinely wrong, others would be appalled, morally scandalized. And if you ask yourself, as Mary Midgley[3] would urge, "what do you really think about this," I am confident you would say the same. Further, I would note that, in the spirit of G. E. Moore's comment that he knows the truth of many propositions the analysis of which he cannot provide,[4] my knowing these first-order moral truths does not require that I be able to provide a full articulation of their grounds. As an epistemic fallibilist, like Audi, I don't think I need to be able to provide a 'full articulation' of these grounds, if by that one means articulating grounds that logically guarantee the truth of my claims: knowledge doesn't require certainty. And as a modest epistemic foundationalist, also like Audi, I think that (i) some of the things I know, I know inferentially, others non-inferentially, and (ii) that knowing that p doesn't require *showing* that you know that p (that's the 'modest' part of my foundationalism).[5] Finally, being an intuitionist, again like Audi, I think that I know some first-order moral truths by *intuition*.

If I am right, then there are epistemic differences in my grounds for knowing first-order moral propositions P1–P4—for example, some I know inferentially, others non-inferentially—but my major concern here will be *the epistemic centrality of the role that moral intuition plays in the epistemic grounds of some of these knowledge claims.* Before addressing moral intuitions directly, however, I want to say a number of things about *what* is known when we know moral propositions of the sort I have been referring to.

2. THE MEANING OF 'FIRST-ORDER MORAL TRUTHS'

Let's first ask this question: What does it mean to say that there are moral truths? The answer depends on a number of things, importantly, on what one means by 'true'. And of course people have meant many things by this. What I mean, however, is captured most fundamentally by William Alston: any plausible conception of the nature (meaning, definition) of (propositional) truth must preserve what he calls the 'T-schema,' which is, "the proposition that p is true *iff p.*"[6] Thus, for example, the proposition 'The Matterhorn has snow on its summit' is true *iff* the Matterhorn has snow on its summit, and false otherwise. This conception of truth is, both by Alston's and my lights, a realist conception of truth, albeit a 'minimalist' conception. It is *realist* because what it means for p to be true is that p says the way of the world is, that p comports with the facts. It is *minimalist* because it doesn't specify the nature of the relation between proposition and world, a task that falls to a correspondence *theory* of truth. But as Alston cogently points out, "Anyone who sees that any instance of … [the T-schema] is analytically true has a firm grasp on the realist conception of truth."[7] Thus, if one sees that, *qua* instance of the T-schema, it is analytically true that the proposition 'There is snow on the summit of the Matterhorn' is true *iff* there is snow on the summit of the Matterhorn, then one sees, fundamentally, what realist truth is. Still, I want to go a bit further than Alston's minimalist account. Some recent work by John Searle is suggestive.[8]

Very briefly, on Searle's view we assess statements as true when we consider them trustworthy, that is, when we think that "the way they represent things as being *is the way that they really are.*"[9] Furthermore, "the criterion of reliability is given by disquotation."[10] Take an instance of (to use Alston's term) the T-schema, the one we have been using:

T1 'There is snow on the summit of the Matterhorn' is true *iff* there is snow on the summit of the Matterhorn.

The left-hand side of T1, 'There is snow on the summit of the Matterhorn,' is trustworthy just in case the right-hand side of T1, there is snow on the summit of the Matterhorn, is the case. If it is not the case that there is snow on the summit of the Matterhorn, then the proposition 'There is snow on the summit of the Matterhorn' is untrue, thus (ultimately) untrustworthy, and *mutatis mutandis* similarly for any instance of the T-schema. Searle urges that, "We need a meta-linguistic predicate for assessing success in achieving the word-to-world direction of fit, and that term is 'true.'"[11] 'True' as a predicate, moreover, is assigned to statements "in virtue of conditions in the world" that are "independent of the statement"; "we need general terms to name these how-things-are-in-the world, and 'fact' is one such term ... [another is] 'state of affairs.'"[12]

This is not, however, the place to get into a detailed discussion of truth. Suffice it to say that when I claim that '*p* is true' I am making a realist claim about the truth of *p* captured fundamentally by Alston's T-schema, but usefully elaborated by Searle's correspondence theory of truth, which explicitly appeals to the notion of extra-linguistic facts.

It will be convenient, given space constraints, to confine my remarks here to first-order moral claims. In short, then, the reason I think P1 is true (i.e. that it's true that it is morally wrong for anyone to shoot me as I'm writing this paper), and that the generalization referred to in P3' is *false* (i.e. that it is always morally impermissible to use physical force in defense against a violent attacker), is that I think that P1 *does* and P3' *does not* comply with the T-schema, and thus that P1 *does* and P3' *does not* say correctly the way world is in the relevant moral respect. That is to say, the proposition:

P1 "It is morally wrong for anyone to shoot me as I sit here writing this paper"

is true *iff* it is morally wrong for anyone to shoot me as I sit here writing this paper.

And similarly, the proposition:

P3' "It is always morally impermissible to use physical force in defense against a violent attacker," is true *iff* it is always morally impermissible to use physical force in defense against an attacker. But to cast the truth or falsity of these propositions in a more metaphysically robust way, I am saying that P1, being true, expresses a *fact*, the *moral* fact that shooting me is wrong, and that P3', being false, fails to express any such fact. P1 does, and P3' does not, then, express the way things are, morally speaking.

Clearly, what I am endorsing here is *moral cognitivism*: first-order moral locutions are propositional, hence true or false. I also mean to reject any form of *moral constructivism*—cultural, linguistic, conceptual, whatever—though space limitations do not permit me to defend this latter commitment, a major undertaking in itself. In short, I mean to endorse a version of *moral realism,* a metaethical view committed to 'unconstructed' first-order moral facts. But given that I am not here defending my realism against constructivism, I can claim no more than that if a cognitivist, non-constructivist morality is defensible—if moral realism is defensible—then this is what I think it should look like in outline. What, then, of moral facts?

3. SENSES OF 'FACT' AND MORAL TRUTHS

Facts in general, and moral facts in particular seem problematic to many, sufficiently so that they would just as soon do without them. One popular reason to eschew facts is Occam's razor-type concerns: Do we really need to posit a type of abstract entity, *facts*, to do the work done by the notion of a 'true statement'? Well, perhaps we don't *if* what is at issue is the necessity of positing facts as *sui generis.* But what seems clearer still is that the notion of a 'true statement' will not do the same work as facts. Searle seems on target when he argues that:

> Facts are not the same as true statements. There are several ways to demonstrate this. ... First it makes sense to speak of facts functioning causally in a way it does not make sense to speak of true statements functioning causally. [For example, says Searle, ' "The *fact* that Napoleon failed to perceive the danger to his left flank caused his defeat' makes good sense, whereas 'The *true statement* that Napoleon failed to perceive the danger to his left flank caused his defeat' either makes no sense at all or means something totally different."] Second, the relation of a fact to

a statement is one-many since the same fact may be stated by different statements. For example, the same fact is stated by "Cicero was an orator" and "Tully was an orator."[13]

Indeed, I am loath to jettison the notion of facts. And *apropos* of our concerns here, I am loath to jettison the notion of *moral* facts, because without them I see no way to account for moral discourse's ability to do what it certainly at times seems to do, namely, to express *how things are, morally speaking.*[14] Thus, for example, I think that the truth of P1 issues from its correctly expressing something about the moral status of someone's shooting me. But this is only to say, roughly, that the truth of P1 issues from P1's expressing, or referring to, or corresponding to the *fact* that it is morally wrong for anyone to shoot me as I sit here writing this paper. What, however, *are* these moral facts, anyway?

Let me first say a bit about facts in general, and on this I find some recent work by Ramon Lemos[15] quite suggestive. And let's start by drawing some distinctions regarding propositions, states of affairs, and facts. Let us understand propositions to be abstract entities, which are expressed by declarative sentence-tokens such as 'There is snow on the summit of the Matterhorn';[16] and let us understand a state of affairs to be, as Lemos puts it, "something's being, doing, or having something."[17] So understood, although propositions are either true or false, truth or falsity does not apply to states of affairs: they either obtain or do not obtain. Thus, while the proposition 'The Matterhorn has snow on its summit' is true or false (it's true: I've been there!), the *state of affairs* of the Matterhorn's having snow on its summit is, *qua* state of affairs, neither true nor false: it either obtains or fails to obtain.

What, then, of facts? There seem to be several different senses of the term 'fact'.[18]

Sense 1: Designates a state of affairs that obtains. For example, there being snow on the summit of the Matterhorn, which is a state of affairs that obtains, is a *fact*. (There being a Catholic Church on the summit of the Matterhorn, which is a state of affairs that does not obtain, is not a fact.)

Sense 2: Designates the obtaining of a state of affairs, as opposed to designating the state of affairs that either does or does not obtain. For example, the obtaining of the state of affairs of my moving my fingers as I write this, is a *fact*.[19]

Sense 3: Designates a true proposition. For example, '*p* is true' and '*p* is a *fact*' say the same thing.

Sense 4: Designates something (anything) that exists independently of (as Searle might put it) human or other intelligent representations. For example, the Matterhorn is a *fact*: no one's representation made the Matterhorn exist.

Now, not all of these senses of 'fact' seem equally useful for our purposes,[20] but I agree with Lemos that these distinctions plausibly point us in the direction of maintaining that the term 'fact' does not denote a unique, irreducible ontological category. Yet this isn't to say that the concept of a fact is otiose. As Lemos remarks, "If there are real entities, states of affairs that do or do not obtain, and true propositions, then there are also facts."[21] And of course I am convinced, as I think it quite likely you are, that there are real entities, that there are states of affairs that do or do not obtain, and that there are true propositions.

The sense of the term 'fact' that seems particularly relevant for us is *Sense 1*: a state of affairs that obtains. Thus, for example, the proposition, 'There is snow on the summit of the Matterhorn' is true in that it is a fact that there is snow on the summit of the Matterhorn, which in this sense of 'fact' is to say that the state of affairs of there being snow on the summit of the Matterhorn *obtains*. Or to take an example more germane to our purposes, P1 (it's morally wrong for anyone to shoot me as I'm writing this paper) is true in that it is a *fact*, in the sense of a moral state of affairs that *obtains*, that it is morally wrong for someone to shoot me. Similarly, but conversely, P3' (being morally impermissible to use physical force in defense against a violent attacker) is *false* because it is *not* a fact that to use physical violence in defense against an attacker is always morally impermissible, which is to say that, in terms of the sense of 'fact' under consideration, the moral state of affairs of its being morally impermissible to use physical force in defense against a violent attacker is not a state of affairs that obtains.

Still, this won't quite do: matters are considerably more complicated than this would suggest.[22] Some states of affairs obtain, such as the Matterhorn's having snow on its summit, and others do not, such as President Obama's being ten feet tall. And similarly, some *moral* states of affairs obtain, others don't. The state of affairs of its being wrong for the government of the People's Republic of China to persecute the Tibetans obtains, or at least so I would argue, but the state of affairs of its being morally wrong that all of the people in the United States have been murdered does not. The reason that this latter moral state of affairs doesn't obtain is quite simply that it is not the case that all of the people in the United States have been murdered. Were they murdered, the moral state of affairs would, alas, obtain. In a similar vein, some moral states of affairs obtained at one time but no longer do, such as the moral state of affairs of its being wrong of the Nazis to incarcerate Jews in Auschwitz-style concentration camps. And of course other states of affairs, moral and otherwise, will obtain in the future, but do not now obtain. How then, do first-order moral propositions like the ones I have referred to express a fact in the sense of 'fact' in question? Roughly, I think, as follows: take P1, 'It is morally wrong for anyone to shoot me as I write this paper.' Given that this state of affairs obtains—this situation of my sitting in my office writing this paper—the proposition just referred to expresses a fact, because someone shooting me as I sit here would instance moral impermissibility and/or some other cognate moral property. On the other hand, P3' ('It is always morally impermissible to use physical force in defense against a violent attacker'), does not express a fact, because it is not the case that there are no states of affairs that obtain (or *could* obtain) wherein physical force is used in defense against a violent attacker that instance moral permissibility.

I have been referring to a 'moral state of affairs': But what *is* a moral state of affairs? What is its status? Here we have to distinguish among types of moral claims.

As noted earlier, I understand a state of affairs to be "something's being, doing, or having something,"[23] and so I take a *moral* state of affairs-*type* to be the *kind* of "something's being, doing, or having something" such that *what* is had is a set of moral properties.[24] A moral state of affairs-type may or may not be instanced, depending on whether a corresponding moral state of affairs-*token* obtains. In contrast to other kinds of states of affairs—for example, *physical* states of affairs, such as the Matterhorn's having snow on its summit, which is a state of affairs such that the physical property 'snow on the summit' is attributable to the physical object 'the Matterhorn';

or *logical* states of affairs, such as a deductive argument's being valid, wherein the logical property of validity is attributable to an argument because it instances a valid argument form, like *modus ponens*—a *moral state of affairs* is a state of affairs such that a moral property is attributable to whatever it is that is (relevantly) capable of taking a moral property. Thus, for example, the property of moral goodness may be attributable to an act of generosity to a suitable recipient, and the property of moral wrongness may be attributable to a policy of enslavement of one people by another.[25]

Now, it is difficult to see how some kinds of states of affairs *per se* can have moral properties directly associated with them. It is difficult to see, for example, how either logical states of affairs or mathematical states of affairs can take moral properties. What would it be to say that the state of affairs of the number 3 being the cube root of 27 possesses, or has directly associated with it, a moral property like permissibility? Physical states of affairs, however, seem to be different. Of course some physical states of affairs don't have moral properties directly associated with them: the Matterhorn's having snow on its summit possesses no moral property *per se*. But some physical states of affairs do. The physical state of affairs of a person's being enslaved—being physically prevented, although relevantly innocent, from pursuing her own ends, etc.[26]—may have, I would say *does* have, associated with it the property of moral wrongness, or injustice, or cruelty, or what have you. But all this needs a bit of unpacking. What is the relationship between physical states of affairs and moral states of affairs?

To address this question, it seems quite likely that in a variety of ways the obtaining of physical states of affairs is *necessary* for the obtaining of moral states of affairs. It seems highly dubious that moral states of affairs could obtain were there *absolutely no* obtaining physical states of affairs —— no physical world, no moral world, which is to say, no morality (or at least so I would argue), though it is too much for me to dispute here radical non-physical conceptions of the world. Further, surely some specific moral states of affairs could not obtain unless corresponding physical states of affairs obtained. The moral state of affairs (-token) of its being wrong for Smith to burglarize Jones's house, for example, couldn't obtain unless Jones's house exists. Thus, the very possibility of this moral state of affairs obtaining is contingent upon the obtaining of a specific physical state of affairs (-token)—one that instances the house in question. Moreover, it seems that physical states of affairs of certain *kinds* are necessary if moral states of affairs are to obtain. A physical state of affairs such as the Matterhorn's having snow on its summit won't do, but a physical state of affairs such as that of one human being shooting an incapacitated, unconscious victim will. What makes the latter sort of state of affairs a suitable candidate is that it involves entities—in this case, human beings—that have moral standing, that is, entities which themselves can instance moral properties like goodness and badness, virtue and vice, or that can be treated in ways that instance such moral properties.

So it appears that at some level the obtaining of a physical state of affairs is necessary for the obtaining of a moral state of affairs. Are they, however, sufficient?

This is a vexed question. Of course they would be sufficient were moral properties identical with physical properties. Notice, however, that physical states of affairs obviously can, and I think must, instance more than merely physical properties. The physical state of affairs, for example, of three apples sitting on a table instances the numerical property of the cardinality of the set of apples, three, and also instances (three times over) the reflexive relational property of each apple being identical with itself. But cardinality and self-identity scarcely seem to be physical properties; so physical states of affairs are sufficient to instance non-physical properties. Well, what about moral properties? Obviously some physical states of affairs don't instance moral properties: the Matterhorn's having snow on its summit does not. But it certainly seems that some do: a man's being stabbed to death on the snowy summit of the Matterhorn appears to qualify. It is dubious, however, that the set of *physical* properties that are instanced would include any of the instanced moral properties. Indeed, it is not the 'physicality' of the stabbing of a man—a physical being acted on in a clearly physical way—that *per se* makes this a 'moral state of affairs.' Something different from physicality seems to be present in such states of affairs. Like the properties of cardinality and self-identity instanced here, any *moral* properties it instances seems to be additive. It seems, in fact, that moral properties are irreducible to physical properties, that they are different in kind. That moral properties can't just *be*, or be reducible *to* physical properties is suggested by an apparent contrast in our epistemic access to them. Physical properties, at least of the most epistemically basic kind, are commonly held to be known via the senses; it is much less clear that we know moral properties in a similar way. But whatever may be the plausibility of various moral sense theories, it is at least highly dubious that we acquire knowledge of moral properties via *the same* (five) senses that ground knowledge of physical properties. And this suggests that, given the anti-skeptical stance I adopt toward morality, moral properties are not to be identified with physical properties.

Still, that moral properties are in some sense related to physical properties seems clear. It is supported by the overwhelming plausibility of claims like the one I made above: were there no physical world, there would be no morality—no 'moral world.' It is also supported by the plausibility of broadly naturalistic theories of mind, theories to the effect that minds are causally related to brains. That minded beings are capable of instancing (perhaps necessarily) moral properties *in virtue of* their mindedness, which is in some sense a 'product' of their physical brain, surely suggests a connection between the physical and the moral.[27] Further, and put very roughly, the association of the physical and the moral is supported by our strong intuition that if two cases share relevant physical properties, then *ceteris paribus* they share relevant moral properties.[28]

But if the moral is neither reducible to nor disassociated from the physical, what sort of relation obtains between them? Along with many others, I think moral properties *supervene* on physical properties: physical properties constitute the *base* set of properties that is necessary and sufficient for the instantiation of supervening moral properties. Furthermore, I favor strong supervenience over weak supervenience: (roughly) a set of moral properties $\{M\}$ *weakly* supervenes on a set of physical properties $\{P\}$ where, if individuals A and B within the *same* possible world differ in their moral properties, they differ in their physical properties; while in *strong* supervenience, even if A and B are in *different* possible worlds, any difference in their moral properties entails a difference in their physical properties. Strong supervenience is preferable to weak supervenience because, among other things, it better captures the intuitions implicit in the case referred to at the end of the previous paragraph: if full specification of the relevant (non-relational) physical properties of two individuals results in isomorphic pairing of these properties, there would *ceteris paribus* be an isomorphic pairing of moral properties, if any, even if the two individuals were in different possible worlds.[29] But I cannot pursue this matter further now; and in any event, I don't want to press here for one type of supervenience over another, principally because for present purposes little hangs on it. Any plausible account of the supervenience of the moral on the physical puts us in the position to hold the broad thesis that moral states of affairs are relevantly associated with physical states of affairs, and that is all I wish to establish at this juncture.

My answer, then, to the question, What is the relationship between physical states of affairs and moral states of affairs?, is that moral states of affairs supervene on physical states of affairs, and consequently, obtain only if relevant physical states of affairs obtain. Furthermore, in some cases the obtaining of a physical state of affairs is *sufficient* for the obtaining of a moral state of affairs, 'sufficient' in the sense that when the physical state of affairs obtains, it necessitates the obtaining of supervening moral properties.

4. KNOWING MORAL TRUTHS NON-INFERENTIALLY

So much for my brief statement of my views on moral facts. Now for how all this bears on moral intuitionism.

I have claimed to know a number of first-order moral truths. I shall now argue that I, in common with almost everyone else, know many such moral truths by *moral intuition*, a view with which Audi certainly concurs and has convincingly argued for in a number of places, pre-eminently in *The Good in the Right*. It will be convenient to concentrate for the moment on my knowledge of P1.

A rough explication of what I know in knowing P1 is this: I know a (non-relativistic) moral truth, namely, that it is wrong for anyone to shoot me dead as I sit here writing this paper, the truth of which derives from its expressing a moral fact—understood to be a moral state of affairs that obtains—that it is wrong to shoot me, etc. This moral state of affairs supervenes on the physical state of affairs that obtains (at the time of the assertion of my knowledge claim). All of this I took pains to outline in sections II and III above. But of course there is another sense, a *non*-explicatory sense, in which my knowing P1 involves none of this. I just know that nobody should shoot me dead as I'm writing this paper! It is in this non-explicatory sense that I know P1 to be true by moral intuition. My knowledge seems to qualify as 'intuitive' according to Audi's criteria.[30] My knowledge is:

Non-Inferential: It is not evidentially based on a premise(s); it is not the result of inference.

Firmly believed: I believe it; I am quite confident it's true.

Comprehended: I understand it fully, or at least quite adequately.

Pre-theoretical: It is not evidentially dependent on a theory or itself a theoretical hypothesis.

Two of these criteria are certainly fulfilled: I am quite confident that I shouldn't be shot to death while sitting here writing this paper; and I am quite clear both on what it would mean to be shot to death while sitting here, and that it shouldn't happen. If I do not believe and understand P1, I believe or understand little if anything. The other two criteria, however, are more controversial.

As to non-inferentiality: note first that we can know the truth or falsity of many propositions on the basis of a variety of sources. Take, for example, the proposition that President Obama addressed an audience at a specific time and place. One might know the truth of this proposition based on direct perceptual experience: one might have been present for the address. Or one might know it based on, as it were, 'indirect' perception: one might have watched the event on live-feed television. Or, perhaps one might know it based on testimony: one may have been told of the address by a highly reliable person who was present for the event, or who watched it on live-feed television, or who was herself informed of its occurrence by a highly reliable eye-witness. It seems that some propositions, however, are knowable on only one basis. For example, perhaps my knowing the proposition that 'I am in pain *now*' admits of no basis other than my own occurrent pain experience. Perhaps no second party evidence or testimony would provide adequate or even relevant evidence for *my* claim to be in pain now. In any event, among those propositions that are knowable on more than one basis, it may be that one in fact knows them in multiple ways. I may have been present for the Obama address, and I may also have read about it in the newspaper. Either basis would be sufficient to possess knowledge. Similarly, it seems that I could know propositions like P1 in more than one way. Perhaps I know that shooting me is wrong because I inferred it from a moral principle I knew to be true—from, say, the second version of Kant's Categorical Imperative, or from a principle of utility. But knowing P1 inferentially does not mean one cannot also know it intuitively. It is simply clear and evident[31] to me that I shouldn't be shot here and now. I am aware of no inference, no occurrent passage in thought from one set of propositions to another.[32] There is no appeal to a grounding principle. The phenomenology of the process by which I arrive at my claim is that it is non-inferential, immediately present to the mind.[33] Yes, I can provide a detailed defense of my claim if called upon to do so, a defense that seems to me quite adequate to fulfill any reasonable evidential requirements for knowledge. But that is not to say that the wrongness of being shot here and now is not evident to me without appeal to inference. I *intuit* its wrongness.

The 'pre-theoreticality' criterion, however, presents a vexed issue that I cannot fully resolve here. There are a variety of perspectives on this matter—a range too extensive to deal with here—but it seems that some would think this criterion cannot be fulfilled in principle, on the grounds that no knowledge claim is 'theory independent,' and that anything with cognitive significance—anything propositional—is theory *de*pendent.[34] But because intuitions are reputed to be cognitively significant, they couldn't be pre-theoretical. I disagree with this, but recognize that my response may be considered question-begging by some potential critics.

Many philosophers believe that there is no meaning in isolation, that the meaningfulness of anything is dependent on the meaningfulness of something else. Thus, proposition *p* could only *be* a proposition in the context of its relationship to a set of other propositions {*q,r,s* ...} or some proper subset thereof. Some of these 'semantic holists' further hold that the term 'theory' should be understood to refer to whatever itself is meaningful, in the sense that *p* is meaningful only relative to the 'theory' comprised of {*q,r,s* ...} or some proper subset thereof. (Thus *q*, *r*, *s*, etc. would in turn be meaningful only relative to some set of propositions, which would perhaps include *p*.) But that is to say that whatever is propositional is theory dependent, hence not pre-theoretical. So the pre-theoreticality criterion for intuitions cannot be fulfilled.

Now, I agree with this as far as it goes. Nothing is meaningful in isolation; and in *this* sense of 'theory dependence,' nothing is pre-theoretical. If *x* is propositional, *x* is propositional in virtue of its situatedness in the context of other propositions. However, the meaning of the term 'theory' I have in mind implies something quite a bit more grand than mere bare-bones propositionality. It is difficult to specify the criteria that must be met to qualify as a theory in a specific domain, much less the criteria for theoryhood *tout court*, and I will not try. What I mean by 'theory,' however, is what seems a much more natural, common-sense reading of the term than that discussed in the preceding paragraph. It is well illustrated by paradigm cases: Einstein's General Theory of Relativity, Russell's Theory of Types, Rawls's Theory of Distributive Justice, and Kant's deontological ethics are clear examples. All of these theories are complexly structured sets of propositions that are (more or less) internally consistent, coherent with other theories, possess explanatory force, are testable in some fashion or other,[35] and are clearly intended to entail truths. If one were to say to a physicist, "Here is my physical theory," and what one presented lacked structure, had no explanatory force, and entailed no relevant truths—well, one can easily imagine the physicist's response. The ethicist would say similar things about any such purported 'ethical theory.' Note too that there is a difference between a set of propositions being a *bad* theory and its not being a theory at all. There are certain minimal conditions that must be fulfilled to qualify as a theory: mere 'meaningfulness' or 'propositionality' is not sufficient. This generally understood sense of 'theory,' then, is what I have in mind when I defend both the pre-theoreticality criterion's possibility of fulfillment, and that it is *in fact* fulfilled regarding my knowledge of P1. So far as I can tell, my knowing P1 does not depend evidentially on appeal to any theory in my sense of 'theory.' It is simply evident to me, without conscious inference, that I shouldn't be shot. True, I can provide elaborate moral reasons why I should not be shot; but that would be inferential and 'theoretical,' and is not what is going on here.

Note further how probable it is that I would have known that P1 is true long before I ever heard of Kant or utilitarianism or of 'normative ethical theory.' Any normal child old enough to comprehend P1 would almost surely see that it is true. We would be worried if the child didn't. Of course I, like virtually everyone else, have possessed 'moral values,' however minimally codified and falling however short of being a theory in my sense of 'theory,' since early childhood. And of course it is only in the context of the possession of such moral values that I or anyone else would see that shooting me was wrong. But still, I would have known it was wrong long before I had in hand a 'moral theory.' My knowledge of P1, then, is pre-theoretical.

In sum, I find that my knowing P1 fulfills Audi's criteria for intuitive knowledge. I now add that (i) I am confident that I know by intuition an indefinitely large number of other first-order moral truths like P1: P1 is hardly epistemically unique for me in any way;[36] and (ii) I haven't the slightest reason to suppose that my case is different from that of an indefinitely large number of other people: my case is perfectly epistemically typical. Consequently, *intuitive moral knowledge is ubiquitous.* I now want to argue that moral intuitions are of special epistemic importance.

First, observe that it seems that some moral intuitions have as their objects *particular* moral facts, others *general* moral facts such as moral principles or moral generalizations. I have already argued at length that I have intuitive knowledge of P1, which expresses a particular moral fact about a concrete, presently obtaining state of affairs. I also believe that I know by intuition the truth of moral principles such as, 'like moral cases should be treated alike,' and moral generalizations such as that expressed by the denial of P3', that physical force used in defense against a violent attacker is at sometimes morally permissible. Both of these instances of knowing seem to fulfill Audi's criteria. So it certainly appears that both general and particular moral facts can be known intuitively.

Now two further claims: First, moral intuitions are 'epistemically central' in the sense that they provide a necessary component in a modest epistemic foundationalism as it applies to moral justification and knowledge. Second, the most epistemically central of moral intuitions are intuitions which have particular moral facts as their objects. I'll take each of these claims in turn.

I began this paper by quoting with approval Sinnott-Armstrong's comment that "everyone relies on moral intuitions ... ." I really see no plausible way to proceed with broad-gauged normative ethical reasoning without appeal to moral intuitions. Indeed, many who have qualms about the efficacy of moral intuitions nonetheless see them as unavoidable.[37] It is nothing new to point out that one of the ways we test a normative theory is to see how its entailments square with our moral intuitions. Nor is it new to note that we are wrong to think our moral intuitions either indefeasible or beyond the reach of moral theory. I assume we all have come to reject once-held moral intuitions; I assume that in many cases this is because of the implications of moral theories which we come to view as more plausible than the moral intuitions. Still, some intuitions asymptotically approach indefeasibility. For example, although in principle I can conjure up first-order moral reasons to believe that P1 is false, it seems about as likely that I am deceived regarding P1's truth as Moore and I are about these being hands before our eyes. Possible, yes, but really ... the indefeasibility of belief in the *falsehood* of P3' seems at least as likely. Assuming the propositionality of first-order moral discourse, if I am wrong about the truth of P1, and wrong about the falsehood of P3', I can only say that I am in such a muddle about what is morally true and what false that I understand nothing. The truth or the falsity of many other first-order moral propositions is, of course, much less clear. Obviously there is a broad range of degree of justification of our first-order moral beliefs, with those such as I have been discussing constituting one pole. Some are exceedingly strongly justified, and if non-inferential, qualify as foundationally justified beliefs. I have argued that moral intuitions are non-inferential, and that some are exceedingly strongly justified. I therefore regard some moral intuitions as foundationally justified beliefs.[38] This is in turn to argue that intuitions can serve as a component in foundationalism regarding the justification of first-order moral beliefs. And because (i) justified intuitions are in principle defeasible, and because (ii) I see no reason to rule out moral intuitions receiving further support from normative theories, the type of foundationalism I am endorsing is of a *modest* variety—the only type that, in view of the tribulations of broadly Cartesian (i.e., strong) foundationalisms, has any chance of survival. So this is one sense in which moral intuitions are 'epistemically central': they are, or can be, *morally foundational*.

Here is another: As I noted several paragraphs above, moral intuitions can serve to test the credibility of normative ethical theories. If a normative theory—Kantian deontology or rule-utilitarianism, say—runs afoul of our moral intuitions, that is *prima facie* ground to re-examine the theory. In some cases, disagreement with our intuitions, such as those I have discussed regarding P1 and P3, would be sufficient ground to reject the theory. What normative ethical theory could stand if it entailed that it was absolutely *never* morally permissible to defend yourself against even the most egregious physical attack? Or that it is morally permissible to just up and shoot somebody? What I think we in fact look for is a kind of *reflective equilibrium* between theory and intuition. Still, intuitions can wield extraordinary epistemic weight: more so, in many cases, than can any normative theory. Thus, moral intuitions are indeed epistemically central as regards guidance of first-order moral deliberation.

But more than that, moral intuitions are, or ought to be, epistemically central in terms of even ethical meta-theory, at least in this sense: It is largely because of the overwhelming cogence of intuitions such as those I have about propositions like P1 and P3 that I endorse, and have developed and defended, a cognitivist, realist metaethics. Surely I am not alone in this motivation. That the moral wrongness of shooting me dead as I sit here, or the falsehood of the universal moral impermissibility of defending oneself against violent attack, is merely, or fundamentally, a function of the a relevant pro or negative-attitude seems preposterous. Such non-cognitivisms are to be accepted only if there are no viable alternatives. I have sketched such an alternative. Moral intuitions, then, are rightfully epistemically central in the determination of one's metaethical views.

Lastly, I want to urge that the most epistemically central of all types of moral intuitions are those we have of *particular* first-order moral facts. First, I suspect that our intuitive knowledge of propositions such as, say, P1, is epistemically prior to our intuitive knowledge of propositions such as P3, a moral generalization. Restricting the discussion to intuitions *per se*, it seems quite likely that we would need to intuit the permissibility of a specific person, or limited set of persons, using physical force in defense against a violent attacker, perhaps in a specific situation, before we could intuit the falsehood of the generalization that it is *always* morally impermissible to use physical force in defense against a violent attacker. Knowledge of the particular moral fact would seem to underlie knowledge of the general moral fact, if not occurrently, at least dispositionally. That is to say, knowledge of the particular would seem to be a necessary part of the 'epistemic background' requisite to have knowledge of the moral generalization. Similarly with knowledge of moral principles. This isn't to say that intuitive knowledge of particulars is *absolutely* epistemically prior to intuitive knowledge of moral generalizations or principles. For there indeed seem to be cases wherein knowledge of moral generalizations and/or principles is part of the requisite epistemic background requisite to intuit particular moral truths. For example, perhaps knowledge, intuitive or otherwise, about the fundamental moral equality of persons is part of the necessary epistemic background for a particular woman S to intuit that *she* should be treated equally to other persons. But I suspect that these cases are not the norm. For the most part, intuitions of particular moral facts are epistemically prior. And second, note that that it is plausible to think that a child may possess intuitive moral knowledge that, say, she should not be hurt when she's done nothing wrong, but may not possess intuitive moral knowledge that this applies across the board, that the generalization to others is likewise true. Perhaps she would not possess this general moral knowledge even under appropriate Socratic questioning. But this again suggests the usual epistemic priority, that is to say, the *centrality,* of particular mortal intuitions.

5. CONCLUSION

I have based my case for the epistemic centrality of intuitive moral knowledge on a defense of a cognitivist, realist metaethics. My defense of moral realism is, in turn, 'bottom up,' based on the overwhelming cogence of the truth or falsity of first-order moral claims. And this 'overwhelming cogence' derives from the fact that we *know* many first-order moral claims to be true and others to be false. But because propositional knowledge requires truth, commitment to first-order moral knowledge commits us to a cognitivist metaethics. I have sketched here a version of moral realism, along with the conceptions of truth and facts in which it is couched. I have argued that we all possess moral knowledge, including *intuitive* moral knowledge, the latter being 'epistemically central' in terms of normative theory construction and testing, in terms of developing a modest moral foundationalism, and in terms even of developing a metaethics. Any version of moral non-cognitivism is, to say the least, unconvincing. Moral intuitions make this clear.[39]

PART II: THE NEW INTUITIONISM AND ADVANCES IN MORAL EPISTEMOLOGY

CHAPTER FOUR

INTUITIONISM AND PERCEPTUAL REPRESENTATION

Ralph Kennedy, Wake Forest University

1. INTRODUCTION

In a recent book Robert Audi cites as one reason for a renewed interest in intuitionism that "a half-century's responses to W. V. Quine's attack on the *a priori*, and indeed on the power of reason to reveal significant truths, have restored in many philosophers a certain sense of epistemological freedom."[1] As a second reason he mentions that "we have recovered from the attack on the possibility of non-inferential knowledge, something that intuitionism in any major form, whether rationalist or empiricist, is committed to positing for certain moral propositions."[2] I will be focusing on this second reason—our no longer being overly impressed by the attack on the possibility of non-inferential knowledge—but in the context of perceptual rather than moral knowledge. Although I am not skeptical about the possibility of non-inferential knowledge, I argue that Audi's own brand of intuitionism, may not adequately address what Peter Markie has usefully dubbed "the mystery of direct perceptual justification."[3]

Consider the belief that a hand is in front of one's face. Audi would maintain that if this belief is based on an apparently normal visual experience of a sort that seems to show that a hand is in front of one's face, then it is normally justified.[4] The experience (normally) gives rise to justification; the justification is intuitive, or direct.

Although I begin by talking of perceptual *justification*, my primary concern will be with perceptual *representation*: what *is* it for a visual experience to seem to show a hand in front of one's face, and how does it do this? I consider what Audi's treatment of non-inferential or intuitive justification appears to entail regarding the representationality of visual experience and I compare that with Ernest Sosa's very different account, arguing that neither approach is without its difficulties. Two key questions posed by Laurence BonJour will help frame much of the discussion.

2. PERCEPTION, JUSTIFICATION, REPRESENTATION

Jack Lyons has argued recently that perceptual beliefs need not be experientially grounded: even zombies could have them.[5] Perhaps this intriguing possibility is actually correct, but I shall take as given for the purposes of this paper both that perception is required for perceptual beliefs and that perception is experiential. As Audi says, "There is something it is *like* [emphasis in original] to see a maple tree ... and here 'like' has its phenomenal, not its comparative, sense."[6] Assume, then, that a being with perceptual beliefs must have perceptual experiences. If one's belief that there is a tree before one is a perceptual belief, it must be at least somehow connected with one's perceptual experiences. Even if zombies had *some* beliefs, they would have no *perceptual* beliefs.

If perceptual beliefs are experientially grounded, one may ask regarding a given sort of perceptual belief what sort of perceptual experience would serve to ground it. Audi's 'visual experience principle' gives at least a partial answer:

> ... when, on the basis of an apparently normal visual experience (such as the sort we have in seeing a bird nearby), one believes something of the kind the experience seems to show (for instance that the bird is blue), normally this belief is justified.[7]

The fact that one's believing that the bird is blue is based (appropriately) on an apparently normal visual experience of the sort we have in seeing a bird nearby generally suffices to justify one's belief that there is a bird there and that it is blue. There is no need to infer that a blue bird is present from premises about the character of one's visual experience.

Audi maintains also that principles like the visual experience principle are *a priori*:

> We cannot know that, in every possible world, conformity with the principles conduces to forming true beliefs; but we can know *a priori* that in any possible world they generate *prima facie*) justified beliefs. For the concept of justified belief is in part constituted by the very principles that license our appeal to these elements.[8]

James Pryor endorses a similar principle:

> An experience as of there being hands seems to justify one in believing that there are hands in a perfectly straightforward and immediate way ... the mere fact that one has a visual experience of that phenomenological sort is enough to make it reasonable for one to believe that there are hands. No *premises* [emphasis in original] about the character of one's experience—or any other sophisticated assumptions—seem to be needed.[9]

Audi and Pryor follow a common practice in characterizing visual experiences in terms of the physical objects whose presence they appear to indicate or reveal. The 'as of' employed by Pryor in the above quote and by Audi and others elsewhere is an economical device for doing this. A visual experience as of an F is an experience in which, as Brentano might have said, an F is intentionally inexistent; it's a visual seeming that an F is present, a visual experience in which an F is—as it were—presented. I say 'as it were' to accommodate the possibility that no F is actually present. An experience *as of* an F may be an experience *of* an F, but—of course—it need not be.[10]

It's at least easier to describe experiences in this way—in terms of the physical objects they appear to reveal—than to describe them directly in terms of their intrinsic features. Perhaps, as Gilbert Harman says, it's the only possible way to describe one's perceptual experience: "Look at a tree and try to turn your attention to intrinsic features of your visual experience. I predict you will find that the only features there to turn your attention to will be features of the presented tree."[11]

Harman's view would provide an answer to two questions Laurence BonJour asks, namely, what is the significance of our characterizing experiences in physical-object terms, and what accounts for the seeming appropriateness of these characterizations?[12] To the first question a good Harmanian answer might be: our characterizing experiences in this way signifies nothing other than a lack of any alternative way of doing so. And if, as Harman says, when we try to attend to the intrinsic features of a visual experience we find *no* features to attend to except features of the presented object, then why should we not find the description of the experience in terms of the features of the presented object perfectly appropriate?

But is it true that when we attend to the intrinsic features of a visual experience we never find anything to attend to other than features of the presented object? It seems at least coherent to suppose that perceptual experiences may have, as Laurence BonJour has suggested, a sensory, non-conceptual core.[13] Such a core might contribute towards determining what the experience 'says' or presents. The view that there is or could be such a core is not without problems, but for present purposes I propose mainly to ignore them. I'd like to consider, on the supposition that there is such a core, how one might go about addressing BonJour's questions.

Let us suppose then that a certain sort of visual experience has intrinsic non-conceptual sensory features which somehow make descriptions of it in terms of a particular sort of physical object 'appropriate'. These features, we might say, contribute to its being apt for presenting, e.g. a sphere as before one—hence the appropriateness of describing the experience in terms of a sphere. BonJour asks how these features do this trick. What is it about the intrinsic sensory features of a visual experience as of a sphere that makes it an experience as of a sphere as opposed, say, to one as of a pyramid, cube, or barbell? This is not a question that can arise for Harman or like-minded thinkers. It may arise for Audi and indicate a difficulty with his approach. So BonJour appears to believe. Audi's 'epistemic realism' is the view that "it is implicit in our concept of a real empirical object that it can impinge on our senses, that, under certain conditions, it tends to affect our senses, and that it is the sort of thing which best explains our spontaneous perceptual experiences."[14] Of Audi's development of this view BonJour writes that it "seems to suggest that there is after all no further reason or explanation as to why the object-experience correlation takes the specific form that it does."[15]

Are BonJour's questions legitimate? They may appear to presuppose that a visual experience has intrinsic qualitative properties such that given those properties alone it is apt for revealing whatever it does reveal, or counts as being 'as of' such and such a kind of thing. In general this is implausible. A sort (as characterized in terms of intrinsic, qualitative properties) of visual experience apt for revealing to human beings with normal color vision the presence of something white might be apt for revealing to some other sort of creature the presence of something green.[16] But although the general claim is implausible, some related restricted claims appear less so. Consider shape, for instance. It seems plausible that the intrinsic sensory character of a visual experience as of a sphere would make that experience *more* apt for revealing the presence of a sphere than the presence of a tetrahedron.

Part of what Pryor claimed was that an epistemic agent needn't reason from premises about the character of her experience in order for her belief to be reasonable. Her mere *having* the experience is enough. But it seems that something more *is* needed, namely that the belief be based on the experience. This suggests a worry well-expressed by Donald Davidson as to whether there is any justifying sense in which a belief could be based on a perceptual experience, or anyway on a 'sensation':

> The relation between a sensation and a belief cannot be logical, since sensations are not beliefs or other propositional attitudes. What then is the relation? The answer is, I think, obvious: the relation is causal. Sensations cause some beliefs and in this sense are the basis or ground of those beliefs. But a causal explanation of a belief does not show how or why the belief is justified.[17]

Davidson here locates the obstacle to there being a logical relation between a sensation and a belief in the *sensation*: sensations are not items of a sort that can stand in logical relations to anything. Something needs to be said about how sensations or perceptual experiences can serve, non-inferentially, as genuine bases or grounds of perceptual belief. There are many actual and possible accounts. We turn to Ernest Sosa's.

3. SOSA ON BELIEF AND VISUAL EXPERIENCE

Sosa takes it that a visual experience can be a reason to believe that an object of such and such a description is present. But his view is markedly different from Audi's or Pryor's. He writes:

... visual *experience as if there is something white and round before one* is a reason for believing that there is such a thing there before one, but only because in the actual world such a visual experience is reliably related to there being such a thing there: that is to say, what is required is that in the actual world such a visual experience *would* in normal conditions reveal the presence of such a thing before the perceiver. Most naturally one would want the state of the perceiver describable as "visual experience as if there is something white and round before him" to be necessarily such that it *would* normally reveal the presence of such a thing before the perceiver. Otherwise that same state would not be properly describable as such an experience. [Emphases in original.][18]

Like Audi and Pryor, Sosa characterizes the visual experience in a way that is non-committal as to the experience's actually being of a physical object of the sort mentioned in the characterization. One difference (from Audi at least) is that Sosa builds an externalist, reliabilist condition into the very conception of what it is to be a visual experience of the given sort. According to Sosa an experience is as if there is something white and round before one only if the occurrence of an experience of that sort would normally (in the actual world) reveal the presence of something white and round before one. For Audi, by contrast, it's not built into the very conception of what it is for a visual experience to be as of a white round thing that occurrences of experiences of that type are reliably correlated with the presence of white round things.[19]

Sosa's approach provides a straightforward response to one of BonJour's questions. BonJour wrote "it seems ... important to ask just what the significance of these characterizations of experience in physical-object terms really is and what it is about the experience that makes them seem so obviously appropriate."[20] Since on Sosa's approach it is essential to an experience as if an F were present that experiences of that sort be reliably correlated (in the actual world, normally) with the presence of Fs, we have the basis of an answer to the first of BonJour's questions. Whether we have, in Sosa's approach, an adequate response to the second—what it is about the experiences that makes the physical-object characterizations of them so 'obviously appropriate'—is less clear, as will appear.

For Sosa, it is *only* in virtue of a reliable connection holding between the occurrence of experiences of a certain kind and the presence of objects of a certain kind that the experiences make it reasonable to believe that such objects are present. This is particularly evident in Sosa's characterization of an alternative to his sort of view:

> Alternatively one might suppose that there is a state with an intrinsic mental character whose intrinsic mental character makes it properly characterizable as a state of experiencing thus (as a state of experiencing a white, round item, or the like), and this with logical independence of any modal relation that such a state, with such an intrinsic character, may bear to the presence or absence of white and round items.[21]

This alternative is like Audi's own view in its internalism: what earns a state a description as a state of experiencing in such and such a way is independent of any relations states of its sort (states with the same intrinsic mental character) bear to the presence or absence of any given sort of physical objects. For just this reason, Sosa says, the view runs into difficulties:

> The problem for this view will be to explain how such states could possibly give a reason to believe that there is something white and round before one. It may be held that *it just does* [emphasis in original]. And now one will face the following prospect: the need for a boundless set of principles each with fundamental status, connecting various intrinsically characterized mental states with paired external facts of specific sorts.[22]

Has Sosa identified a serious problem for Audi-style accounts of these matters? Certainly Audi is committed to the view that when one believes, on the basis of an apparently normal visual experience, something that the experience seems to show, one's belief is normally justified. This is essentially his visual experience principle. Sosa is not, of course, saying that the principle is false. He is suggesting rather that it may be, for the internalist, inexplicable, or—what may come to the same—explicable only by reference to a 'boundless' set of fundamental principles. Sosa's thought appears to be that since on the view under discussion there need be no reliable relation that occurrences of a given sort of experience bear to the presence of, say, round and white objects, there is simply no possible explanation (on that sort of view) of how such an experience can be a reason to think a white round object is present. In each case the fact that a given sort of visual experience gives a reason to think that an object of such and such description is present would simply be a brute fact. ('It just does.') If indeed all these facts were in this way brute there would be some justice to the claim that one would be faced with the need for a boundless set of fundamental principles. Each pairing would come under its own 'principle,' which, being applicable only to one case, would be a principle in name only.

It is not clear, however, why all the relevant facts would have to be brute. Sosa is in effect simply assuming that the only possible explanation of how visual experiences can provide (or be) reasons to believe that an object of such and such description is present must be given in terms of reliable connections between the occurrences of visual experiences of a certain character and the presence of objects of a certain description. If this is true, then Audi-style views may be in trouble. Further, what Sosa says here is not implausible. How else would a visual experience come to have this 'authority' about how things are?

One might say in defense of an Audi-style approach that only a relatively few fundamental principles would be needed, of which the visual experience principle might be a typical example: when you believe that p on the basis of an apparently normal visual experience that seems to show that p, your belief is normally justified.

I don't find this defense entirely convincing. We may get down nominally to just a few principles in this way, but something could still be amiss. Might it not be that every fact of the form *such and such a sort of visual experience seems to show that p* is brute? For Sosa, clearly not, but I do not see that Audi has said anything that would rule this out.

4. AUDI AND THE SELLARSIAN DILEMMA

Wilfrid Sellars is often taken to have argued against the possibility of beliefs being supported solely by perceptual experience by posing roughly the following dilemma. First horn: if a perceptual experience is non-conceptual it will not suffice to justify any belief because it won't stand in any particular logical relation to the content of any belief. Second horn: if a perceptual experience is conceptual it will itself require justification, and will therefore again not by itself suffice to justify the belief.[23]

'Seeing as' is conceptual, so the second horn should apply. Audi once wrote of "seeing a green arrow as such" that it

> ... may require conceptualizing what one experiences in terms of the concept of an arrow. It does not follow that the grounding visual *experience* [emphasis in original] needs or even admits of justification, and neither seems to be the case. The conceptual, as opposed to the doxastic (the belief-constituted) need not admit of justification.[24]

Audi is not alone in holding that perceptual experiences neither need nor admit of justification. Some go further. For instance, Michael Huemer writes: "It does not make sense—it is a category error to say—that an experience is justified or unjustified."[25] This is a plausible view. Can we make sense of the idea that seeing a green arrow as a green arrow is justified—or unjustified?

If seeing a green arrow as a green arrow required *believing* there to be an arrow present or believing there to be a green arrow present, etc., that would be a different story. But does it? Isn't it possible for a person looking at a green arrow to see it as a green arrow and yet not believe that there is a green arrow present?

If seeing a green arrow as a green arrow does not require believing there to be a green arrow present, then it is unclear how this seeing-as could require epistemic justification. It seems then that there is reason to doubt (at least on Audi's reading of it) the truth of the second horn of the Sellarsian dilemma, which says: if a perceptual experience is 'conceptual' it will itself require justification, and will therefore not by itself suffice to justify the belief.

However that may be, Audi does see a role for the non-conceptual in the justification of belief, so it looks as if he must attend to the first horn of the dilemma as well. A non-conceptual experience won't stand in any 'logical' relation to any belief-content; how then can it play a justificatory role in relation to a belief?

Audi's answer goes something like this. Suppose you say that it is foggy. When asked (say, over the phone) how you know this, you say "I *see* dense fog." In making this claim you express, Audi claims, "a belief whose content is 'conceptualized'."[26] He continues:

> But that the *expression* or indication of one's ground is conceptual does not necessarily mean that one's ground itself is. Citing a

ground in this justificatory way is intrinsically conceptual. Citing it in this way, however, constitutes giving it as a *reason* in defense of the claim being supported or explained; the reason, though it indicates the source of one's ground (vision), is not itself that ground (visual experience). The *fact* that I see it is my reason— and a good one—because it identifies my ground. [Emphases in original.][27]

For Audi, the non-conceptual experience serves as a ground, not a reason. The reason (the fact that I do see a dense fog) "identifies" that ground and in turn justifies the belief that it is foggy. But what exactly is the role of the non-conceptual experience? What role does its being 'identified' by the fact that I see a dense fog play? Is the suggestion that the fact that I see a dense fog is a good reason for my belief insofar as it 'identifies' the grounding non-conceptual experience? But this seems quite mysterious. What is it to 'identify' the grounding experience, and how does such identification contribute to making the fact that I see a dense fog a good reason for my belief?

Audi may have good answers to these questions. I confess to some uncertainty as to what his argument here actually is. But for my part I cannot see that he has made much headway against the non-conceptual horn of the dilemma. The epistemic role presumably played by non-conceptualized experience continues to mystify. Perhaps the following will help:

> ... an experience may have *qualities*, such as the visual sense of the dense grey of fog, that—quite apart from whether they are believed to belong to it—*can* stand in 'logical' relations to the content of the proposition believed [emphases in original]. The phenomenal property of my having a visual impression of grey is in a certain way appropriate to the property of being grey: the internal instantiation of the former is at least arguably best explained by causation by the external instantiation of the latter.[28]

Thus, even if I do not experience the dense grey of the fog *as such*—even if I do not conceptualize my experience as being as of a dense grey something—nevertheless the experience itself may have properties that stand in 'logical' relations to, for instance, the property *dense grey*, a content of the proposition believed.

But can we make sense of a non-conceptual experience having properties that stand in logical relations to contents of the believed proposition in the required way?

A naïve thinker might be tempted by the notion that his visual experience was itself a dense grey in color just as is the fog he believes to surround him. If this were correct, a quality of the experience *would* stand in a 'logical' relation—identity—to a content of the proposition believed: *dense grey* would be both a property of the experience and a content of the believed proposition. But even on this naïve view it is hard to see what reason there would be to think that the internal instantiation of the property (the experience's being grey—whatever that might mean) would be best explained as an effect of its external instantiation (the fog's being grey).

Of course, Audi does not think of the visual experience as being literally grey. He does not take experiences to be concrete objects. In his theory of perception the *concrete* objects are just the perceiver and the thing perceived.[29] The thing that does the internal instantiating is the perceiver. The internal, phenomenal, property that is said by Audi to be appropriate to the grey of the fog is the property of the perceiver's having a visual impression of grey, which may be understood adverbially as perceiving in a certain way. But we are still left in the dark. In what way is my having a visual impression of grey particularly appropriate to or best explained in terms of the external instantiation of the property grey in the fog that surrounds me?

For Sosa, having a visual impression of grey is necessarily such that one's instantiations of it are, in the actual world, normally reliably connected with instantiations of grey in one's immediate vicinity: nothing would count as being a visual impression of grey if it were not so connected with such environmental conditions. Is this enough to show that having a visual impression of grey is best explained in terms of grey's being instantiated in one's immediate vicinity? Moliere's doctor might have thought so, but we know better. This is not a criticism of Sosa, who is not committed to the possibility of such explanations. But Audi does seem to be so committed, and it's even less clear on his internalist view how having a visual impression of grey could be explained in terms of the instantiation of grey in one's immediate vicinity.

Could this be an empirical question, unsuited for investigation from the armchair? It depends on how one thinks about the properties involved. If with Sosa we think of a property like my having a visual impression of grey as being *necessarily* such that its instantiations are, in the actual world, normally reliably connected with instantiations of grey in my immediate vicinity, then the question may not be empirical. If the necessary connections aren't there, how could the property be the property of my having a visual impression of grey? Perhaps in Audi's way of thinking about such phenomenal properties the question is empirical. I think we cannot tell until we know more about how Audi thinks of such properties than he has told us so far. For now we're in no position to say more than that Audi's best-explanation claim *could* be true. We cannot say how it could be true, or what it's being true would amount to.

5. AUDI VS. SOSA

Earlier I attributed to Sosa the assumption that the only possible explanation of how visual experiences with such and such a character can provide or be reasons to believe that an object of such and such description is present must be one in terms of reliable modal relations in the actual world between occurrences of visual experiences of a certain character and the presence of objects of a certain description. Audi's response to the non-conceptual horn of the Sellarsian dilemma, if successful, would by being a counter-example, show Sosa's assumption to be false. But although Audi's best-explanation claim, like Sosa's assumption, *could* turn out to be true, we are not in a position to see that it is true or how it could be true. Have we then reached an impasse?

Sosa may not have succeeded in showing that an Audi-style approach to perceptual justification is defective. He has, however, presented a straightforward alternative account in terms of reliability of what it is for a visual experience to be as if, for example, something white and round were before one. Further, Sosa's account includes an explanation of why it is that such a visual experience can provide a reason for believing that something white and round was before one. Sosa's account is elegant, comprehensive, relatively simple, and seems to leave little unexplained. Should we think on balance that it is superior to Audi's? There are two reasons one might think so. First, Audi appears to have little to say of a systematic nature about what it is for a visual experience to be as of such and such. And the second is the obscurity of what Audi does have to say about why it is that a visual experience, e.g. as of something white and round before one, provides a reason for believing that something white and round is present.

How damaging to Audi's position are these two points? I'll begin with the second. I think it's tantamount to the complaint that Audi presents no convincing argument for the visual experience principle beyond a possibly ill-considered feint in the direction of inference to the best explanation. This is true, but note that the principle's being non-inferentially justifiable would certainly comport well with the intuitionist epistemology Audi advocates. It could be that belief of the principle based on an adequate understanding of what it says is simply—non-inferentially—*prima facie* justified.

The first point may present a greater difficulty. Audi does not appear to have much to say of a systematic nature about what it is for a visual experience to be as of such and such, or what it is for a visual experience to 'seem to show' that *p*. Some remarks of Audi's in a reply to a paper by BonJour seem rather to illustrate the difficulty than to point the way to a solution. Audi writes:

> But I am not committed to holding that the kinds of arboreal experiences we normally have are only contingently related to the *concept* of a tree ... it is essential to the concept of a tree that trees have, for example, branches, and it is essential to an arboreal visual experience—one *as of* a tree (a non-committal expression I use to cover both veridical and non-veridical experiences)—that it exhibit, for example, branches.[30] [Emphasis in the original.]

Thus, on Audi's view, it's essential to an 'arboreal' visual experience—one as of a tree—that it 'exhibit branches,' and hence normal arboreal experiences are not merely contingently related to the concept of a tree: since the concept of a tree is among other things the concept of a thing with branches, a visual experience as of a tree *must* 'exhibit branches.' But this thought is helpful to one puzzled about what it is for an experience to be as of a tree, or 'arboreal,' only to the extent that it is clear to her what it is for a visual experience to exhibit branches. Audi does not make it clear what this would be. Might one say that it is for branches to be a part of what the visual experience represents? One might well (and perhaps truly) say this, but to say it to one puzzled about what it is for a visual experience to be as of a tree, or "arboreal," would obviously not be helpful.

Recall BonJour's questions. He asked first what the significance of characterizing perceptual experiences as Audi and Pryor (and others, of course) do in terms of physical-objects really is, and he asked secondly what it is about the perceptual experiences that makes these characterizations 'seem obviously appropriate.'[31] On Sosa's view it is essential to an experience's being as if an F were present that it is of a kind such that in the actual world occurrences of experiences of that kind are reliably connected with the presence of Fs. This addresses *a* question about the significance of giving physical-object characterizations of experiences: at least part of the significance of characterizing a particular visual experience as being 'as if' an F were present is that its occurrence is a defeasible but reliable indication of the presence of an F. But how well does it respond to the further question what it is about perceptual experiences of a given sort that makes certain physical-object characterizations of them seem so obviously *appropriate* (and, one could add, makes certain others obviously inappropriate)? Sosa is not without resources here. Experiences of such and such an intrinsic qualitative character just are normally connected with one's being affected by objects of such and such a description. Why not say that this connection is all that's needed to explain why characterizing the experiences in terms of the objects seems appropriate? They're the sorts of experiences we have in the presence of those kinds of objects. So naturally—whatever their intrinsic qualitative character—it seems 'appropriate' to describe the experiences in terms of those objects.

As ingenious as Sosa's approach is, it seems less than fully satisfactory. The sorts of experiences that are in the actual world experiences 'as if' spherical things were present could have been reliably correlated instead with the presence of, say, pyramids, cubes, barbells—anything, actually, but we'll stick with pyramids for simplicity. Such experiences would in that case have been experiences 'as if' (in Sosa's sense) pyramids were present even though in the actual world experiences of the same intrinsic qualitative character are experiences as if spherical things are present. This raises the question whether the correlations to which Sosa's account adverts fully account for or explain the *representational* character of the experiences—especially if, as seems plausible, intrinsic, qualitative characteristics of experiences do play *some* role in determining their representational character. In a defense of the theory of appearing, William Alston touches on this concern:

The most fundamental component in our concept of perception is that it is an *intuitive*, rather than a discursive, cognition of objects;

it is a matter of having objects *presented* to one's consciousness, rather than a matter of thinking about them, or bringing them under general concepts, or making judgments about them. Much less is it just a matter of a causal relation between the object and one's experience of something else or of nothing ... It is the *presentational* feature of perception that gets lost in externalist accounts of object perception.[32]

Whatever one's estimation of the theory of appearing or of Alston's defense, one may find it plausible that a visual experience 'as if' (in Sosa's sense) a white round thing were present could fail to be an 'intuitive cognition' of anything, even if a white round thing *were* present. It's a reliable indicator of the presence of a white round thing, but is it more than that? Perhaps nothing more is to be expected, but it may well be worth trying to work out a conception that does justice to the idea that perception is an "intuitive cognition of objects."

6. CONCLUSION

Why does a visual experience as if a white, round thing is present normally justify one's believing that a white, round thing is present? Sosa has this answer: visual experiences, in order to qualify as being in his sense 'as if' white, round things are present, must be of a sort reliably correlated (in the actual world) with the presence of white, round things. This entails that visual experiences 'as if' (in Sosa's sense) white round things were present are in the actual world good indicators of the presence of white round things. So far so good. But if we take 'as if' to have representational import—if we think of an experience 'as if' a white round thing is present as one which presents a white round thing as being there before one—then it seems the correlations mentioned by Sosa fail to clarify how the experience can do this, how it can make a white round thing present to consciousness.

As for Audi, he seems rather to presuppose than to offer an account of what it is for a visual experience to present a white round thing as there before one—to be, as we might put it, genuinely 'as of' a white round thing in front of one. Such an account would complement the visual experience principle and could play a key role in a satisfactory intuitionist view of direct perceptual justification.

CHAPTER FIVE

MORAL PERCEPTION AND KNOWLEDGE BY PRINCIPLES[1]

Carla Bagnoli, University of Modena and Reggio Emilia

Some intuitionists hold that there are moral truths that we know in the same way we know other facts about the world, via the perception of properties that constitute its fabric or structure. To emphasize that moral knowledge is a rather ordinary kind of knowledge, intuitionists often advocate the idea of moral perception, not as a mere metaphor or as a *façon de parler*, but in strict analogy with sensory perception. Supporters of the perceptual model of moral knowledge claim that it has the advantage of being true to facts and common-sensical. This is supposed to be an advantage over anti-realist views, which deny that there is any genuine moral knowledge. In contrast to such views, the perceptual model of moral knowledge has the merit of confirming (or, at least, not disconfirming) our common experience that 'one sees injustice in the world,' or that in such and such occasion 'one felt wronged by somebody else.' Critics of the perceptual model object that this is no (common) experience at all: we do not perceive wrongness in the world, which makes the appeal to moral perception rather counter-intuitive.

Not all supporters of the perceptual model argue that moral knowledge is solely perceptual. Some defend a less demanding and more plausible claim that some moral knowledge is perceptual, or that it is like perceptual knowledge in relevant respects.[2] Supporters of moral perception are not oblivious to the main difference between the moral and the sensory case, which is that moral perception is not equivalent to the perception of sensible properties. Advocates of the perceptual model counter that this difference is not crucial. Arguably, not all perception is perception of sensory properties;[3] furthermore, in spite of the fact that there are no moral analogues of sensible properties, the similarities with sensory perception are still striking, and the perceptual model of moral knowledge is useful.

In this essay, I will focus on the epistemological import of the model of moral perception by taking into consideration Robert Audi's recent defense of it. For Audi moral perception qualifies as a ground for objective moral knowledge. On Audi's perceptual model, some moral knowledge is neither inferential nor basic, since it rests on perceiving non-moral properties. We perceive moral properties such as wrongness by perceiving other sorts of properties from which moral properties result. In accounting for moral perception, Audi thus invokes consequentiality as the relevant ontic relation.

My argument will be that Audi's version of this relation crucially brings into play moral principles, and raises the issue of their distinctive epistemic role. Since the main epistemic purpose of the perceptual model is to account for a non-inferential sort of knowledge, it is unclear what sort of role moral principles can be accorded. This question can take the form of two objections, which are moved from opposite philosophical perspectives. On the one hand, particularists such as Jonathan Dancy deny that moral principles play any epistemic role in the perceptual model of moral knowledge. Accordingly, Dancy objects that the ontic relation of consequentiality holds at the ontological level, but it does not hold at the epistemological level.[4] On the other hand, Kantians object that moral principles should be regarded as much more important than the consequentiality thesis allows: they are nothing less than 'the form of knowledge'. Interestingly, many Kantians may agree that not all sorts of moral knowledge are inferential, and reject deonto-logical forms of justification, deductivism, and proceduralism. But they object that intuitionism fails to account for the crucial epistemic role of principles. In particular, they argue to carry on the project of objectively grounding moral knowledge we need a more robust conception of the epistemic role of principles. Key to this dispute is the practice of moral judgment, or so I will argue.

1. MORAL PERCEPTION: ITS PROSPECTS

The analogy with perception is invoked to bring to light the ontology and epistemology of moral claims. As far as moral ontology is concerned, the idea of moral perception has been one of the *foci* of the debate about the viability of moral realism.[5] Furthermore, to construe moral knowledge according to the perceptual model allows us to take moral beliefs at face value, and thus avoid the challenges that many anti-realist accounts of moral discourse face. Anti-realists deny the veridical valence of these seemings and thus bear the burden of showing that our moral grammar and phenomenology are misleading. For instance, Simon Blackburn's way of drawing the analogy between moral properties and secondary properties does not lead to any significant conception of moral perception as the ground of moral knowledge. This is a sufficient basis for a metaethics that mimics realism, but it does not allow for moral judgments as carrying cognitive import.[6] By contrast, John McDowell uses the analogy in support of qualified forms of realism, and argues that our moral sensibility provides us with veridical moral experiences.[7] This is because values, like sensory secondary properties, are genuine properties even though they cannot exist independently of the sensibility that generates them.

McDowell's claim about the ontological status of ethical properties carries significant consequences. First, it shows that any sharp division between realist and anti-realist metaethics ought to be abandoned. If the ontological status of moral properties is hybrid as McDowell claims, it does not make much sense to situate moral language within a realist or anti-realist camp. An adequate metaethics should make room for concepts that cannot be understood otherwise than in terms of dispositions to give rise to subjective states. Because ethical concepts depend on the subjects' appropriate affective responses to a given situation, to master an ethical concept requires a specific sort of moral sensibility. It is open to the sensibility theorist to accept that the development of this sort of moral sensibility is paired with or even requires a certain perceptual sensibility. The thrust of the argument is that a plausible account of objectivity cannot dispense with references to subjective aspects of our agency.

Second, the analogy with visual perception seems promising in accounting for the ontological relation between moral and non-moral properties, facts and values. The notion of moral perception has been routinely deployed to counter the non-cognitivist claims that our moral convictions are completely separable from our beliefs about the world.[8] According to the non-cognitivist view, values are projected onto a realm of bare and brute facts. By invoking the notion of moral vision, philosophers intend to undermine this dichotomy and suggest that facts and values are inextricably entangled, and thus resist the metaphors of detachment and projection. This claim about the entanglement of facts and values is importantly related to the claim about the inextricability of contents and concepts, but this is a further complication that I must set aside.

The appeal to the analogy with sensory perception, then, also has important epistemological consequences. First, it points out that an adequate account of moral knowledge must overcome traditional dichotomies such as those between the subjective and the objective, and the affective and the cognitive. Perceptual judgments reflect a certain response (that is, a visual experience) to some genuine property, given a certain sensory equipment, and "somewhat similarly," John McDowell argues, "we can learn to see the world in terms of some specific set of evaluative classifications, aesthetic or moral, only because our affective and attitudinal propensities are such that we can be brought to care in appropriate ways about the things we learn to see as collected together by classifications."[9]

Second, and as a consequence, the perceptual model vindicates the immediate or non-inferential character of (some) moral knowledge. At least in some cases, we immediately see that an act is wrong. Hearing an abusive vulgarity screamed at a conference speaker strikes us as morally wrong;[10] and it is hard to imagine what sorts of considerations could excuse such an objectionable act, or make it right.[11] Likewise, we see that there is something wrong about a woman stoned to death because accused of adultery, a girl chained at a sewing machine to ensure her productivity, or a boy conscripted as a soldier. We simply see that these are rather 'obvious' ways of wronging others. The perceptual model accounts for the immediacy of this sort of moral knowledge. Lengthy reasoning is not necessary to figure out that these acts are wrong, even though we can discuss and sharply disagree about why they are wrong. Morally competent valuators may endorse different accounts of why child labor is wrong, for instance. Some may invoke respect for humanity and denounce a violation of autonomy; others may invoke our duty to protect the weak and the vulnerable. Moreover, morally competent evaluators may have significantly different philosophical accounts of autonomy and vulnerability. It is argued that the perceptual model has the distinctive virtue of making these differences apparent and salient.[12]

Third, the perceptual model allows for a developmental understanding of moral competence, agency, and sensibility, and it is best fit to account for phenomena such as improvement and corruption in moral vision. Evaluators are differently attuned to moral reality. The appeal to moral vision serves the purpose of emphasizing that moral visions differ in quality, some are better than others, and they are susceptible to change and improvement. To use a famous example, Iris Murdoch invokes the metaphors of moral perception and vision to describe the moral change of a woman who slowly, by particular acts of attention, changes her attitude toward her daughter-in-law. This is a moral change, even though it is not noticeable from outside. It is an improvement in moral vision. The woman in Murdoch's example slowly becomes more discerning than she was at the outset. Perhaps her emotions become more attuned to reality, and she has become more attentive to and perceptive of the features of the world that are morally significant.[13]

Finally, the perceptual model of moral knowledge makes sense of error in a straightforward way. It takes certain moral errors to be akin to perceptual errors, where we fail to notice or misperceive some relevant properties of the object, and mistakenly judge the case. If someone pauses to figure out whether there is something wrong or morally disturbing about child slavery, there must be something amiss with him. The case of child slavery allows for no perplexity. Many different normative theories are hospitable to this substantive claim. For instance, Aristotelians would say that the practically wise, judges the case more accurately and more swiftly than the wicked or unwise. The wise may not need to spend too much time in deliberating and processing information. They see right away that something went wrong. Some Kantians accept that the practice of moral judgment requires moral education and sensibility, and agree that deliberation is not always needed, even though they hold that it is always true that moral judgments are to be reflectively endorsed in order to be genuinely authoritative.[14] Such normative theories propose different conceptions of moral education and of its roles. Apart from differences in normative theoretical frameworks, however, there is a fairly large agreement that moral perception requires some degree of moral training, skill, and education.[15]

2. MORAL PERCEPTION: SOME RESERVATIONS

Despite the apparent broad commonalities between moral knowledge and non-moral knowledge,[16] the perceptual model has been severely criticized. At the ontological level, critics object that such broad commonalities are not sufficient to preserve adequate constraints on what is perceived. What is the relevant object perceived in moral perception, which is an external constraint on thought? Taken literally, the idea of moral perception is ontologically problematic. Thus, some critics of the model of moral perception advise not to take the perceptual analogy too seriously, and they prefer to bear the burden of proof of showing that the surface grammar of moral discourse is misleading.

It is an open question, however, whether the availability of this proof is sufficient to assuage the worries of those who care about moral phenomenology. Even if anti-realists offer a credible reconstruction of the grammar of moral discourse, they still have to explain why we experience morality as objectively as we do. One may argue that moral perception is not dispensable on the basis of epistemological considerations. For instance, some intuitionists hold that refraining from talking in terms of moral perception for fear of metaphysics prevents us from explaining in a straightforward way ordinary acts of knowledge, such as seeing the dangerousness of a cliff, which would become 'unobservable.'[17]

To be sure there are more complicated cases of immorality that we do not detect as immediately as seeing that a cliff is dangerous. For the intuitionist this is no proof that the perceptual model is mistaken. Rather, it shows that such cases require more attention and careful observation. Some hold that to perceive such cases as cases of moral wrongness, evaluators need a specific form of sensibility, appropriate training, and moral education.[18] The question arises, however, whether such cases show that the perceptual analogy is misleading or incomplete. It is misleading for those who think that sensory perception does not need special training and education to function correctly. If not misleading, the analogy with sensory perception is incomplete and ought to be supplemented with a differentiated account of the specific form of moral sensibility and moral concepts that are at work in each domain, respectively.

Perhaps the most important objection, though, is that morally competent evaluators disagree about moral matters, and some seem to be 'morally blind,' that is, they do not perceive wrongness at all.[19] These are important objections to the perceptual model of moral knowledge. Whether these objections are fatal depends on the specifics of the model. In particular, I will argue, it depends on whether moral perception is understood as an active or a passive phenomenon, an issue that interestingly relates to the epistemic role of principles. The relevance of this issue becomes apparent as we consider Robert Audi's recent attempt to defend a sophisticated model of moral perception.

3. ROBERT AUDI ON MORAL PERCEPTION AS RESPONSIVENESS TO REASONS

Robert Audi has recently argued that moral perception suitably defined qualifies as the ground for objective moral knowledge. Audi focuses on "the *prima facie* constitutive cases of moral perception," because they appear to be more similar to the sorts of everyday perceptions that ground perceptual knowledge. I assume we agree with Audi that "hearing an abusive vulgarity screamed at a conference speaker" strikes us as morally wrong.

> Given our psychological constitution, we may normally be unable to witness these things without a phenomenal sense of wrongdoing integrated with our perceptual representation of the wrong-making facts.[20]

Audi adds that "certain perceptions of moral wrongs are virtually irresistible," and I take this to mean that these cases strike us as self-evident. This is not to say that there are some kinds of wrong perceived as self-evidently wrong. Rather, the point here is that, for morally competent (normal adults), one can't help morally seeing a wrong, as opposed to amorally merely visually experience, e.g. a stabbing. The intuitionist would say that normal adult moral evaluators take these singular cases as plainly (or even irresistibly) wrong; this is not to say that they will also form a general belief about the kind of deed.[21] In contrast to classical intuitionism, Audi is committed to a soft kind of self-evidence, which is non-axiomatic. Moral perceptions of this sort have epistemic weight but are fallible:

they can be corrected, defeated by countervailing intuitions, or even withheld given comprehending reflection.[22] Intuitions are typically of non-inferentially known propositions, and held neither on the basis of premises nor as theoretical hypothesis, but they are neither necessary nor *a priori*. They are firm, but their firmness is based (at least) on a minimally adequate understanding of their propositional objects. They might be complex enough that to see their truth requires practical reflection.

4. THE POWERS OF REFLECTION

In Audi's view, then, the appeal to moral perception does not dismiss or discount the role of practical reflection. On the contrary, Audi emphasizes that the correctness and coherence of intuitions can be achieved by reflection. While intuitions are exempt from proof, reflection might play an important role in their justification. Intuitions can be corrected or improved, but also defeated by reflection and comparison with the intuitions of others.[23] This is no concession to proceduralism, the view that moral claims are the outcome of a rational decision procedure. In contrast to proofs and inferential reasoning, whose conclusions are inferentially grounded on premises, reflection in the relevant cases is a non-linear and global kind of reasoning. Conclusions of reflection emerge from thinking of the case as a whole. It is a rather different operation than deriving moral claims from evidential premises. As Audi remarks, "drawing a conclusion of reflection is a kind of wrapping up of the question, akin to concluding a practical matter with a decision."[24] More precisely, judging upon reflection is like a response, and we respond to patterns. The point is that at least some moral knowledge is not inferential, but amounts to the formation of a belief that is a response to a recognized pattern.[25]

To make certain cases of moral perception akin to the conclusion of reflection or judgment has some important consequences. First, it implicitly emphasizes that moral perception is in some cases an exercise of practical reason that does not exclude, but it instead often follows practical thinking or deliberation. Second, such a construal of moral perception significantly broadens the modes of moral perception beyond the bounds of the emotional sensibility. On several perceptual models, responses to recognized patterns are said to be attitudinal or emotional.[26] In the debate on moral realism the analogy with visual perception serves the purpose of investigating the nature of the relation between moral properties and emotional responses.[27] In the debates on character and deliberation, it is deployed to highlight the importance of emotional life for a plausible account of moral agency, in contrast to action theories that focus on the outward performance of acts.[28] By contrast, for Audi 'moral perceptual seemings' are not necessarily emotional. I take this to be a significant descriptive advantage of his model. In broadening the scope of its application it becomes relevant for a larger class of epistemic facts.

Third, Audi's claim that moral perception is sometimes akin to moral perception is proposed in contrast to another sort of phenomenal representations, which are said 'cartographic,' or 'pictorial.' For Audi moral perception is best construed as a non-pictorial phenomenal representation, which is constituted by a response to moral properties, for instance, injustice via perception of the relevant base properties, e.g. unequal distribution. This construal presents obvious advantages at the ontological level. In particular, it points out that in perceptual moral judgment, ordinary and moral aspects of perception are phenomenally integrated. This sort of phenomenal integration explains why it is inappropriate to separate evaluative and factual elements. At the same time, this claim about the inextricability of evaluative and factual elements and their phenomenal integration is defended as a straightforwardly naturalistic proposal.

When we perceive that child labor is wrong,[29] we perceive some natural properties, for instance, about the psychological make-up of children and their vulnerability. The perception of such natural properties is ordinary perception. However, such ordinary perception is phenomenally integrated with a sense of the wrongness of child labor. This integration importantly makes sense of the experiential element in moral perception.[30] Because of its constitutive feature, it is both useless and methodologically inadequate to try and separate the evaluative and factual elements of moral judgment. It should be noted, however, that the claim about the inextricability of evaluative and factual elements and their phenomenal integration does not encourage any mysterious metaphysics and is defended as a straightforwardly naturalistic proposal.

On Audi's account, moral perception can be an adequate basis for framing a general view. To perceive that children have some features that make child labor wrong is phenomenally integrated with the moral perception that child labor is wrong. This means that one cannot perceive the wrongness of child slavery unless one does not perceive those features of child slavery that make it wrong. Moral evaluators "may normally be unable to witness these things without a phenomenal sense of wrongdoing integrated with our perceptual representation of the wrong-making facts."[31] In other words, where we perceive the natural properties, and understand them as bases for wrongness, our perception of them can count as perception of the wrongness itself. That is, the moral evaluator discerns moral reasons by discriminating the base properties, and this act of recognition is integrated with a specific phenomenology. This is to say that wrongness is consequential on some other properties. Furthermore, Audi holds that when one perceives an instantiation of wrongness, which is grounded in instantiations of other properties, one perceives the former by perceiving the latter.

5. CONSEQUENTIALITY AS A GROUNDING RELATION

In advocating for the relation of consequentiality, Audi aims at (non-reductively) naturalizing moral perception.[32] The experiential responses are causally explainable in terms of the natural responses, regardless of whether moral responses have causal power. It is interesting that Audi takes this construal to be a non-reductive way of naturalizing moral perception, since it closely resembles G. E. Moore's definition of non-naturalness as consequentiality.[33] As I take it, for Moore 'non-natural' means 'consequential,' 'derivative,' or 'supervenient.'[34] A property is non-natural when it cannot exist by itself in time and it is not a part of anything of which it is a property. To claim that ethical properties are consequential is also to claim that they are not intrinsic properties, but result from or depend on some relations among intrinsic natural properties. That is, moral properties are not intrinsic, in Moore's sense. Natural predicates stand for natural intrinsic properties and describe the nature of an object while value predicates do not.[35] Moreover, for Moore consequentiality names the necessary and *a priori* non-reductive relation of dependence between properties. Since this relation is *a priori*, it cannot be a causal relation. Since it is synthetic, it cannot be a logical relation. Since it is necessary, it cannot depend on the preferences and interests of the evaluator.

It is exactly the grounding relation of consequentiality that J. L. Mackie objects as ontologically queer and epistemologically problematic and redundant. Audi may seem to eschew this objection because he does not take consequentiality to be a necessary and *a priori* relation. However, Mackie's objection is not formulated to target consequentiality as a necessary and *a priori* relation. It is, instead, an objection against any non-reductive normative relations: "The wrongness must somehow be consequential or supervenient. [An action] is wrong *because* it is a piece of deliberate cruelty. But just what in the world is signified by this 'because'? And how do we know the relation that it signifies?"[36] If Audi's construal of moral perception as involving consequentiality eschews the objection of queerness, this is not because Audi endorses a weaker conception of consequentiality than Moore. Rather, his reply to Mackie must be that consequentiality does not belong to the world because it is a normative relation, and no normative relation 'belongs to the world.' In other words, normative relations are not reducible to intrinsic natural properties. It follows that consequentiality cannot be susceptible to naturalistic reduction because it is a normative relation, a claim about reasons. To say that an action is wrong because it is an act of deliberate cruelty is to say that the fact that an action is a piece of deliberate cruelty is a reason to consider it wrong. The reason states a normative relation between something being an instance of deliberate cruelty and something being wrong. To argue that a normative relation is either reductive or vulnerable to the objection of queerness begs the question about normativity. The (empiricist) reductivist assumes that the only credible explanation of the normative relation between the descriptive features of an object and its evaluative characteristics must be reductive and naturalistic. The issue is more complex than I can say here,[37] but I will take for granted that Audi's theory has resources to adequately respond to the objection of queerness. My main interest lies in the epistemological import of his model of moral perception.

As Audi construes the grounding relation of consequentiality, the dependence of moral consequential properties on other natural properties is stable across time. We perceive rightness and wrongness insofar as they are consequential properties, properties that actions have in virtue of having other properties. Whenever there are properties such as provoking pain, for instance, there is wrongness, *ceteris paribus*. Moreover, when we see that something is wrong it is because we perceive the properties upon which wrongness is consequential. Audi holds that this position on perceptual moral knowledge "is sufficient to ground the possibility of a major kind of ethical objectivity: it accounts for the intersubjectively accessible grounds for a wide range of moral judgments."[38] Child slavery is wrong in virtue of other properties, such as causing suffering, under-mining the child's status, impairing child's development, and so on.

To achieve the kind of objectivity that Audi promises, the grounding relation between the wrongness of child slavery and their natural bases must be a stable in time and across evaluators. But this is to say that such grounding relation is patterned or principled, and this implication is problematic. Some may reject the view that the grounding relation is principled. For instance, Jonathan Dancy has objected to Audi's view that one can perceive a consequential property, such as the dangerousness of the cliff or the wrongness of child abuse, without perceiving the base features that make the cliff dangerous or child abuse morally hideous. The general point is that even if at the ontological level moral wrongness depends on other properties, at the epistemological level they may be unrelated: "the epistemology of resultance need not follow its metaphysics."[39] This objection raises an important issue about the epistemological role of principles in the practice of moral judgment.

In contrast to Dancy, I will argue with Audi that moral principles should be should be accorded a crucial epistemic role. Focus on the role of principles in the practice of moral judgment allows us to show that Audi's theory importantly agrees with some features of Kantian moral epistemology. In the final sections, I will attempt to show that this agreement reveals a more interesting disagreement about the function of practical reason.

6. PRINCIPLES AS PATTERNS

Audi starts with *prima facie* constitutive cases of moral perception, such as hearing a vulgarity screamed at a conference speaker.[40] To be sure, not all moral cases are as straightforward as this one. It may be difficult even to detect the moral relevance of a case. For instance, buying milk in the store may seem to be morally indifferent, until one apprehends several other kinds of facts about the modes of production, the rules of fair trade, the country of provenance, the chemical composition of products on the shelves, and so on. In virtue of these facts, even the ordinary choice of buying milk can be morally perplexing.[41]

As this example indicates, some might worry that moral principles may be unavailable, and therefore we should reject the claim that moral perception requires principles. If so, the perceptual model of moral knowledge becomes less interesting and inapplicable in complex cases of moral evaluation. However, supporters of the perceptual model may respond that the case moral perplexity simply shows that moral knowledge might require a great deal of deliberation and reflection. This is something that intuitionists have seldom denied, and Audi's epistemic model is designed to accommodate this possibility.[42] In fact, so-called 'methodological intuitionists,' such as J. O. Urmson, have argued that the expectation that ethical theory should meet the standard of normative and epistemic completeness is misguided.[43] This is not because ethics is not up to high standards of objectivity and completeness, but because to accept such standards is to misunderstand both the aims of ethical theory and its practical relevance. The interesting worry, then, is not the availability of ready-made principles that resolve all moral quandaries. The issue is how to conceive of reflection for perception to be an objective ground of moral knowledge.

Traditionally, the epistemic model of moral perception is offered in contrast to the inferentialism and proceduralism, which are (mistakenly) associated with the Kantian model of principled justification. Intuitionists such as Dancy use moral perception exactly to discount the epistemological role of moral principles. This disagreement may go very deep. Dancy considers moral principles not only epistemologically inert, but also morally pernicious. In his view, reliance on moral principles is akin to moral negligence as it "encourages the tendency not to look hard enough."[44] Kantians (of all sorts) certainly have resources to respond to this critique by distinguishing between the practice of principled justification and a pathological fetishism of the rule. Nonetheless, intuitionists are right to insist that moral knowledge is not available to us effortlessly, *via* the mere application of a decision procedure, but instead requires attention, appropriate training, and skill.

When we take into account Audi's ethical theory, however, the contrast with Kantians must be drawn differently, as it is not obvious that it is as stark as the one drawn above. Audi holds that principled intuitionism is a coherent doctrine, and he has forcefully argued for a complex integration of intuitionism and Kantian ethics.[45] In his view, both normative theories have something to gain from this integration. In particular, intuitionism is expected to profit from the Kantian appeal to principles. Audi takes principles as devices that provide structural integrity, systematization, integration, coherence, and the possibility of completeness. These are clearly important functions that principles perform in ethical theory, and may seem enough to establish a general agreement between intuitionist and Kantian theories. But this is not so. There is a more interesting philosophical disagreement between the two perspectives, which emerges as we refocus the discussion on the epistemic role of moral principles in the practice of moral judgment. In contrast to intuitionists such as Dancy, the Kantian view of practical reflection is both non-linear *and* guided by principles. In contrast to intuitionist such as Audi, the Kantian view is that practical reflection provides genuine knowledge *because* it is guided by principles.

7. KNOWLEDGE BY PRINCIPLES

Arguably, both the Kantian and the Intuitionist theories represent practical reflection as a non-linear form of reasoning, which differs from the mechanistic application of algorithms and functions, deduction from premises, or subsumption under generalizations. In short, both camps distinguish practical reflection from practical reasoning understood as solely involving our inferential capacities. Contrary to the received view, the Kantian defense of principles commits neither to legalism nor to codifiability. In fact, Kant distinguishes between the mere conformity to principles (legality), and morality understood as acting on principles, which he takes to be equivalent to acting for the sake of duty.[46] Moreover, the appeal to principles does not take the form of a defense of moral code. It follows that the interesting sort of disagreement between the intuitionist and the Kantian view does not concern the availability of principles or codifiability of ethics. As Audi argues, intuitionism can coherently appeal to principles. As large debates in Kantian scholarship show, it is misleading to consider the categorical imperative as a mere decision-procedure. First and foremost, it is the form of knowledge. If the perceptual model is proposed in contrast to the legalistic view of morality as a codified system of norms, then Kantians may readily endorse it.[47]

While this is an important point of convergence that deserves notice, it builds on a deeper and more interesting. To highlight the form of knowledge is not yet to account for the fact that there is genuine knowledge. This is to say, first, that the laws of practical reason could be empty, that is, not applicable to anyone. In this case, there would be no ground for objective practical knowledge. Second, the question of what is a plausible ground of genuine knowledge introduces a further distinction concerning the function of reason. In its practical function, reason does not presume that there is an object of knowledge that exists prior to and independently of the activity of knowing; hence, practical knowledge is not knowledge of something external to the practice of moral judgment. This marks the distinction between practical and theoretical knowledge. As it appears, this is also a significant difference between the Intuitionist and the Kantian models of moral epistemology. This disagreement should be the focus of further discussion.

The Kantian view is that practical reflection provides genuine knowledge *because* it is principled. The mind is active when governed by principles. Thinking and acting are principled activities. Insofar as they are principled activities, they are the key modes in which we exercise our autonomy. Kantians think that a necessary condition for self-governance is to be guided by self-legislated principles rather than being driven by external laws. Therefore, Kantians identify the chief role of principles from a different perspective than the one Audi identifies, which concerns the structure of reflective consciousness or rational agency. Principled justification is distinctive of reflective consciousness because appeal to principle warrants a distinctive kind of epistemic authority, which is internal to the practice of judgment and is marked by autonomy. To hold that principles are self-conscious is to say that they exhibit a specific form of reflexivity, which commands both self-agreement and agreement with all rational agents capable of knowledge.[48]

Traditionally, intuitionists have not availed themselves to the notion of agential autonomy.[49] In this regard, Audi represents an important exception, as he invokes the idea of autonomy and insists that an action based on moral judgment is not a mere effect of, but also a response to moral judgment. "Autonomous actions," he writes, "are done in part from appropriate judgment or belief, not merely in accordance with its content."[50]

Here comes an interesting difference, though. The Kantian claim is that moral action is never a mere response to reasons; rather, it is the effect of thinking that there are reasons for action. That action is an effect of thinking is an important thesis, which is tantamount to the very idea of the objectivity of practical reason. Reason is shown to be objective when it is regarded as a subjective motive, and this means that it drives the agent to action. This is not to say that acting is the only or the chief mode of realizing value. Rather, it means that in order to qualify as agents we are required to be susceptible to practical reason, and thus directly driven by it. To say that the rational or autonomous action is a response to a practical judgment is a very different thing than claiming that it is an expression of such judgment.

Whereas Kantians claim autonomy to be "a metaphysical property of the will" and yet a normative capacity,[51] Audi takes the autonomous agent as primary,[52] and then defines autonomous action in relation to it. Autonomous actions are those that express the autonomy of the agent insofar as they are grounded in some reasons of the agent.[53] What is, then, necessary for an agent to be autonomous? Audi apparently deploys a Kantian notion of autonomy, which names a specific form of self-government, that is, government by norms. It is not simply that the autonomous agent follows rules of conduct. Most importantly, she governs herself by self-legislated norms. It is not simply that the autonomous agent follows rules of conduct. Most importantly, she is supposed to govern herself by self-legislated norms. Understood as the absence of external control, freedom is not sufficient for autonomy: "The thoughtlessly self-indulgent person, like one who acts entirely on whims, may be quite independent without being autonomous."[54] This is to say that there are both external and internal threats to autonomy. Phenomena such as compulsion, self-deception, dissociation, and weakness of the will are categorized as cases where the agent lacks autonomy. Likewise, "arbitrary power over oneself is not autonomy."[55] Principles, ideals, and standards protect against arbitrariness and provide "a regime and a coherent pattern in which one can locate and evaluate oneself."[56]

There are many points of agreement between Audi's view and the Kantian conception of practical knowledge as grounded on autonomy. First, Kantians agree that reason is a discursive and cognitive capacity. Second, they also agree that judgments convey genuine knowledge. In particular, logical judgments involve representations of objects, and convey knowledge produced by reason.[57]

The capacity to think, and understand in general, amounts to the capacity to judge.[58] The capacity to judge is thus a cognitive capacity; in the ethical case, it is the capacity to know the good. Differently than theoretical knowledge, practical knowledge is efficacious.[59] But formally practical knowledge is not different than theoretical knowledge: in both cases, their form is principled. This is because there is, ultimately, one single capacity to reason. Third, Kantians would agree that principles are a barrier to arbitrariness. Universal communicability and non-arbitrariness are the key features of genuine knowledge. These features are warranted by principles.

However, from a Kantian perspective, these marks of genuine and objective knowledge depend on another key feature of judgment, which is that it is a cognitive *self-conscious* act produced by reason.[60] Reason refers to the active rather than passive or receptive aspect of the mind, and exactly in this sense it is opposed to perception. In order to avoid arbitrary relations of objects, judgments must be determined. However, they cannot be determined from outside or result in something that lies 'out there' before judging. In order to deliver genuine knowledge, the activity of reason must be governed by principles that do not originate outside but are internal or constitutive of reason itself.[61] This is not to say that the activity of reason is inferential. The point is that there is a form of practical knowledge.

But to identify a form does not amount to identifying a set of axioms or generalizations from which to derive normative conclusions. The claim is more general. Reason is identified with the employment or conformity to principles, such as principles of logical inference, what Kant calls the principles of understanding, canons for the assessment of evidence, mathematical principles, and principles of practical reason. Principles are not the decision-procedure for selecting reasons, but constitute instead the very structure that governs the activity of the mind.[62]

When it is successful, this activity delivers reasons in the substantive sense, which are considerations that count in favor of something or rational motives that justify action.

Audi takes principles as devices of systematization and integration. Their function is not different from generalizations, rules of thumb, or any other kind of criteria. Audi does not deny knowledge of principles. In fact, he takes knowledge of principles to be *a priori*. For Kantians, this distinction should not hold, however. The point of identifying the form of practical knowledge is exactly to identify a universal form in any singular act of judgment. Practical cognition is cognition of universality itself: we cognize the particular in the universal.[63] Again, the claim is that to take practical cognition to have the form of a law does not commit one to inferentialism.[64]

According to Kantians, practical principles are normative criteria of a specific kind, that is, internal to the very activity they govern: they play a constitutive role. Hence, we run a significant risk in treating principles as simply improving the coherence or integration of our intuitions. The risk is to downplay the crucial epistemic role of principles. Ultimately, the Kantian objection is that the Intuitionist view reduces practical reason to a receptive faculty. For instance, Christine Korsgaard objects: "if this is all there is to rational agency, then, of course it does not involve the exercise of any specifically human power which we might identify with the faculty of reason: it is just a way we describe certain actions from outside, namely the ones that conform to rational principles or to the particular considerations we call 'reasons'."[65] By contrast, to reason is to engage in an activity, being governed by specific normative criteria, which are internal and constitutive of that activity itself. It's not merely a matter of being motivated by considerations about what makes an action good; rather, it is a matter of being motivated by the consciousness that the action is good. This is not a distinction that can be captured by invoking the subjective/objective reasons dichotomy. The key point concerns the reflective structure of reasons, and to account for this feature we need to refer to self-consciousness.[66] Judgment is a self-constituted type of thinking, whose key feature is that it is self-conscious. It is not an awareness of something prior and external to the very act of judging. Arguably, this is one sort of judgment, but from the epistemological point of view it is the privileged sort of judgment. In contrast to aesthetic judgment, which depends on our sensibility, moral judgment is produced by the spontaneous activity of reason.[67]

The feature of spontaneity seems to be dispensable in the perceptual account of moral knowledge. For instance, Audi says that:

> moral sensitivity may run ahead of judgment. We may sense a duty to help someone ... We may thus respond to appropriate grounds before forming a belief that they are present or

making the corresponding judgment, here the judgment that we should help. Emotion, here compassion or indignation, can be both morally evidential and morally motivating. Emotions may reveal what is right or wrong before judgment articulates it; and may both support ethical judgment and spur moral conduct.[68]

Even when moral sensitivity does not precede judgment, "judgment may be produced by its grounds without our recognition of the process or even of the grounds."[69] This is not to say that there is no awareness of the grounds, but only that such awareness is not conceptualized or conceived under moral concepts or as grounds.[70] The agent might conceptualize such awareness afterwards, and upon reflection identify the grounds of duties as such, but he does not have to. A justified moral judgment does not require that the action be categorized as an action of a certain kind and subsumed under a principle. Rather, moral knowledge may arise from a specific response in a specific case, providing a direct justification without recurring to principles or application of procedures. For instance, emotional awareness of moral duty conveys justified moral knowledge independently of the recognition of its grounds.

Kantians do not merely object that such an account of the emotions bypasses reasoning, but they argue that such an account lacks the specific reflexivity that is essential to rational judgments. Lacking reflexivity, there is external determination of judgment, which does not qualify as an adequate ground for objective practical knowledge.

8. OBJECTIVE KNOWLEDGE AS KNOWLEDGE BY PRINCIPLES

Kantians argue that the idea of moral perception is misleading because in responding to patterns the mind is not active. Responding to reasons is not the same as generating objective moral knowledge, which requires spontaneity or activity of the mind. Kantians do not deny that our receptivity to moral reasons plays an important part in our moral life. Instead, they argue that such receptivity cannot be the basis for *objective* moral knowledge. From this argument, two distinct conclusions follow. First, the perceptual model of moral knowledge fails to account for objectivity insofar as it fails to account for the activity of the mind in the process of knowing. Second, if the mind is not passive in moral perception, it is because it is governed by principles. Then, even in the perceptual model of moral perception, the epistemic work is done by principles. The question arises as to what the distinctive purpose of the model of moral perception is, since it does not interestingly discriminate between principled and non-inferential accounts of moral knowledge.

Supporters of the perceptual model may simply reject the Kantian standard for the objectivity of moral knowledge. Indeed, it is not obvious where the burden of proof lies. A more interesting reply, however, would require the intuitionist to show that the Kantian argument assumes a simplistic account of perception. Some supporters of the perceptual model doubt that there is a sharp distinction between activity and passivity, and suggest a more complex account of perception where the mind is partly actively engaged. On this sophisticated view, moral perception is more 'conception' than 'reception';[71] it "involves exercising an inculcated capacity to be reliably sensitive."[72] Jonathan Dancy has explicitly argued that responsiveness to reasons is not reducible to "gazing at in a receptive frame of mind."[73] Indeed, this is what he means by equating perception and judgment.[74] Audi also is inclined to this sort of reply.

Kantians are prepared to accept that perception is not totally passive or receptive, that "the perceived world does not merely enter the mind," and even that "in sensing and responding to the world our minds interact with it."[75] They concede that moral perception is not perception of "brute moral facts." They also recognize that we are rationally required to be responsive to practical reasons. But they would add that while responsiveness is crucial to our functioning as moral agents, it is not the key feature that constitutes us as rational animals. In contrast to sophisticated forms of moral perception, which are not reducible to mere receptivity, Kantians still hold that "reasoning is self-conscious, self-directing activity, through which we deliberately give shape to the inputs of receptivity."[76] While moral perception may be recognized to have some aspects of activity, it cannot be the paradigm of objective moral knowledge. To account for the objectivity of moral knowledge starting with such peripheral cases is misleading, as it misses the source of objectivity. If in moral perception the mind is active, then moral perception can be the ground of objective moral knowledge. In order for the mind to be actively engaged, it needs to be governed by principles. If this is so, then the objectivity of moral knowledge is not due to any strict sort of direct perception, but to its principled structure. In other words, in generating genuine moral knowledge it is the principles that do the epistemic work. The epistemic import of moral perception thus depends on moral principles. This is not to say that all the cases of knowledge by moral perception are cases of suppressed inferences. As I argued in section 7, on a Kantian view justification by principles is not equivalent to proceduralism or inferentialism. Thus understood, then the appeal to moral perception does not finely discriminate between Kantian and Intuitionist accounts of moral knowledge. From a Kantian perspective, it is a mistake to hold both that perception is not completely receptive and yet not informed by principles.[77] This is because the activity of reason is always informed by principles; and consequently, the form of genuine and objective perceptual knowledge is knowledge by principles.

Suppose one accepts the Kantian argument. Does a model of moral perception, which recognizes the epistemic role of principles, retain its original polemical force? It can be objected that it is a deflated conception of moral perception, which has lost its purpose. This model is still useful to point out that we do not achieve objective moral knowledge solely by the exercise of our inferential capacities, but also as the result of non-linear and non-algorithmic reasoning. In this respect, the perceptual model clearly marks a departure from legalist conceptions of morality and the proceduralist conceptions of deliberation.

Audi and Kantians agree that to grant these results it is not necessary to dispense with moral principles because reflection and justification by principles does not amount to drawing inferences. In fact, it should be noted that prominent supporters of the perceptual model of moral knowledge, such as Lawrence Blum, have argued that "moral perception is formed and informed by general principles."[78] Kantians further argue that the paradigmatic case of objective moral knowledge is knowledge by principles. Why must there be one paradigm for knowledge, given that there might be different sorts of knowledge?[79] The Kantian answer is that there must be one paradigm insofar as knowledge is the product of reason, which must exhibit autonomy and unity. The Kantian claim is that principles warrant the reflexive unity that is the mark of genuine knowledge, that is, knowledge produced by the autonomous activity of reason. This is where the disagreement with the intuitionist ultimately lies.

9. CONCLUDING REMARKS

I have argued that the perceptual model of moral knowledge presents important merits in accounting for moral phenomenology, but it does not provide with objective grounds of moral knowledge. In sections 1–2, I examined the prospects of the model of moral perception. In sections 3–5, I took into account Robert Audi's sophisticated model of perception, focusing on his claim that some moral knowledge is neither basic nor inferential. In section 6, I suggested that this more sophisticated perceptual model relies on the acknowledgment of principles as patterns to which moral competent evaluators appropriately respond. In section 7, I drew some important contrasts between conceiving of principles as patterns and as the basic form of knowledge. In section 8, I brought to light the interesting aspect of disagreement, which concerns the standard for objective moral knowledge.

CHAPTER SIX

ETHICAL INTUITIONISM AND MORAL SKEPTICISM

Clayton Littlejohn, King's College, London

In this paper, I want to defend ethical intuitionism from some recent skeptical attacks.[1] As the view is understood here, intuitionism is a foundationalist view on which it is possible for some of our moral beliefs to be non-inferentially justified and good candidates for knowledge. We don't need independent justification from our non-moral beliefs to justifiably believe, say, the fact that something would fulfill a promise counts in its favor or the fact that something would seriously harm another counts against it. Moral intuitions give us reason to hold our moral beliefs and there's no principled reason to think we need any more reason to justifiably believe moral propositions than the reasons provided by intuition.[2]

What are intuitions? Some authors identify intuitions with judgments or beliefs or say that having such and such an intuition involves having a belief.[3] Others prefer to think of intuitions as distinct from beliefs, the sorts of things that provide the reasons or grounds for well-grounded beliefs without themselves being held for reasons or being well-grounded.[4] My preference is for the latter view.[5] It seems possible for two subjects with the same moral intuitions to end up with very different moral beliefs if, say, one of these subjects does not take her intuitions at face value and comes to hold beliefs backed by principles she concedes are counterintuitive. Intuitions, I'll assume, have representational content and dispose you to form beliefs with that content. In having an intuition (e.g. that it's wrong to turn the trolley in such and such a circumstance), things seem to you a certain way. When taken at face value, we form the belief that things are that way. The intuitionist view I'll defend is modeled on a familiar account of perceptual judgment, one on which there are non-doxastic, representational states that dispose you to believe that things are the way that they make them seem.[6]

Foundationalists who think that we have some non-inferential moral knowledge might defend an intuitionist view on which properly basic moral beliefs are based on intuitions, but intuitions are not the only possible basis for immediate moral knowledge. Some have recently defended views on which it's possible to have non-inferential moral knowledge based on perceptual experience.[7] My hope is that the defense I offer of the intuitionist view will help the perceptualist fend off skeptical attacks. Skeptics will say that the difference between the intuitionist and perceptualist models won't save either of these views from their objections. The difference in wiring that would determine whether intuitions or experiences serve as the basis for moral judgment is not the sort of difference we could cite in fending off some skeptical challenge. Like the skeptic, I think little of normative significance turns on whether our moral beliefs are based on intuition or experience. Unlike the skeptic, I think that this means that there are no principled objections to either view.[8]

The moral skeptic thinks that we shouldn't take our moral intuitions at face value. She doesn't think moral knowledge is possible and thinks it's not possible for our moral judgments to be justified. Her target is broader than the intuitionist's view, but it includes that view. Her skepticism doesn't derive from a more general skepticism that applies to non-moral belief. Her concerns have to do with the epistemic standing of moral judgment. The moral skeptic defends two theses:

ST1: Moral knowledge is impossible.
ST2: Justified moral judgment is impossible.

The intuitionist denies both. We'll start by looking at three lines of skeptical argument. I don't think any of these arguments give us compelling reason to abandon the intuitionist view. In the final section of the paper, I'll offer an explanation as to why intuition justifies moral judgment.

1. THE SKEPTICAL ARGUMENTS

We shall look at three skeptical arguments, each designed to show that it's not possible to have non-inferential knowledge based on moral intuition. Each is also intended to show that it's not possible to have non-inferentially justified moral judgment or to offer defeaters that undermine whatever justification intuition would otherwise provide. I cannot provide a refutation of the skeptic's view, but I'll do my best to rebut the arguments for the skeptical view. Either these arguments are too weak to establish ST1 or ST2 or they beg the question against the intuitionist in subtle ways.

1. 1 The Empirical Case Against Intuitions

In this section, I want to look at some of Sinnott-Armstrong's arguments for moral skepticism. The first of these arguments draws upon recent empirical research into moral intuition and judgment:

> Until the last decade of the twentieth century, philosophers and psychologists usually engaged in their enterprises separately. This was unfortunate, because it is hard to see how to determine whether certain moral intuitions are justified without any understanding of the processes that produce those intuitions. We are not claiming that psychological findings alone entail philosophical or moral conclusions. That would move us too quickly from 'is' to 'ought.' Our point is different: moral intuitions are unreliable to the extent that morally irrelevant factors affect moral intuitions. When they are distorted by irrelevant factors, moral intuitions can be likened to mirages or seeing pink elephants while one is on LSD. Only when beliefs arise in more reputable ways do they have a fighting chance of being justified. Hence we need to know about the processes that produce moral intuitions before we can determine whether moral intuitions are justified.[9]

Let's suppose that the available evidence does strongly suggest that moral intuitions can be influenced by factors that we take to be morally irrelevant. Specifically, let's suppose that the evidence does support the hypothesis that our intuitive moral judgments are subject to framing effects. When this happens, we might classify equivalent options as morally different as a result of how these options are presented.[10] Because of this, Sinnott-Armstrong thinks that the intuitionist view is sunk. The intuitionist says that our intuitions can justify our moral beliefs without needing any independent support from non-moral beliefs. If they're subject to these effects, he thinks that the justification of judgment depends upon whether we can provide independent support that's not dependent upon our unreliable intuitions.

It seems that Sinnott-Armstrong has this sort of argument in mind:

P1   The empirical evidence suggests that your moral intuitions are unreliable.

P2   Thus, your moral intuitions can neither justify your moral judgments nor serve as an adequate basis for moral knowledge.

One way to take the argument is as resting on the implicit assumption that intuitions must be reliable if they are to justify our moral beliefs and a further assumption that knowledge requires justification. It's not clear whether the argument rests on (i) the claim that intuition is unreliable, or (ii) the claim that the evidence suggests that (i) is true. Let's bracket (ii) for now and suppose that (i) is true.

One problem with this argument, if taken as an argument against ST2, is that it assumes that justification requires reliability. This is a matter of some controversy, but many epistemologists are moved to reject the reliability requirement on justification on the basis of this rather simple thought experiment:

> I think the evil demon hypothesis (or its contemporary neurophysiologist version) uncovers a defect in the Reliabilist position. We can see this by supposing the hypothesis to be true. Imagine that unbeknown to us, our cognitive processes (e.g. perception memory, inference) are not reliable owing to the machinations of the malevolent demon. It follows on a Reliabilist view that the beliefs generated by those processes are *never* justified.

Cohen offers these remarks concerning his example:

> It strikes me as clearly false to deny that under these circumstances our beliefs could be justified. If we have every reason to believe e.g., perception, is a reliable process, the mere fact that unbeknown to us it is not reliable should not affect it's justification ... My argument hinges on viewing justification as a

normative notion. Intuitively, if S's belief is appropriate to the available evidence, he is not to be held responsible for circumstances beyond his ken.[11]

If Cohen is right (more on this later), the argument I'm attributing to Sinnott-Armstrong fails because the justification of a belief doesn't depend upon whether the methods that led to its adoption are reliable.

Suppose, however, that reliability is necessary for justification and for knowledge. The hypothesis that intuition is unreliable might be true, but the empirical evidence gives us no reason to think it's necessarily true.[12] So, even if we assume that (i) is true, it couldn't support an argument for ST1 and ST2 since these theses imply that moral knowledge and moral justification are *impossible*, not simply unattainable as a matter of contingent fact.

Does the argument do any better if we read it as relying on (ii)? Suppose there is relatively strong evidence that intuition is an unreliable guide. Evidence of unreliability (which is misleading evidence, since we're assuming (ii) is true, not (i)) can defeat justification, but only if someone has it or ought to have it in her possession. There are certainly some moral philosophers who have this evidence in their possession and it might be that some of them ought to know better than to trust their intuitions. The folk, however, don't have this evidence and it is counter-intuitive to say that they should have known better than to take their intuitions at face value before consulting the literature. So, I don't think the argument for ST2 is persuasive if we assume (ii).

Our first skeptical argument doesn't succeed as an argument for ST1. Evidence of unreliability (which isn't the same thing as unreliability) doesn't defeat someone's knowledge unless that evidence is in someone's possession or ought to be in her possession.[13] If this is right and ordinary folk cannot be blamed for failing to take account of the recent literature on framing effects, the best that the argument could do, assuming that (i) is correct, is show that we don't have moral knowledge as a matter of contingent fact. It doesn't tell us anything about the epistemic status of moral judgments made by those who don't have the empirical evidence that suggests that moral judgments are subject to framing effects.

1. 2 The Threat of Moral Nihilism

In this section, I want to look at another of Sinnott-Armstrong's arguments against intuitionism. He endorses moral nihilism, the view that there are no moral properties or moral facts. If this view is correct, our moral judgments are systematically false. Even if this view isn't correct, it still poses a significant epistemological problem. Moral realists often say that moral facts or properties provide the best explanation of our moral judgments, but the nihilists have their own non-moral explanations as to why we make the moral judgments that we do. The nihilist's explanatory hypotheses are skeptical hypotheses that threaten our moral judgments much in the way that, say, the hypothesis that we're deceived by a Cartesian demon threatens our perceptual judgments.

Sinnott-Armstrong's second skeptical argument can be stated as follows:

(P1) You're not justified in believing that moral nihilism is false.
(P2) You know that if it is wrong to torture babies just for fun, moral nihilism is false.
(P3) If you know moral nihilism would be false if it is wrong to torture babies just for fun and you justifiably believed that it's wrong to torture babies just for fun, you would be justified in believing that moral nihilism is false.
(C) Thus, you're not justified in believing that it's wrong to torture babies just for fun.[14]

How does this skeptical argument fare?

In his discussion of the arguments for external world skepticism, some have argued that the claim that we're not justified in believing skeptical hypotheses are false is the sort of claim that the skeptic should have to argue for.[15] It's not the sort of thing they should be allowed to argue from until they earn the right to do so. I agree. A similar point applies here. Sinnott-Armstrong does offer this justification for (1):

> To be justified ... the believer must have some way to rule out moral nihilism. To try to do that, moral intuitionists might simply cite a moral belief that is contrary to moral nihilism ... Here's one example:

> (T) It is morally wrong to torture innocent children just for fun ... But suppose that a moral nihilist appears on the scene and denies (T). What could the moral intuitionist say against such a moral nihilist? Not much. Moral intuitionists can point out

that (T) seems obvious to them ... However, to appeal to such a moral belief in an argument against moral nihilism clearly begs the question ... Such moral beliefs appear obvious to almost everyone who is not a moral nihilist, but that appearance is just what would be predicted by the moral nihilist's hypothesis that all moral beliefs are evolutionary or cultural illusions ... When both of two hypotheses would predict an observation, that observation cannot be used as evidence for one as opposed to the other.[16]

Should the intuitionist say that we could rule out nihilism? It depends upon what it takes to rule out the nihilist's view.

There are two natural ways of reading this talk of ruling out a view. First, we might say that you can rule out views that you know are incompatible with propositions you know are true. Second, we might say that you can rule out views that you know are incompatible with your evidence. On the first reading, the justification offered for (1) comes to this: you don't know that (T) is true. Doesn't this beg the very question at issue? The intuitionist view is that we have some non-inferential moral knowledge. The selection of (T) was arbitrary. It was chosen because it was thought that if we know anything non-inferentially about morality, it would be (T). To say that we cannot rule out (~T) is to say, in effect, that we have no non-inferential moral knowledge. Not only does this justification for (1) beg the question, it misses its mark. On this reading, you can't justifiably believe something unless you can rule out being mistaken. In other words, you can't justifiably what you do not know.[17]

On the second reading, the justification offered for (1) comes to the claim that your evidence is consistent with (~T). On this second reading, the argument is still question begging. To see why, think about what the intuitionist should say about the evidence you have for your non-inferentially justified moral beliefs. Suppose, for example, that you think your evidence consists of all and only those propositions that you know.[18] If E=K is correct, the argument is identical on its first and second reading. To avoid the problems with the argument on its first reading, you have to reject E=K. While E=K needs revision, the differences between E and K are relatively minor. Suppose you know p non-inferentially and you know that q is a logical consequence of p. Does your evidence for q include p? It's clear that p stands in the right support relation to q to be potential evidence for q. The question is whether p is part of *your* evidence for *q*. According to Conee and Feldman, your 'ultimate' evidence consists of those things that provide evidential support where you don't need independent evidence to treat these things as evidence.[19] Given this gloss on ultimate evidence, it seems anything you know non-inferentially belongs to your stock of evidence. Thus, in order to show that your evidence is consistent with (~T), you would have to show that your evidence includes nothing that entails (T). Since (T) entails (T), it looks like Sinnott-Armstrong can only say that your evidence doesn't rule out (~T) if your evidence doesn't include (T). So, his skeptical argument gets off of the ground only *after* establishing that you don't know (T) non-inferentially. But, the intuitionist view just is that you know things like (T) non-inferentially.

I suspect that the root of the problem is that he's assuming a dialectical conception of evidence, a conception of evidence on which your evidence against a theory is limited to facts that would be acceptable to either proponents of the theory or some neutral arbiter.[20] I think this is a defective conception of evidence. It's one thing to say that it's not sporting to appeal to obvious mental facts in a public debate with eliminativists and another to say that you oughtn't treat such obvious facts as the basis for judgments about whether to head to the medicine cabinet for aspirin. If ruling out moral nihilism required citing evidence acceptable to the nihilist, ruling out nihilism would require demonstrating that nihilism is internally inconsistent. It is unlikely that this is so and unclear why the justification of your view is lost if you cannot demonstrate that competing views are internally inconsistent. Logic alone does not conspire against the nihilist.

There might be a fourth way of understanding this talk of ruling out, but I'll wager that the fourth way will suffer from one of two defects. Either it would beg the question against the intuitionist to say that she cannot rule out the nihilist's view (as with the first two readings) or the fact that the intuitionist cannot rule out the nihilist's view tells us nothing about whether the intuitionist's moral beliefs are justified (as with the third reading).

1. 3 Cosmic Coincidence

I want to consider one final skeptical argument. This argument's intended target is not intuitionism *per se*, but the combination of intuitionism with non-naturalism about moral properties. It's not clear what the commitments of naturalism are, but it's often thought there's more to moral naturalism than just the thesis that the moral properties supervene upon the natural properties. Let's assume that the non-naturalist agrees that this supervenience relation holds. In this section, I'll defend a version of intuitionism on which moral properties supervene upon natural properties from the argument from cosmic coincidence:

(P1) Your intuitions are physical events or states.

(P2) The physical world is causally closed.

(P3) Thus, your intuitions are fully causally closed.

(P4) Ethical facts or properties are non-physical facts or properties.

(C1) Thus, ethical facts or properties do not cause anything in the physical world.

(P5) Your physically caused intuitions accurately represent non-causal ethical facts or properties only if there exists a 'cosmic coincidence' between the causal order and the non-causal facts or properties.

(P6) The need for cosmic coincidence, once realized, constitutes a defeater.

(C2) Thus, whatever intuitive justification for beliefs in ethical facts or properties you have is defeated once you realize the need for cosmic coincidence.

For the sake of this discussion, I'll grant (P1)–(P4). The real work is done by (P5) and (P6).

Bedke says this in support of (P5):

> If one's ethical commitments are psychological, physical, and so part of the casual order, and if ethical facts or properties are not part of the causal order, how, exactly, do the causal forces of the world conspire to ensure that one's ethical commitments, including intuitions and beliefs, accurately represent the ethical facts or properties? After all, the latter are not part of the causal order and so they cannot causally influence one's commitments.[21]

So as to clarify the guiding intuition that supports (P6), he adds:

> One could argue that there is a kind of coincidence foreclosed by metaphysical necessitation. Consider the possibility that some

natural fact in the causal order N causes me to have an ethical intuition and a subsequent ethical belief that *p*. Suppose that N also metaphysically necessitates the ethical fact that *p*. In such a case, it would not be *metaphysically* coincidental that my intuition and belief reflect the ethical fact, for both hold in virtue of N, where the in virtue of relation is causal in the case of the intuition and belief, and the in virtue of relation is metaphysical in the case of the ethical fact. This is true enough, but it does not eliminate the kind of coincidence central to this paper. *For notice how lucky I am that the metaphysical necessitation was tailored to necessitate the very fact my ethical belief represents.* After all, N could have necessitated some non-*p* fact, *q*. To be clear, it couldn't do so metaphysically speaking, by hypothesis, but it certainly is conceptually possible that it necessitate *q*, and more importantly, it is evidentially possible that it necessitate *q* or any other non-*p* fact given that my intuitive evidence of the ethical fact depends only on the causal order.[22]

I'm not convinced that intuition supports the case against the intuitionist. In fact, I think we can use this to run a thought experiment that supports intuitionism.

Let's imagine that a being with vast power and little better to do creates a series of planets populated by creatures that are in many ways physically and psychologically similar to us. On each planet, these creatures are wired up in such a way that they're disposed to attribute moral properties when they take it that certain natural properties are present. So, for example, there's a planet on which the creatures are disposed to think that if some action would cause someone pain, that counts against it. There's another where the creatures are wired up so as to think that there's something wrong with sodomy. There's another where the creatures are wired up to think that non-human animal pain counts for little compared to human pain. There's yet another where the creatures are very concerned with the welfare of plants. Internally, some of these creatures are similar to you. No matter how strange your views might be you have a counterpart out there somewhere. Your counterpart has similar beliefs, experiences, wants, desires. None of these creatures knows how they came to be. They have the same sorts of creation stories we do.

The argument from cosmic coincidence doesn't rest on the thought that we don't have moral beliefs, that there aren't moral facts, or that our beliefs don't fit the moral facts. Since the argument doesn't assume these things, let's stipulate that there are some creatures that have beliefs that fit the facts. We've just crossed off two of the conditions necessary for knowledge. Some of these creatures have moral beliefs that fit the facts.

There are lots of creatures wired for failure, but let's focus on the creatures wired in such a way that they are the lucky ones that get things right. Just so we're clear, these creatures aren't wired this way because someone chose them to get things right. They happen to be the ones who get things right. Given the sheer number of different wirings, the odds were that someone would get things right. We can imagine that the creator responsible for the wiring doesn't know which natural properties are the natural properties on which the moral properties supervene. She wanted to cover her bases and make sure that 'wherever' the moral properties are found, there's some group out there that judges that they are where they take them to be. To give this group a name, let's call them the 'Rossians.'

Do the Rossians have moral knowledge? If they don't, it's not because they lack true beliefs about moral matters. And, because they're wired in such a way that they reliably attribute the correct moral properties when their non-moral judgments are correct, they would seem to satisfy any reliability condition on knowledge. So, if they don't have knowledge, it's not because they don't have a reliable basis for their moral judgments. It's perfectly consistent with everything that we've said that their beliefs are sensitive and safe. Given the way that they are wired, in the nearest possible worlds where their moral beliefs wouldn't be true, they wouldn't have those beliefs. Given the way that they are wired, if they have a moral belief, that same belief is true in the nearby possible worlds. So, why shouldn't we say that they have moral knowledge?

One reason might be that nothing we've said thus far shows that their beliefs are reasonable. For all we've said, they might be in the same epistemic position as the chicken sexers. Of course, you might think that chicken sexers know the sex of the chicks that they sort and so might think that this just provides further support for the claim that the Rossians have moral knowledge.[23] If, however, you think chicken sexers don't have knowledge, this is easily remedied. We can add that the Rossians have good wiring *and* that when they take the relevant natural properties to be present, it seems intuitive to them that the moral properties are present as well. Surely if they can be wired up to track the right properties, they can be wired up to have the 'right' intuitions. If they take their intuitions at face value, aren't they reasonable?

Now we can exert some additional pressure on the skeptic. The intuition that underlies the new evil demon objection to reliabilism suggests that if someone is the same on the inside as someone who has knowledge, no matter how bad things are external to her perspective, we can still say that she's reasonable in her judgments and she is justified in making them.[24] At this point, we've effectively silenced the moral skeptic. The moral skeptic wants to say that *our* moral beliefs aren't justified and don't amount to knowledge. If ST1 is off the table, there's little the moral skeptic can say about our moral judgments.

The moral skeptic cannot say that we don't have moral beliefs. She doesn't derive her view from non-cognitivism. She cannot say that none of our beliefs fit the facts. She doesn't derive her view from moral nihilism. She cannot say that there are moral beliefs for the facts to fit and that none of our beliefs fit the facts. If I judge that giving to charity is either permissible or obligatory and she judges that that's false, she's committed to saying both that giving to charity is impermissible *and* that she doesn't know that it is. This combination of attitudes constitutes a Moorean absurdity. Such thoughts are deeply irrational.[25] Similarly, she cannot say that our moral beliefs fail to constitute knowledge and fail to be justified for purely Gettierish reasons. If she did, she'd have to concede that our beliefs are true and would be committed to the Moorean absurd thought that she does not know that they are true. Moveover, beliefs are justifiably held in Gettier cases, so this wouldn't matter to assessing the justificatory standing of our moral beliefs.

It looks like the skeptic would have to say that we're not the same on the inside as someone who has moral knowledge and argue for ST1 by arguing for ST2. The trouble she faces is that the thought experiment above suggests that ST1 is false, assuming that our standard accounts of knowledge are approximately correct. In this case, she can only argue that we're not the same on the inside as someone who has moral knowledge by arguing that our moral beliefs couldn't be true. Again, the skeptic cannot argue that our moral beliefs are mistaken without committing herself to the Moorean absurd thought that, say, giving to charity is impermissible and nobody knows what that is.

At this point that the skeptic would remind us that we haven't addressed the argument from cosmic coincidence. Yes, the Rossians have good wiring and it's true that if *they* take their intuitions at face value, they get things right as a rule. But, doesn't this miss the point? The creatures I've described get things *wrong* as a rule when they take their intuitions at face value because it's only in the rarest case that someone gets things right as it's only in the rarest case that someone is wired up in the way that the Rossians are. So, as noted above, it looks like the Rossians are lucky to get things right and this sort of luck precludes knowledge. If it does, then even if the intuition that underlies the new evil demon objection to reliabilism is correct, we have no reason to say that those who are the same on the inside as the Rossians have justified moral judgments. We have no reason to think that they're the same on the inside as someone whose moral judgments constitute knowledge.

The skeptic's argument is too crude if it rests on the thought that epistemic luck precludes knowledge. Some luck is malignant, but some is benign. Let's contrast two kinds of epistemic luck. First, there is *veritic* epistemic luck. In cases of veritic luck, the subject is lucky, so her belief is true, but she's lucky, so it easily could have been false. To sharpen this up just a bit, it's lucky that the subject gets it right given what her evidence is. Second, there is *evidential* epistemic luck. In cases of evidential luck, the subject is lucky, so her evidence is good, but she's lucky, so it easily could have been that she had worse evidence.[26] Evidential luck is thought to be benign because it's not lucky that the subject has a true belief given her good evidence. Veritic luck is thought to be malignant because it is lucky that the subject gets it right given the accidental link between her evidence and the truth.

If the case of the Rossians is a case of veritic luck, the anti-skeptical strategy outlined here is a failure. If, however, the case of the Rossians is a case of evidential luck, the anti-skeptical strategy looks pretty good. While I don't know if I can make a compelling case for the claim that the case we're dealing with is a case of evidential luck, I also don't think the skeptic can make a compelling case for the claim that it's a case of veritic luck. The intuition that underlies the argument from cosmic coincidence is a kind of anti-luck intuition. If the skeptic cannot show that the luck at issue is malignant, we're at an impasse.

The problem is this. Suppose we take the Rossians and all the other creatures and say that their evidence for their moral beliefs differs in content, not kind. By this I mean the evidence that they (i.e. the Rossians and the rest of our creatures) have for their moral beliefs is basically this: it seems that some feature of the situation calls for a certain sort of response or counts against a certain sort of response. This evidence would consist of propositions about how things seem to them and given only *that* evidence, the Rossians are lucky to get things right. This would be a case of veritic luck and that kind of epistemic luck is malignant. Suppose instead that the evidence they have for their moral beliefs differs both in content and in kind from the evidence the other creatures have. By that I mean the evidence that the Rossians have includes the propositions about how things seem *and* true propositions about which features call for certain kinds of responses. The Rossians wouldn't be lucky to get things right given that their beliefs were based on this sort of evidence. The rest of the creatures wouldn't have these facts at their disposal because their moral beliefs and intuitions don't fit the moral facts. But, if the Rossians enjoy an epistemic advantage over the others, there's no reason to think the Rossians' beliefs are veritically lucky. This would be a case of evidential luck and that kind of epistemic luck is benign.

What evidence do the Rossians have for their moral beliefs? The intuitionist should say that their evidence includes both psychological facts (e.g. that it seems that such and such a feature counts for or counts against) *and* normative facts (e.g. that such and such a feature counts for or counts against). The intuitionist should also say that this second kind of evidence isn't available to the others. If this is right the Rossian's evidence differs in content and kind from the evidence the other creatures have and so our case is a case of evidential luck, not veritic luck.

Earlier I said that your evidence includes the proposition that p if you know p non-inferentially. Non-inferential knowledge is all you need to have p as a reason for belief. I didn't say what it takes for p to *be* a reason for belief. There's currently some controversy as to whether *false* propositions can constitute evidence or reasons to believe.[27] (There's no question that they can be treated *as if* they are evidence or reasons to believe, but that's not the same thing.) If only true propositions can constitute evidence, the Rossians' evidence differs in kind from the evidence the other creatures have for their moral beliefs because their intuitions misrepresent the moral domain.

There are two promising lines of argument for the claim that false propositions do not constitute evidence. First, there's the linguistic evidence that suggests that evidence ascriptions are factive. As Unger noted long ago, the following remarks are clearly defective:

(1) What was his reason for believing that he was out of milk? It was that his fridge was empty. Of course, he didn't know that the fridge was empty.[28]

Those who deny the evidence ascriptions are factive have to offer some explanation as to why (1) seems defective. If something can be your reason for believing even if it's not true, something can be your reason for believing even if you don't know it's true.

Why then does (1) seem contradictory? Those who deny that such ascriptions are factive will have to offer some explanation as to why (1) seems defective even if it is correct. The explanation will have to say that there's something weaker than entailment that holds between the reason-ascription and the further claim that the proposition ascribed by the that-clause is true. One way to test to see if a connection is weaker than entailment is by considering the reinforcement data.[29] You can properly reinforce information that is merely pragmatically implied, but not information that is entailed. If you try to reinforce an obvious entailment, the result is a statement that seems defective, a redundant conjunction:

(2) I have a dog. In fact I have just one dog.
(3) He knows he has a dog. Not only that, he believes he has a dog.

If (1) weren't a contradiction and it didn't follow from the fact that his reason was that he was out of milk that he was out of milk, then this should seem felicitous:

(4) His reason for believing that he was out of milk was that his fridge was empty. Not only that, his fridge was empty.

Intuitively however, it seems (4) is a redundant conjunction along the lines of (3). This is some evidence that the relation between the first sentence and the second is not weaker than entailment. So, the linguistic evidence suggests that the reason (1) appears contradictory is just that it is a contradiction.

The second line of argument focuses on the relation between evidence and explanation. Our evidence or our reasons for belief can figure in explanations in two ways. When we know that p is part of our evidence, we know that so long as p is not a brute fact, there's some explanation as to why p. We also know that if p is part of our evidence, p explains certain support facts. It explains, for example, why it's likely that q if, say, the probability of q on p is high. Whether a piece of evidence figures in an explanation as the explanans or the explanandum, since we know that only facts figure in (correct) explanations, only facts constitute evidence. Views that deny that evidence consists of *true* propositions cannot account for these connections between evidence and explanation.[30]

With this in place, we can now see why the intuitionists ought to say that the Rossians have evidence that differs both in content and in kind from the evidence that the other creatures might have for their moral beliefs. It differs in content because these other creatures attribute moral properties in different situations than the Rossians do. It differs in kind because the Rossians have true moral propositions as part of their evidence and the others do not. So, the intuitionists should say that the case described is a case of evidential luck rather than veritic luck, in which case the skeptical argument isn't all that threatening.

I can anticipate two objections to the view developed here. The first is that the intuitionists don't have anything good to say about cases of error. It's a consequence of this view that the Rossians are the only subjects that have moral propositions as part of their evidence, so how can the intuitionist say that the rest of these subjects are justified in their beliefs? The second is that the account I've described is only available to the naturalists.

Let's think about some of the creatures that get things reliably wrong. These poor subjects attribute moral properties when they take certain natural properties to be present when and only when it's incorrect for them to attribute these moral properties. To give them a name, let's call them the 'Randians.' Intuitively, the Randians are just as reasonable and just as rational as the Rossians since they both form their moral beliefs by taking their moral intuitions at face value, they are internally coherent, they reason just as carefully, and so on. It's true that the Randians get things wrong as a rule, but they are no worse off than those systematically deceived by a Cartesian demon and the demon's dupes count as rational in their beliefs. I don't think it's difficult for the intuitionist to accommodate the intuition that the Randians are rational. While their beliefs aren't based on (genuine) evidence, this isn't due to a failure on *their* part. They count as rational, in part, because they respond in the way that they should have responded if the evidence had been the sort of evidence they took themselves to have. What about the intuition that their beliefs are justified? The intuitionists might go in one of two directions here. There's a difference between saying that something is rational and saying that it's justified. If someone's actions or beliefs are justified, it's not true that they should have been otherwise. If someone was rational or reasonable, it doesn't follow from the fact that they should have done things otherwise that they are anything less than perfectly virtuous. If the intuitionist wants to explain why the Randians' beliefs are just as justified as the Rossians', they can say that the justification of a belief doesn't depend upon whether it's based on evidence but whether it's formed in such a way that the believer formed the beliefs she should if her evidence was what she took it to be. Myself, I'm not inclined to say that the Randians' beliefs are just as justified as the Rossians' beliefs. Surely the Rossians' behavior is better justified than the Randians' behavior. The Rossians do what they're obliged to do and the Randians don't. If, however, the Randians really believed what they ought to have believed, it seems that they'd be justified in acting as they judged that they ought to act. Since they're not, I'd rather classify both their actions and their attitudes as excusable at best.

There is a second worry that arises for the intuitionist. The intuitionist view has to juggle two commitments. The first is that it's possible for some subjects to have moral facts as part of their evidence. The second is that these facts are not natural facts. You'll recall that the argument from cosmic coincidence assumed that moral intuitions are physical states or events. If we assume that that's so and we say that intuitions provide us with our reasons or our evidence for our basic moral beliefs, how could we also say that our evidence for these beliefs includes moral facts?

To deal with this worry, it's important to stress that intuitions can provide reasons even if the intuitions aren't themselves the reasons and aren't constituted in part by those reasons. On the account of evidence defended earlier, if you know p non-inferentially and p is a reason, p is a reason you have that you can rely on in your reasoning. To have a reason is for the thing you have to be a reason and for you to have the right to treat it as such. If you think intuitions or experiences by virtue of which it seems to you that p justify believing p to be true, these give you the right to treat p as a reason. Whether p is a reason depends upon whether p is true. There's no obvious inconsistency here in saying that the intuition is not part of the non-natural order but gives you a right to reason from premises that are true by virtue of how things stand in the non-natural order.[31]

Let's take stock. I've reviewed a few of the recent arguments for moral skepticism to see if any compels us to reject the intuitionist view. So far, the arguments we've considered don't force us to say that it's not possible to have non-inferentially justified moral belief or non-inferential moral knowledge based on intuition. In this next section, I want to gesture towards an explanation as to how intuitions justify.

2. JUSTIFYING BELIEF-FORMING METHODS

If the intuitionist is right, the belief-forming method that consists of taking our moral intuitions at face value justifies the beliefs based on those intuitions. There's a question as to why intuition justifies belief. In this final section, I want to explain why this is.

I want to begin by looking at a recent attempt to justify some of our basic belief-forming methods, one that builds on earlier work of Reichenbach's. Reichenbach once tried to justify the habit of relying on induction where that justification took the form of a kind of dominance argument.[32] Do we know that induction works? Perhaps we don't. While we don't know whether induction works or not, we know that if we're in a world where induction would work, we're better off for relying on it and if we're in a world where it doesn't, we're no worse off than we would be if we didn't rely on it. By way of analogy, he offers us this:

> A blind man who has lost his way in the mountains feels a trail with his stick. He does not know where the path will lead him, or whether it may take him so close to the edge of a precipice that he will be plunged into the abyss. Yet he follows the path, groping his way step by step; for if there is any possibility of getting out of the wilderness, it is by feeling his way along the path.[33]

In a similar way, Enoch and Schechter have suggested that a basic method of belief formation will confer justification upon our beliefs if there is a project that is rationally required for the thinker to engage in where it's possible for the thinker to succeed in this project by employing the method in question and it's not possible to successfully engage in this project if the method is ineffective. The basic structure of their justification is this: We're required to pursue some end and can only do so successfully if we, say, rely on inductive reasoning or inference to the best explanation. Thus, the use of these methods of belief formation is justified since these methods are for doing what we're rationally required to do.

They apply their approach to the method of forming beliefs based on intuition:

> ... [C]onsider the method of relying on our normative intuitions. The project of deciding what to do is quite plausibly one which is rationally required for us. Moreover, it is plausible that we can only successfully engage in this deliberative project if we have some way of coming to know normative truths. Given our constitution, our only hope for coming to know such truths is if our normative intuitions are at least reasonably reliable; if relying on these intuitions is not at all reliable, the project of deliberating about what to do is doomed to systematic failure. According to our account, it is in virtue of these facts that we are *prima facie* epistemically justified in relying on our normative intuitions (or on some privileged subclass thereof).[34]

One of the problems with using Reichenbach's approach was that he identified practical goals that we might pursue and even if pursuing those goals required relying on certain belief-forming methods, it seems he's identified the wrong sort of reason to offer epistemic justification. Enoch and Schechter try to deal with this worry by saying that there's some *epistemic* project that we're rationally required to engage in that we can only engage in if we place our trust in our normative intuitions. The trouble they face is that it's plausible that our epistemic obligations are negative rather than positive.[35] If theoretical reason only requires us not to form certain beliefs or not to form certain beliefs in certain ways, the requirement to pursue the project doesn't become a requirement to rely on intuition in belief formation.

Rather than hunt around for rationally required projects that can succeed only if we rely on intuition, let's aim lower. You can justify something by showing that it's required for something that is itself required because anything required is permitted and anything permitted is justified. If that's the strategy, why don't we call of the search for this rationally required project and find one that's rationally permitted instead?

What we're trying to do is offer a kind of theoretical vindication of making the move from a moral intuition to a moral judgment based on that intuition, to explain how these intuitions can justify. The first part of my attempted explanation is to explain why it's rational or reasonable to take intuition at face value in believing the content of that intuition rather than, say, believing the negation of that content or suspending judgment. My suggestion is that it is rational to Φ if, from the agent's perspective, Φ-ing would serve a goal the agent has (where that goal is intelligible).[36] Trying to count the moon isn't an intelligible goal, so I doubt there are rational ways of trying to do that. Trying to settle questions about moral matters is an intelligible goal. I don't have a view of the intelligible/unintelligible distinction to offer, but I assume that the skeptic's arguments aren't designed to show that the goal of settling a question about moral matter is unintelligible in the way that trying to count the moon is.

The first step in the explanation is this. If the goal of Ψ-ing is an intelligible goal and it makes sense to you to Φ as a means to that end given your perspective, Φ-ing is rational as a means for pursuing that goal. A consequence of this is that if it seems, given your perspective, that Φ-ing is a way of Ψ-ing, Φ-ing is a rational way of pursuing your goal. Next, we apply this to the case of theoretical reasoning. If it seems to you that p where the mental states by virtue of which it seems to you that p dispose you to believe p, it's *prima facie* rational to believe p. If the goal of doxastic deliberation is to settle the question whether p is true correctly, when it seems to you that p, it seems given your perspective that taking the seeming at face value just is a way of correctly settling that question, in which case it seems rational to settle the question this way.

Some authors take it that Φ-ing is justified if it is rational or reasonable, but this is a mistake. Rationality is a component or condition of justification, but it is not a sufficient one. There can be decisive reason not to pursue your goals in ways that make sense given your perspective, so assuming the gloss on rationality is right, there's more work to be done in explaining how intuitions justify than just securing agreement that intuitions rationalize or make reasonable. What has to be added, then, to turn the rational belief or the reasonable belief into the justified belief? Nothing.

I've chosen my words carefully. What we have to add to the reasonable and the rational belief to get a justified belief is nothing further, by which I mean we have to add no further reasons. If you add in extra reasons that constitute reasons not to believe, you can foul everything up, but if you add in no further reasons, you add in no further reasons not to pursue your goals in a way that's reasonable given your perspective and with no reason not to believe, nothing stands in the way of your beliefs being justified. We ought never believe without sufficient justification for our beliefs This is trivially so. To justifiably believe something is to permissibly believe something. If you don't justifiably believe or permissibly believe, your epistemic obligation is to change your beliefs. Since 'ought' implies 'reason,' if you oughtn't believe p, there's a reason not to believe p. Thus, if there's no reason not to believe p, there's no obligation not to believe p, so you're in the clear when it comes to believing p.

What reasons might there be *not* to believe something by taking a seeming (memorial, intuitive, perceptual, etc.) at face value? One reason might be that the goal that you're pursuing is unintelligible or the intelligible goal is pursued in an unintelligible way. This needn't worry us. It's reasonable to take seemings at face value so the goal of trying to settle moral questions is pursued in an intelligible way and that goal is itself perfectly intelligible.

Another reason not to believe might be that the goal is pursued in a way that is too risky. It's plausible to say that epistemic risks make for epistemic wrongs, but how is risk to be understood here? Because our concern is with justification, some will want to assess risk *subjectively*. If we assess risk this way, since there's nothing available to ordinary subjects to indicate that the seemings that support their ethical beliefs are more suspect than the seemings that support their perceptual beliefs or their mathematical beliefs, I don't think the subjectively characterized risks constitute wrongs in the case of belief based on intuition. Those with more externalist sympathies will want to assess risk *objectively* and *subjectively*. It's a contingent matter whether our intuitions score lower in terms of reliability than, say, our experiences do, so there's not much fodder here for the skeptic's argument for ST2.

Finally, some authors think that if your beliefs contravene some epistemic norm such as the truth norm or the knowledge norm, there's a reason not to hold those offending beliefs.[37] We've not seen any compelling reason to deny that our moral beliefs can constitute knowledge and no reason to deny that our moral beliefs could be true. I think we've run out of potential reasons. If there's no reason not to form beliefs on the basis of moral intuition, *that's* the theoretical justification we're looking for, the explanation as to how intuition justifies. It makes belief reasonable by virtue of its representational content and functional role. If we get lucky, the rest just takes care of itself.

CHAPTER SEVEN

PSYCHOLOGICAL CAPACITY AND POSITIVE EPISTEMIC STATUS

Peter Graham[1], University of California, Riverside

More epistemologists than ever recognize and appreciate the plurality of positive epistemic statuses. Knowledge, of course, is the central case. But there are many others. In general, positive epistemic statutes are goods or successes understood in terms of promoting truth and avoiding error. Knowledge is clearly such a good. True belief itself is another. Over the last forty or so years epistemologists have uncovered a number of such statuses—just think of all of the various theories of 'epistemic justification' they've proposed. Nearly every one isolates and at least partially explicates a good or success understood in terms of promoting truth and avoiding error.

An analogy may help. In the first half of the twentieth century philosophers of language widely held that singular terms—definite descriptions, names, indexicals, demonstratives and demonstrative phrases—all worked in the same way; they all worked the way definite descriptions work: 'singular reference' was just one thing. We now recognize that singular reference is many; singular terms don't all work the same way. Likewise there isn't just one kind of positive epistemic status.

Traditionally epistemology investigates the natures, powers and limits of our psychological capacities (Hatfield 1998). Different positive epistemic statuses correlate with different psychological capacities. Some apply, in the first instance, to believers, while others apply, in the first instance, to beliefs. Some apply to higher non-human animals like apes and maybe dolphins, as well as small children and ordinary human adults. Others apply only to reflective, mature humans. To paraphrase Adam Leite, just as mature humans have abilities animals and young children lack, mature humans enjoy positive epistemic statuses animals and children lack. "Different abilities allow for different statuses" (Leite 2008: 422).

Given the plurality, many epistemologists now self-consciously see 'epistemic justification' as a largely technical term (BonJour 2001: 49; Feldman 2008: 346). They use it as shorthand for a particular positive epistemic status they are interested in isolating and explicating. Many use it functionally for the normativity constitutive of knowledge; on this use, knowledge analytically entails justification. Many externalists tend to use 'justification' this way, in part because of the general recognition that knowledge involves a number of externalist elements or factors (e.g. Alvin Goldman, John Greco, and Ernest Sosa).

Though some internalists also insist that justification is necessary for knowledge internalists tend to connect their use of 'justification' to evidence, good reasons, rational procedures, justifying arguments, or responsible inquiry and reflection (Robert Audi, Carl Ginet, Adam Leite).

On internalist uses it is at least an open question whether knowledge entails justification. Indeed, a number of externalists grant the internalist use of 'justification' and then go on to argue that knowledge does not entail justification (Unger 1968; Dretske 1981; Kornblith 2009). Some internalists do so too. With the advent of reliabilist theories of knowledge, Robert Audi was one of the first to draw a sharp distinction between knowledge and justification (1987; 1988; 2011). On Audi's view, the externalist has the upper hand when explicating knowledge. But when it comes to justification, the internalist wins the day.

Since Audi's and other like-minded proposals in the 1980s, matters have grown more complicated, for two reasons. First, as I've already noted, there's the growing recognition of the plurality of positive epistemic statuses; there isn't just 'externalist knowledge' and 'internalist justification.' Second, for each positive epistemic status, one may naturally query whether it is entirely externalist, entirely internalist, or somewhere in between (BonJour 2001: 51; Kornblith 2010: 8).

A complete epistemology would sort out the whole plurality of positive epistemic statuses relying on a firm understanding of our psychological capacities and kinds, then isolate and explicate each one in turn, laying bare their internalist and externalist elements or dimensions. It would explicate knowledge, rationality, reason-ableness, warrant, evidence, justification, virtue, responsibility, reliability, and others, including wisdom and understanding.

I shall not attempt a complete epistemology here; that would take a rather large book if not an entire career. Instead I shall undertake a more modest task. I shall sort out four levels of mind or psycho-logical capacity and then focus on just one distinctive positive epistemic status, paradigmatically enjoyed by perceptual belief. The idea is to isolate a distinctive role for an epistemic status to play, an open spot for a good or success understood in terms of promoting truth to occupy. I shall call it *warrant* (cf. Burge 1993; 2003).

I shall discuss in some detail four levels of mind or psychological capacity. I do this partly for its own sake; getting the psychology right is philosophically worthwhile. But also for epistemology, for different epistemic statuses correlate with different psychological capacities. If one fails to appreciate psychological differences, one is apt to miss, blur, misunderstand or misconstrue various positive epistemic statuses. And it is by appreciating some of the details that one appreciates the differences. And by appreciating the differ-ences one is more likely to appreciate the point of isolating warrant, especially perceptual warrant.

1. FOUR LEVELS OF PSYCHOLOGICAL CAPACITY

Human and non-human animals use all sorts of psychological mechanisms with various degrees of complexity and sophistication for various purposes. Providing a taxonomy of possible psychological mechanisms and their relations would probably require a textbook, and given the state of our knowledge in cognitive and comparative psychology it would surely be incomplete. Regardless, relying on results in the cognitive sciences and some armchair reflection, we can roughly distinguish a handful of psychological mechanisms or capacities. Reflection on cases, experiments, philosophical theory and psychological science all contribute to advancing our under-standing of our psychological capacities and correlated epistemic statuses.

In this section I sort out four levels of psychological capacity: functional sensory-registration of information; objective perceptual representation of distal objects, attributes and relations; propositional thinking and reasoning; and critical reasoning (Burge 2003; 2009; 2010).

1.1 Sensory Registration

So there is a sense in which steel 'carries information' about the presence of oxygen in the environment: the steel wouldn't rust unless it was in contact with oxygen (Dretske 1981). Rusting obviously isn't a psychological process. Psychology doesn't begin with information carrying. Psychology begins with information used to guide biologically useful behavior.

Changes on the amoeba correspond to changes in heat, light, and acidity. The surface of the amoeba carries information about features of its environment. The surface, however, doesn't just carry information. Unlike steel, the amoeba makes use of the information carried. For unlike steel, organisms behave. Change the acidity of the water and the amoeba will change direction. Heat up one side or shine a bright light and it will turn away. The movements of the amoeba have obvious functional benefits. Heat and acidic water isn't any good for the amoeba. To fulfill its biological needs the amoeba needs to move in various ways in response to changes in its environment. The amoeba thus recruits information carried about its environment by changes on its surface—its sensory receptors—to guide its behavior in fulfilling its biological needs. To sense isn't just to carry information, but to make use of information carried by proximal stimulation in the control of biologically useful behavior.

In general a sensory system carries or 'registers' information about the whole organism's environment that assists the organism in fulfilling its whole organism biological needs. Sensory systems are systems whose function is to carry information about the environment that in turn controls or contributes to biologically beneficial behavior of the whole organism. A sensation or sensory registration is then a state of such a system; it's a state that's supposed to carry specific information about the organism's environment (Burge 2010; Dretske 1986; Godfrey-Smith 1996). Proximal information-carrying stimuli produce biologically useful behavior.

Many philosophers connect sensation with conscious sensory experience. From the first-person perspective, this can seem rather obvious, for only conscious sensations are accessible to first-person reflection. But is phenomenal consciousness present whenever sensory registration occurs? Is there something it is like for the amoeba to sense the presence of light or a physical obstacle that impedes its movement? I have my doubts. The science of consciousness does not, to my knowledge, have an answer. Sensory registration may occur long before the onset of phenomenal consciousness. Though phenomenal consciousness often accompanies human sensory registrations, it often occurs, in particular cases, without phenomenal consciousness. The connection between functional sensory information carrying and phenomenal consciousness is, to my mind, unclear. Sensory *registrations* are not always sensory *experiences*.

Sensory systems are ubiquitous in the animal kingdom; you're not a member of the kingdom unless you sense your environment, in one way or another. They are present in all species of mammals, reptiles, amphibians, birds, fish, insects, and arachnids. Having a sensory system is one way an organism fulfills its biological needs. And for many organisms sensory systems are enough; there is no need for further capacities or faculties to functionally adapt to its environment.

1.2 Perceptual Representation

Many animals also perceive distal objects, attributes, and relations; they perceptually represent their world. The amoeba only *senses* the warmth of the water. The eagle *sees* its prey emerging from the water.

What's the difference between a sensory system and a perceptual system? What else is involved in perceiving the environment beyond sensing it? What's the psychological mechanism perceptual systems deploy that sensory systems lack?

One crucial element involves *perceptual constancies* (Walsh and Kulikowski 1998; Burge 2003; 2010). Imagine a box moving towards you. As it gets closer, the two-dimensional image on your retina—the proximal stimuli on your sensory organs—will continually grow: a series of differing proximal stimuli follow one after another. But nonetheless the three-dimensional size of the box continually looks exactly the same size to you. You continue to perceptually represent the distal object—the box—as having the same attribute—the same size—despite continual changes in proximal stimulation. This is an example of what's called size constancy. Your perceptual representation is *constant*—it keeps representing the box as having the same size—despite changes in the sizes of the images on your retina. And for every type of thing we perceive—objects, size, shape, motion, location, distance, color—we rely on constancy mechanisms, mechanisms that produce representations of distal objects, attributes and relations as being the same despite various changes in sensory, proximal stimuli. It also works the other way. Two identical sensory stimuli in different environmental conditions can produce differing perceptual representations. Perceptual systems thus involve transitions from sensory stimuli that underdetermine the features of the distal stimuli to perceptual representations of the distal stimuli. Understanding these transitions is in large part what perceptual psychology is all about. Perceptual psychology asks how we form representations of a stable world from ever changing sensory input.

Sense perceptual systems involve constancy mechanisms, but mere sensory systems do not. Hence the idea: perception differs from sensory registration in 'distalizing,' in transitioning from proximal stimuli to representations of distal objects, attributes, and relations.

Sensory systems and sense-perceptual systems are two psychological mechanisms with obvious biological benefits. Many organisms only have sensory systems. Many have both. We certainly do. Fish and frogs do too. Bees do. Fleas? Worms? I don't know. Amoeba? Definitely not.

Perceptual systems produce perceptual representations. These are representations of particulars: of particular objects, particular attributes, or particular relations. But they also group or categorize the particulars as instances of groups or categories. That object is represented as *that brown body*. That physical object is represented as *that cube*, or as *that moving round body*. Perceptual representations are accurate when the particular represented has the attribute or relation the representation represents it as having (Burge 2003; 2009; 2010). Many philosophers connect perceptual representation with phenomenally conscious perceptual experience. From the first-person perspective, this can seem rather obvious, for only conscious perceptual representations are accessible to first-person reflection. But is phenomenal consciousness present whenever perceptual representation occurs?

Is phenomenal consciousness present whenever perceptual representation occurs? Is there something it is like for the bee to perceive the direction of food? I have my doubts. The science of consciousness does not, to my knowledge, have an answer. Perceptual representation may occur long before the onset of phenomenal consciousness. Though phenomenal consciousness often accompanies human perceptual representation, it sometimes occurs, in particular cases, without phenomenal consciousness. Just think of blindsight. The connection between sense perception and phenomenal consciousness is, to my mind, unclear. Not every perceptual representation is conscious, and probably not every perceptual representation that is conscious is necessarily accessible in mature humans to reflection. Perceptual *representations* are not always perceptual *experiences*.

There is a rather large literature on the form and content of perceptual representations. Are they analog or digital? Do they represent like pictures, maps, or images, or more like sentences? Do they have non-conceptual content, or is all content conceptual? Are their contents abstract Fregean *Sinn*, sets of possible worlds, or structured Russellian propositions?

Burge (2009; 2010) argues that perceptual representations have non-propositional structures or forms. Their forms are more like singular noun phrases—e.g. *that round ball, that moving blue cube*— as opposed to singular subject-predicate sentences—e.g. *that is a round ball*, or *that is an object and is moving and is blue and is a cube.* And so, in a sense, a perceptual representation with one kind of structure may have the same 'worldly' veridicality condition or the same 'content' as a sentence with a different kind of structure, e.g. *that round body* is accurate just in case the referent is round and is a body, and *that is a round ball* is accurate just in case the referent is round and is a ball. Though, in another sense, because they have different structures they have different contents, and so different veridicality conditions.

Having this kind of structure or form means that perceptual representations are non-propositional; they have non-propositional structure. Propositional structures are like the structures of indicative sentences. A representation with a structure like a singular noun phrase doesn't have that kind of structure. Propositional thoughts and other propositional attitudes, on the other hand, paradigmatically have propositional structures. Perceptual *representations* thus differ from perceptual *beliefs* in having different structures. I accept this view.

1.3 Propositional Thinking

What is propositional structure? It's not just reference and predication, for in a sense that's present in perceptual representations.

They refer to or single out a particular and group or categorize the particular as having various attributes.[2]

One difference between representations with propositional structure involves the ability to reason or draw logical inferences. Logical constants like OR and NOT operate on representations with propositional structure; they are basic connectives in truth-functional, propositional logic. If you attribute the psychological capacity to reason or draw logical inferences to a creature, then you are attributing to the creature the capacity to reason using logical constants, and so attributing to the creature representations with propositional structure. So one contrast between perceptual representations and propositionally structured representations involves the capacity to reason, to draw logical inferences, and so to represent logical relations.

Capacities to reason may come in degrees or in various packages. That is, one may only have the capacity to draw simple propositional inferences like disjunctive syllogism and simple forms of conditional reasoning, without the capacity to represent generality in the form of existential and universal quantification. The capacity may be domain specific. One creature's inferential capacity may have severe limitations. Another creature may enjoy an unlimited, universal inferential competence, limited only by time and energy.

If we use 'reasons' rather narrowly to denote representations with propositional structure—so that only reasons are involved in propositional reasoning—then it follows that the transition from a non-propositional perceptual representation to a propositional perceptual belief is not reasoning. On this usage, only propositional thinking constitutes reasoning.

Is all propositional thinking phenomenally conscious? No. A good deal is fast and automatic, beneath the level of consciousness. Some is slow and ponderous but still below consciousness. What about conscious thinking? Is it always phenomenally conscious? I don't know. But I do know the issue is currently disputed.

There is a lively debate with a very long history over the rational (logical reasoning) capacities of non-human animals (Hurley and Nudds 2006; Rescorla 2009). In the contemporary debate, it is universally agreed that animals employ both learned and innate strategies for getting around their environments. A principle capacity involves the capacity to associate stimuli. Ring a bell often enough in the presence of food, and the animal will associate a perceptual representation (or perhaps, for the behaviorist, just an auditory stimuli) of the bell with an anticipatory representation of food (or, again, just a salivating response). Associating is one 'intelligent' capacity for learning about and navigating one's environment. And it is widely thought that no matter how much representation actually goes on in animals when associating, associating isn't reasoning or relying on inference. Logical reasoning is a different kind of psychological capacity. So the contemporary debate concerns, in large part, the reasoning or inferential abilities of non-human animals. Do they, or don't they, reason?

There is some experimental evidence that suggests that apes and chimpanzees reason. In front of chimpanzees, Premack and Premack (1994) took two boxes and placed an apple in one and a banana in another. Later the chimpanzee would witness the experimenter eating the banana. Then when given the opportunity to go pick a fruit from the two boxes, the chimps would go right to the box with the apple. They concluded that the chimps reasoned something like this: there is an apple in box A and a banana in box B. But there is no longer a banana in B, so there's just an apple in A. That's why they went right for A. Animals that don't reason like this, but presented with the same information, might still look for a banana in box B, or might only slowly make their way to box A.

Josep Call (2006) set out to extend this research with experiments involving apes. But this time he wanted to compare and rule out the rival associative hypothesis. So he put two opaque cups in front of an ape, one with food and the other without. He then shook them. One made noise because of the food; the other did not. Shake the one with food, and the apes tended to pick that one. Shake the one without food and the apes tended to pick the other one. Call thinks they reasoned causally. In the first case, 'it's the food making the noise, so grab the shaking cup'. In the second 'when there's no noise, there's no food in the shaking cup, so grab the other one'.

Call ruled out the rival associative hypothesis by again placing two cups in front of the ape, one with food and one without. But then he conditioned a sound stimulus with the cup with food. Perhaps he tapped the cup with the food instead of shaking it, or played a recorded sound. It turns out that the apes performed worse in the 'associative' condition; they didn't reliably tend to pick the cup with food, despite the conditioning. They were worse at associating the stimuli than reasoning from the cause-effect relationship between the food, the shaking, and the sound. According to Call, the "apes do not simply associate a sound with the presence of food, but attribute the sound to the food itself, they understand that the food is the cause of the noise" (2006: 222). Apes, he argues, are able to "reason about their physical world" (2006: 220).

Dogs, despite their obvious intelligence, fail these tests. Though they can use sound to detect the presence of food, when you shake the empty cup before them they don't move to the unshaken cup where the food is hidden.

Additionally Watson *et al.* (2001) found that dogs (at least for some tasks) seem to deploy associative search strategies and do not rely on reasoning, where children to the opposite. They predicted that if you trained a dog to search for a ball behind three different screens, then later set the dog off to search behind the screens in the test situation when a ball was not hidden behind any three, the dog would slow down its search. The time taken to move between 1 and 2 would be less than the time taken between 2 and 3; the dogs would slow down as they searched behind the screens. Why? Because if they were relying on association, each time they failed to find a ball the experience would be an extinction trial. 'No ball here? Well, then less likely a ball there'. They then predicted that if you trained children between four and six years of age to perform the same task, the time taken to move between 1 and 2 would be more than the time taken between 2 and 3; the children would speed up their search. Why? Because if the children are reasoning logically then they are reasoning like this: 'there is a ball behind 1, 2, or 3. If there is no ball behind 1, then more likely there is one behind 2 or 3. And if not behind 2, then definitely 3'. And their predictions turned out to be right. They concluded that "dogs rely on associative guidance and children rely, to some degree, on logical guidance when searching for objects that have recently disappeared" (2001: 225). Though very smart, dogs may lack the capacity to reason. Animal intelligence doesn't require the capacity to draw logical inferences.

Non-human animals have a number of surprising cognitive abilities. But only some reason—engage in propositional thinking and propositional inference. When they do, they enjoy propositional thoughts, representations with propositional structure. Paradigmatically beliefs have propositional structure. Though many animals form perceptual (and other kinds of) representations, only some animals reason and form propositional beliefs. And since epistemology (traditionally conceived) only begins with beliefs, epistemology only begins with animals that reason.

Our first-order representational perspective on the world is largely made up of current and stored perceptual representations and propositional beliefs. Some of these states are phenomenally conscious and some are not. Some are accessible in humans to conscious reflection; some are not. Our first-order representational perspectives are formed and sustained by sub-personal and person-level systems that transition from sensory and perceptual representations to other representational states.

1.4 Critical Reasoning

Many primates reason. We reason all the time. We often reason without much awareness of what we are doing, of what our reasons are for our conclusions, and whether our reasons are any good. We often reason blind (Burge 1996: 99). Blind reasoning isn't blank or empty. It is reasoning that isn't critical reasoning. What's the difference?

Critical reasoning involves an appreciation of reasons *as reasons* (Burge 1996: 99–101). When we critically reason, we weigh and appreciate reasons for or against a proposition or a course of action. When you wonder whether something is true, or whether something is a good idea, you are reasoning critically. When you tell me why something is so, or ask me why I believe what I do, you are reasoning critically. As you read this paper and nod attentively or shake your head in disagreement, you are reasoning critically.

Critical reasoning involves an appreciation of good and bad reasons. We have an appreciation of what follows from what, when something is a good or bad reasons for a conclusion or a course of action. We have a sense of validity, a sense of good or rational support. We have a sense of when something is good evidence for something else.

When reasoning we are normally reasoning about the world, about a first-order subject matter. I'm reasoning about the library's hours and whether I should call first or just set out. But we also think about our reasons as reasons in critical reasoning, and so we think about our propositional attitudes. We assess them as true or false, as well supported or unreasonable. And so crucial to critical reasoning is the capacity to think second-order thoughts, thoughts about thoughts as reasons, as true or false, as well-evidenced or not, both thoughts about our own thoughts and thoughts about the thoughts of others. In critical reasoning we are aware of reasons as reasons, and relations of reasonable or rational support among reasons.

Critical reasoning involves conscious states and events of the agent. Critical reasoning can only engage accessible states and events. Critical reasoning reviews states currently conscious, such as a current conscious perceptual representation (is the ball really that color?) or current conscious thoughts (I thought Reno was east of Los Angeles, but maybe I am wrong). It might also bring to consciousness stored states and events, or current states and events that are currently just below consciousness. But it cannot review states and events that cannot be made conscious. Much cognitive activity is sub-personal and inaccessible to conscious review. Phenomena like blindsight suggest that even some current perceptual represen-tations—non-sub-personal outputs of the perceptual system—are beyond the purview of critical reason.

When we critically reason we often reach evaluations of our reasons that reinforce our reasons, beliefs, and decisions, but that also lead to changes or revisions in our reasons, beliefs, and decisions. Critical reasoning often leads to changes in our propo-sitional attitudes. It's one way we change our minds. It is how we regulate, revise, and review our perspective or point of view.

Critical reasoning thus involves psychological capacities not present in many higher non-human animals, as well as children, especially three-year-olds and younger. Very young children cannot represent propositional thoughts as thoughts; they cannot represent reasons as reasons; they cannot evaluate reasons as good reasons. They cannot critically reason. When they reason, they reason 'blind.'

Critical reasoning as such only requires the capacity to appreciate reasons as reasons and the ability to criticize reasons and reasoning as reasons and reasoning. Reflective critical reasoning involves more. Reflective critical reasoning "makes use of all the main concepts necessary to a full understanding of essential or fundamental elements in reasoning" (Burge 1996: 98, n. 4). We approximate reflective critical reasoning as we mature and also become more reflective about our reasoning. There is a whole range of critical reasoning between the degree exercised by children five to six years old on the one hand, and fully mature humans who have taken the time to develop their skills at critical reasoning on the other.

A good amount of our critical reasoning may be considerably less than ideal. We're subject to all sorts of biases, and we make any number of regular mistakes. Critical reasoning courses, especially those informed by current research in social psychology, aim at improving our skills at critical reasoning.

To review: steel rusts but does not sense; amoeba sense but do not perceive; bees perceive but do not reason; some primates and other animals reason but do not critically reason; mature humans sense, perceive, reason, and critically reason.

I have gone on at some length sorting out these four levels of psychological capacity in the conviction that different epistemic statuses correlate with different psychological capacities. If one fails to appreciate psychological differences, one is apt to miss, blur, or flatly misunderstand or misconstrue various positive epistemic statuses. And it is by appreciating some of the details that one appreciates the differences. And by appreciating the differences you'll appreciate the point of isolating warrant, especially perceptual warrant.

2. PERCEPTUAL WARRANT

Epistemologists have used 'epistemic justification' to denote a large number of distinct, though often related, positive epistemic statuses. It's been used to denote responsible belief, belief that results from (or is tied to) the fulfillment of epistemic duties, belief based on the exercise of intellectual virtues, reliable belief, belief based on or supported by evidence, and the normativity constitutive of knowledge. In this section I isolate a spot for the distinctive epistemic status I call warrant, and then briefly sketch my account of perceptual warrant. Warrant arises with perception and the capacity to reason. But first I want to say a few words about another epistemic status that requires the capacity to critically reason.

Call *being justified* the status you achieve when you are in a position to justify your belief. Justifying is an activity that involves the ability to adduce grounds, evidence and reasons as grounds, evidence, and reasons, and so requires the capacity to critically reason. Animals and small children can't do that. And so only those in a position to justify a belief are justified in believing it.

What occurs when we justify a belief? At least three things. First we cite some property or feature of the belief. We may cite accompanying sensory experiences: it feels hot, that's why I think we left the heater on. We may cite memories: I recall meeting Richard last week; that is why I think I know him. We may cite perceptual experiences:

look, it looks as green to me as a green apple; that's why I am sure his new car is green, not blue. We may cite various facts: the earthquake disrupted oil production; that's why prices are about to go up. We are aware of what we cite; we can't cite something we aren't aware of. Just try. As soon as you do cite it, you're aware of it. And if you're not aware of it, you can't cite it. Being able to justify requires conscious access to justifying states, events, and their justifying properties.

Second we appeal to some norm or standard. What kind? One that has to do with truth. When we give a justification, necessarily we aim at citing facts or reasons that provide good grounds or reasons for thinking the belief we are justifying is true. Since we aim at truth when justifying, justifications (*qua* arguments given when justifying) aim at truth. So when we cite a property of the belief in justifying it, and at least implicitly appeal to a standard that the belief falls under, we are implicitly if not explicitly claiming that beliefs that meet that standard are likely to be true. If we didn't think meeting that standard somehow counted towards truth, we wouldn't cite the fact that the belief meets that standard when justifying it. The process of justifying necessarily has truth as its aim (Audi 1988).

And just to be clear, these two are connected; we are aware or claim that the belief meets that standard in virtue of possessing the property cited. Justifying then cites three things: the property of the belief, the norm or standard, and falling under or conforming to the standard.

Ordinarily this is done in language in conversation with others. But we might justify a belief to ourselves, perhaps even non-linguistically. Regardless, justifying exercises our capacity to critically reason, often reflectively so. We do it a good amount of the time. Animals and small children never do, because they can't. Being in a position to justify, and so being justified, only emerges with higher-order, reflective capacities.

Being justified contrasts with being warranted, or warrant. Being justified is a positive epistemic status that correlates with critical reason. Warrant arises prior. Why should we assume, in general, that there exists such a positive epistemic status?

If higher non-human animals and small children have beliefs, then they have true and false beliefs. So trivially their true beliefs enjoy a positive epistemic status: *truth*. And surely also they know things. And so their beliefs enjoy at least two positive epistemic statuses distinct from the property of being justified. Are these the only two? Or is there another positive epistemic status their beliefs might enjoy?

Yes. Epistemologists in general are willing to attribute to animals and small children a positive epistemic status. Focusing on perceptual belief, one may ask whether relying on a perceptual representation is an epistemically proper response, or whether there's nothing epistemically special about relying on perceptual representations when forming perceptual belief. Put that way, it clearly seems there is. To paraphrase Richard Feldman, we can assess beliefs in terms of whether they are proper responses to the information the individual had to go in when forming the belief. A belief that responds properly to the information is an'epistemically proper' belief. When it comes to perceptual belief, relying on a perceptual representation is the 'proper response.' Responding in the proper way confers a positive epistemic status. And this is so even if the belief formed falls short of knowledge, and even if it falls short of truth. And since children and animals rely on perception, their beliefs enjoy such a status.

Feldman recognizes that different epistemologists will offer different accounts of what constitutes the proper response. Still they agree on the general idea. "Reliabilists, proper functionalists, evidentialists of various stripes, and others, all agree that there is some notion of a proper response to information (or evidence or stimuli), and that paradigmatic epistemic evaluations are about this. A belief is favorably evaluated when it is a proper response and unfavorably evaluated when it is an improper response" (Feldman 2008: 347).

As I use 'warrant,' a warranted perceptual belief is an 'epistemically' proper response to a perceptual representation, a response that does not entail truth and may fall short of knowledge. Epistemologists may happily agree that perceptual beliefs enjoy warrant, while disagreeing over its constitutively necessary, or constitutively sufficient, or constitutively necessary and sufficient, conditions.

So I think once we have a rudimentary grasp on the nature of perception and perceptual belief, we're all willing to recognize that perceptual beliefs have an epistemology, and so enjoy various positive epistemic statuses, but not just knowledge and true belief. Warrant is an intermediate status; a warranted belief is a 'proper' response to a perceptual representation.

I shall therefore assume that perceptual beliefs paradigmatically enjoy warrants, and that perceptual beliefs are warranted, in part, by perceptual representations. Perceptual warrant is empirical warrant; empirical warrant essentially depends on sense-perceptual representations for its warranting force. Perceptual warrant depends upon the exercise of perception and essentially relies on perceptual representation. Perceptual warrant partly consists in being a proper response to a perceptual representation.

Perceptual belief involves a transition from non-propositional perceptual representation to propositional perceptual belief. Ordinarily the perceptual representation plays a constitutive role in the individuation of the perceptual belief. Perceptual warrant thus partly turns on the transition from the perceptual representation to the perceptual belief. Insofar as we are warranted when relying on perception, both the perceptual representation and the transition from representation to belief contribute to the warrant for the perceptual belief.

I have also assumed that perceptual representations lack propositional structure and so are not reasons, and so not warranting reasons. The transition from a perceptual representation to a perceptual belief is then not an instance of good or warranting reasoning. I know that a number of philosophers tend to use 'reason' more broadly so that non-propositional perceptual representations count as reasons for perceptual beliefs, or that even non-representational facts or worldly states of affairs count as reasons. The word does not matter. What matters is the distinction between representational structures and capacities. Perceptual representations are non-propositional and do not require the capacity to reason. Perceptual beliefs are propositionally structured representations and require the capacity to reason.

Following Burge's terminology, I call non-propositional warrants and contributions to warrant *entitlements*. Perceptual representations entitle perceptual beliefs; they contribute to the overall warrant for a perceptual belief. The transition from a representation to a perceptual belief also plays a role. We are entitled to rely on the normal transition from perception to belief. The normal transition thus contributes to the overall warrant for a perceptual belief; not just any old transition will do. Since the perceptual representation and the transition from representation to belief are both non-propositional, they are both entitlements: non-propositional contributions to warrant.[3]

So far this is mostly terminology. Epistemologists of different persuasions should find nothing objectionable in the terminology.

This is especially true for epistemologists that recognize the existence of positive epistemic statuses that apply in the first instance to beliefs, especially the perceptual beliefs of animals and small children.

But now we can see the point of the terminology. Being justified or justified belief only arises with critical reason. Warrant arises prior, with perception and the capacity to reason. But not all warrant arises from reasons—other warranted beliefs. Entitlements are non-propositional warrants, warrants that are not themselves other warranted beliefs.

There are two contrasting tendencies in most theoretical explications of warrant. One is associated with reliabilism. Reliability theories of warrant emphasize *mind-world* connections, *vertical* connections between the outputs of the belief-forming process or system, on the one hand, and the stretch of the world that comprises the subject matter of the process or system, on the other (Burge 2010: 50–1). Warrant, on this view, entails reliability; most warranted beliefs, necessarily, are true. Warrant actually results in truth, at least for the most part. This first tendency sees warrant as a good route to truth. Like substantive views of justice, good outcomes constitute good procedures.

The second tendency emphasizes good procedure or correct processing in belief-formation; it emphasizes *mind–mind* connections, *horizontal* connections between input representations to the belief-forming system or procedure and the resulting outputs. Rational procedures in logic, mathematics and experimental science provide the model. John Pollock and Joseph Cruz have championed this tendency (Pollock and Cruz 1999; Pollock 1999). Applying the models to perceptual belief formation, the perceptual beliefs of animals and small children would enjoy warrant for perception is a good or correct epistemic procedure. Warrant, at best, properly aims at truth, even if it doesn't actually result in true beliefs. Like procedural views of justice, good procedures stand on their own two feet.

Though contrasting, these two tendencies are not necessarily opposing. I see the value in understanding warrant as first and foremost the result of conforming to correct procedures. However, I agree with the first tendency that warrant is, fundamentally, constitutively associated with reliably getting things right; that's where the connection between truth and warrant lies.

Robert Audi drew a similar contrast (1988). *Ontological* conceptions of 'justification' tied it to reliably connecting with truth. *Teleological* conceptions, on the other hand, tie 'justification' to properly aiming at truth. The first emphasizes outcomes, the second emphasizes goals.

In the remainder of the paper I shall sketch my own account. It explicates perceptual warrant in terms of reliably getting things right in normal conditions. And so in a sense I've got a reliabilist view. But it will also emerge that my account is rather friendly to second tendency views.

This is not the place to argue in detail for my account of perceptual warrant, or to argue against different accounts. It's a big project, only partially completed (Graham 2010a; 2010b; 2011a; 2011b; in preparation-a and -b). But sketching the account should provide an existence proof for the role. A simple de facto reliability theory might have done the same thing, but in a way less plausible, at least to my mind, in part because it would fail to capture the horizontal tendency in explicating warrant, especially perceptual warrant.

My account of perceptual warrant exploits four main ideas: the connection between functions and norms; the connection between goods or successes and the fulfillment of functions or the meeting of norms.

Perceptual warrant is just one kind of warrant. Different kinds may require different accounts. Recall the methodology: I have isolated a role for a positive epistemic status by distinguishing perception and reason, on the one hand, and critical reasoning, on the other. So there is a role for a positive epistemic status that applies, in the first instance, to the perceptual beliefs of animals and small children, a status that falls short of knowledge and like many other statuses does not entail truth, despite being understood in terms of promoting truth and avoiding error. I have also assumed that perceptual beliefs enjoy this status. So we are looking for a good or success understood in terms of promoting truth and avoiding error that perceptual beliefs clearly enjoy, a property of perceptual belief that fills that role.

My account of perceptual warrant and entitlement exploits four main ideas: the connection between functions and norms; the connection between goods or successes and the fulfillment of functions or the meeting of norms; the etiological theory of functions associated with Larry Wright (1973) and Ruth Millikan (1984), among many others; and the empirical claim that human perceptual systems have, as one of their functions, the function to reliably induce true beliefs.

The first idea is straightforward. Functions are norms or standards for what a functional item is supposed to do (what effect it is supposed to produce). Your car is supposed to take you to work. Your stapler is supposed to staple papers together. Your heart is supposed to pump blood. When your car gets you to work it has fulfilled its function. When you heart pumps blood it does what it is supposed to do.

Cars, hearts and staplers are all also supposed to work or operate a particular way. Functioning (operating, working) normally is another norm or standard your car, heart and stapler may fulfill. Here are two examples that illustrate the difference between function fulfillment and normal functioning. Suppose you take your car into the shop for inspection. Your mechanic may put your car up the lift and then run it at maximum speed. Up the lift your car may be functioning normally (it's in perfect shape) but since it is not taking you anywhere, it is not fulfilling its function. In order to do that it needs to be in normal conditions. You'll have to take it down the lift and drive off the lot to use it to take you where you want to go. Here's the second example. Suppose a surgeon removes your heart from your chest in a complicated, futuristic surgery, and then places it in a vat where it's chemically and electrically stimulated so that it continues to beat and function normally. Now your heart is, as it were, up the lift. But no blood is flowing through; maybe it's orange juice instead, or nothing at all. Your heart is functioning normally but not fulfilling its function. So there are two norms or standards for functional items: function fulfillment and normal functioning.

That's the first idea. The second asserts that fulfillments of functions or the meeting of norms are goods or successes for functional items. It's a good for the heart to pump blood. It's a good or achievement for a heart to function normally. These goods are not necessarily goods for the whole organism, though biological functions are constitutively associated with whole organism goods. Functional goods are not necessarily moral or aesthetic goods either. From the moral point of view, it might be a bad thing for a morally bad creature's heart to function normally. Architecture might fulfill its functions, despite any political and aesthetic consequences.

The third idea is the etiological theory of functions and normal functioning. On the etiological theory, the function of an item is its selected effect. Crudely, the function of a type T is F just in case F is a selected effect of ancestors of T, where descendants exist because ancestors did F. Think of your eyes. They help you see. And why do we have eyes? Because precursors of our eyes helped our ancestors see. Seeing helped them fulfill their biological needs so that they might produce offspring and thereby produce descendant eyes. The selected effect of ancestors of the type explains why the functional item type exists. Natural selection is one kind of selection. Much learning involves another kind. The item can be a trait like an organ but also a form of behavior or an acquired skill.

The distinction between a function of an item and an 'accidental' side effect partly motivated the etiological account. It's the function of the heart to pump blood, but it also makes regular thumping noises. We have hearts now because they pump blood, not because they make regular noises. Pumping blood is the selected effect, not making noise.

When an item has an etiological function there is a historical explanation for why the item has that function (Millikan 1984). Look at why ancestors were selected for a particular effect. The explanation will include how the item operated in its circumstances so as to produce the selected effect. The way the item worked or operated according to the explanation then counts as *normal functioning*. The circumstances in which it was selected for producing that effect while working that way then count as *normal circumstances*. When an item has an etiological function it is then *a priori* that *ceteris paribus* it will produce its selected effect (it will fulfill its function) often enough in normal conditions when functioning normally. If it didn't produce the effect often enough in normal conditions when functioning normally then it would not have been selected for that effect (selection can't work on effects that don't occur), and then it wouldn't have that effect as a function.

An important consequence follows. Normal functioning (working or operating the way the item is supposed to work or operate) is then constitutively associated with function fulfillment. If it didn't produce the functional effect while working normally, then it wouldn't have that function, and nothing would count as normal functioning. Normal functioning is then partially understood and individuated in terms of function fulfillment; normal functioning *just is* operating the way it operated in normal conditions when fulfilling its function. Normal functioning thus 'encodes' function fulfillment; the latter *types* the former. What makes the transition within the trait, system or behavior a normal or correct transition involves producing functional outcomes in normal conditions. 'Horizontal' correctness within the trait or system requires 'vertical' correctness, often enough, in normal conditions; those inner transitions wouldn't be 'horizontally' correct unless they resulted in 'vertically' correct outcomes.

Even so, normal functioning and function fulfillment are token distinct, for one can function normally without function fulfillment. Don't forget the car up the lift. The car functions normally but it doesn't take you where you want to go.

Putting the first three ideas together, an item with a function can meet or satisfy two standards: it can fulfill its function and it can function normally. And when an item has an etiological function, normal functioning is constitutively associated with function fulfillment. And so when an item has an etiological function, both norms that it may meet are constitutively associated with function fulfillment. That's obvious when it fulfills its function; function fulfillment is trivially associated with function fulfillment. It requires understanding the constitutive association between normal functioning and function fulfillment to see why this is so for normal functioning. Since normal functioning 'encodes' function fulfillment, normal functioning is a good or success understood in terms of function fulfillment. Horizontal correctness 'encodes' vertical connections; horizontal correctness is a good or success understood in terms of vertical connections.

So here we have a general theory of goods constitutively associated with functions and norms, especially norms for items with etiological functions. My account of perceptual epistemic entitlement emerges when this general theory is applied to our perceptual belief-forming capacities.

Perceptual beliefs result from transitions from perceptual representations. Perceptual representations are formed through the operation of our sense-perceptual organs and the workings of the perceptual system. Suppose empirically that an etiological function of the primate perceptual system is to form veridical representations reliably. Suppose empirically that an etiological function of the perceptual system in humans is to form true perceptual beliefs reliably. Suppose it does the latter, in part, by doing the former. Then when the human perceptual system is functioning normally in normal conditions it will, *ceteris paribus*, reliably induce true perceptual beliefs. Normal functioning for the system is then constitutively associated with reliably forming true beliefs; our normally functioning perceptual belief-forming process 'encodes' reliably getting things right. The mind-mind procedure 'encodes' mind-world relations.

Two goods constitutively associated with reliably promoting true belief then apply to our perceptual belief-forming systems. One arises from normal functioning, the other from function fulfillment. In previous work I emphasized the good that arises from normal functioning. I have concluded that *prima facie pro tanto* perceptual epistemic entitlement consists in the normal functioning of the perceptual system and the perceptual belief-forming process, for the overall process has forming true beliefs reliably as an etiological function. Normal functioning is then a good or success understood in terms of promoting truth and avoiding error—a paradigm case of a positive epistemic status—that does not involve reasoning, and so counts as an entitlement, a warrant supporting the resulting perceptual belief (Graham 2010a; 2011a). But for the same reason fulfillment is also a positive epistemic status for the perceptual belief-forming system. One kind or dimension consists in normal functioning, and the other consists in function fulfillment.

And so I have advanced a 'proper function reliabilist' account of perceptual entitlement. Other accounts in the ballpark include Plantinga's 'intelligent design' reliabilist account (Plantinga 1993), and Tyler Burge's account that relies on his distinctive anti-individualist account of the natures of perceptual states (Burge 2003). I discuss Burge's account elsewhere (Graham in preparation-b).

Plantinga's use of 'warrant' suggests that he is really talking about knowledge, and not about the positive epistemic status I have used 'warrant' to isolate. But in fact this is not entirely so. Though Plantinga is not explicit about this, his account involves three grades of warrant. The first requires that the belief-forming process be designed to promote true beliefs in normal conditions, and that the plan be a good one, so that if it were in normal conditions it would reliably promote true beliefs when operating according to the design plan. A brain-in-a-vat might operate according a good design plan, and so enjoy the first level of warrant. It's at this level that his use agrees with mine. The second requires being in normal conditions too, and so requires globally reliably producing true beliefs. The third requires the absence of 'local relevant alternatives' like fake barns, and so requires 'local' reliability. When all three are in place, 'warrant' entails truth. And so when his followers say that warrant entails truth, it's the positive epistemic status that involves all three levels that they are talking about. I compare and contrast his view with mine elsewhere (2011c; in preparation-a). Since his first level accords with mine, he too would recognize the role, despite his focus on knowledge.

An objection Plantinga and many others would lodge against my account is that it wrongly assumes that Mother Nature cares about truth. She only cares about what contributes to survival and doesn't care one whit about truth. So long as it works, it doesn't matter if it gets things right. Though there's an obvious truth in this point, it does not touch my view. The obvious truth is that it's not *a priori* that natural selection would select for true beliefs or reliable belief-forming systems; it's not *a priori* necessary that any representational system have the evolved or learned function of getting things reliably correct. But a representational system could still, empirically, have, as a matter of fact, been selected for reliably getting things right. Just as it's not *a priori* that Mother Nature select for hearts, but it's empirically entrenched that she selected for them nonetheless; it's empirically well-established that Mother Nature selected our eyes, among other things, for reliably informing us about the properties and attributes of distal objects in our natural environments. I discuss these issues at greater length elsewhere (Graham 2011a; 2011b).

I have sketched distinctions between different levels of mind or psychological capacity out of the conviction that different epistemic statuses sometimes correlate with different psychological capacities. This is surely true of being justified as I defined it; it's a status that requires the capacity to exercise critical reflection. It's also true of warrant. For warrant arises with perception and the capacity to reason, but doesn't require the capacity to critically reason. That's not to say that beliefs formed and sustained through critical reason lack warrant, but only to say that warrant emerges prior to the development and exercise of critical reasoning.

My methodology focused on carving out a role for a distinctive epistemic status. I've relied on a four-level account of psychological kinds, the general idea of a positive epistemic status, and a general theory of functions and goods in order to isolate both a distinctive epistemic role and a realizing property. You can accept the role without accepting the realizing property.

CHAPTER EIGHT

REASONABLE DISAGREEMENT: SIDGWICK'S PRINCIPLE AND AUDI'S INTUITIONISM

Roger Crisp, St Anne's College, Oxford;
Dept of Philosophy, Boston University

1. DISAGREEMENT AND SUSPENSION OF JUDGMENT

Consider the following case.[1]

Birds. You and a friend are wandering together in the countryside. The light is good. Both of you have recently been attending a course for novice ornithologists, and each of you knows that the other is roughly equally good at bird-identification. At the same moment, each of you sees a bird on a tree-branch about ten meters away. You believe it to be a redwing, while your friend says it is a song thrush.

What is the rational response to this disagreement? Here is Henry Sidgwick:

Since it is implied in the very notion of Truth that it is essentially the same for all minds, the denial by another of a proposition that I have affirmed has a tendency to impair my confidence in its validity ... And it will easily be seen that the absence of ... disagreement must remain an indispensable negative condition of the certainty of our beliefs. For if I find any of my judgments ... in direct conflict with a judgment of some other mind, there must be error somewhere: and *if I have no more reason to suspect*

151

error in the other mind than in my own, reflective comparison
between the two judgments necessarily reduces me temporarily to a
state of neutrality. And though the total result in my mind is not
exactly suspense of judgment, but an alternation and conflict
between positive affirmation by one act of thought and the
neutrality that is the result of another, it is obviously something
very different from scientific certitude. (Sidgwick 1907: 341–2;
italics added)

Sidgwick's language here is self-referential and descriptive: he
tells us that *he is* reduced to a state of neutrality rather than that
anyone in such circumstances *should* be. But given the context—he
is explaining the fourth of a series of conditions which an apparently self-evident proposition is required fully to meet if it is to
count as having attained 'the highest degree of certainty' (1907:
338)—it is clear that he is to be understood as making the latter,
general, normative claim. His principle is something like the
following:

Sidgwick's Principle: A person who judges that *p*, if she finds that
some other person judges that *not-p*, and if she has no reason to
believe that other person to be in a worse epistemic situation than
her, should suspend judgment on *p*.[2]

Now *Birds* of course does not concern apparently self-evident
principles. But Sidgwick's principle in fact gives a plausible answer
as to what would be the rational response: moving to a 'state of
neutrality.' Sidgwick says that the 'total result' will not be *exactly*
suspension of judgment, but 'an alternation and conflict' between
positive affirmation and neutrality. What I take Sidgwick to be
recognizing here is that you will—and may—continue to affirm
that the bird *appears to you* to be a redwing, while in response to
a question by a third-party about the bird's identity you should
say, "Redwing or song thrush—I really don't know which." The
reason for this is quite simple. Since you believe your friend to be
your 'epistemic peer,'[3] you take her to be as likely as you to be right
about the case at hand. What she says gives you no reason to doubt
her epistemic status (things would have been quite different if she'd
identified the bird as a green woodpecker or a wren, or indeed
if another ten or twenty onlookers had agreed with you). Your

epistemic circumstances are symmetrical, and hence suspension of judgment is the only rational response.[4]

What is an intuition? Robert Audi (2005: 33–6) notes four conditions for a belief or belief-like state to meet if it is to count as an intuition:

(1) The *non-inferentiality* requirement (insofar as the proposition is intuitively held, it is not believed on the basis of any premise).

(2) The *firmness* requirement (intuitions must be accompanied by a reasonably strong sense that the proposition in question holds).

(3) The *comprehension* requirement (intuitions must be held on the basis of an adequate understanding of their content).

(4) The *pretheoreticality* requirement (intuitions, *qua* intuitions, are neither dependent on theoretical evidence nor held as theoretical hypotheses).

Now consider the following case.

Categorical Imperative. You are a well-trained and highly-regarded professional moral philosopher, working in an outstanding philosophy department. For many years, you have studied historical and contemporary works of philosophy, considered the various positions available in ethics, and published many books with excellent university presses and articles in top journals. You believe that you should '[a]ct in such a way that you always treat humanity, whether in your own person or in the person of any other, never simply as a means, but always at the same time as an end.'[5] This belief of yours is non-inferential and pre-theoretical: you see it as stating a fundamental principle of ethics on the basis of which any reasonable ethical theory must be developed. You have thought hard about each of its elements—what an act is, what the scope of 'humanity' covers, what a person is, and what treating someone as an end consists in. And you are utterly convinced. With your view now finally worked out to your satisfaction, you decide to discuss it with a colleague in the same department. This colleague has a similar background to you, is equally well trained, and has an equally impressive publication record. She listens patiently while you explain your Kantian principle, reflects seriously upon it, and rejects it. Her own position—which she has developed after a period of reflection similar to yours—is that we should act to produce the greatest overall good, good being understood to consist only in the welfare of sentient beings. She explains her view to you, equally patiently, including its implication that it can be acceptable to treat someone as a means, and you reject that view.

This case is directly analogous to *Birds*, and so, according to Sidgwick's principle, you should—at least for the time being—suspend judgment on the Kantian principle.[6] As you would (or at least *should*) admit, you have no more reason to suspect that your colleague is making a mistake than that you are, and of course she is in the same position regarding you. You are not required to suspend judgment entirely on the question of how to act. But, despite the way things appear to you, you are required—for the moment, anyway—to give equal credence to both the Kantian and the utilitarian positions.

Does this case suggest that no ethical intuition can be said to be of the 'highest certainty,' and hence that no ethical intuition can plausibly be said to constitute knowledge? In a previous paper (2007: 34), I suggested the following candidate as a piece of ethical knowledge:

Pain: Non-deserved suffering of any agent A that would be caused in or by some action of A counts (though not always decisively), for A, against the performance of that action by A.

Not everyone, I admit, will accept *Pain*. Some will reject the terminology of counting for and against; others—particularists—will deny *Pain* 'on principle,' as it were.[7] It is true that complete consensus would strengthen *Pain*'s claim to the highest degree of certainty. But those who deny *Pain* are a *tiny* minority, and there is, I suggest, sufficient consensus here for those who accept it not to be required to suspend judgment on it. So as long as one's epistemic state meets Audi's conditions, we have here a candidate for intuitive knowledge.

Unfortunately for ethical theorists, however, the opposite is the case when it comes to the kind of first-order principles which form the basis of 'ethical theories' as usually understood. Indeed, even if we use capacious categories (utilitarian, Kantian or deontological, virtue-ethical, contractarian, feminist, or whatever), any theorist will almost certainly find herself not only in a situation regarding other thinkers analogous to that described in *Categorical Imperative*, but in a minority in any controversy at the level of ethical principle. That was really the claim I wanted to press against Audi in my earlier paper: any ethical intuitionist is required to suspend judgment on first-order ethical theory. This is not to say that philosophers cannot continue to report on how things appear to them, and to debate with one another in the usual way. But it does mean—on the plausible assumption that one cannot have knowledge of any proposition on which one is epistemically required to suspend judgment— that, in ethical theory as it is usually understood in contemporary philosophy, we know almost nothing.

In response to my paper, Audi (2007a) offered several suggestive and interesting arguments. He made further points about disagreement in a slightly later paper (2008a). In the present paper, my main aim is to continue the debate. Since the arguments in the first of these two papers by Audi were directly in reply to my own, I shall focus primarily on those, bringing in the later arguments as appropriate. But before that I wish briefly to defend the application of Sidgwick's principle to issues in ethical theory against some recent and powerful criticisms by Ralph Wedgwood (2010).

2. WEDGWOOD ON SIDGWICK'S PRINCIPLE

Wedgwood draws a distinction between *general* and *specific* epistemic principles (2010: 230). The former apply to all beliefs, and include, for example, principles of logical consistency; the latter specify the rational response to some particular type of mental state, a possible such principle being that we should take our sensory appearances at face value.[8] Wedgwood's view is that special principles require special justi-fication. And, he suggests (232), Sidgwick's principle is clearly special, since it tells us how to respond to a particular sort of mental state—that of the belief that another thinker accepts *p* when one accepts *not-p*.[9]

One might seek to construe Sidgwick's principle as applying to all beliefs, and hence as general. Just as, in the case of any belief, it should be consistent with all other beliefs, so, in the case of any belief, it should be suspended if it is inconsistent with that of an epistemic peer. (Likewise, of course, one might seek to construe an allegedly paradigmatically general principle as special. So the principle that one's beliefs should be consistent applies to any specific belief which is found to be inconsistent with some other.)

But the real weight of Wedgwood's argument rests on the claim that there is a much simpler way to understand the epistemic significance of information about the beliefs of others (233)—as just one more item of information to be understood in terms of general epistemic principles, without any need for Sidgwick's principle. This, Wedgwood suggests (233–4), is a more economical position, since all we have in play are general epistemic principles and particular beliefs.

Wedgwood's point about economy is well taken. But an advocate of Sidgwick's principle can respond with the claim that—whether or not that principle is to be seen as general or specific—it is in fact derivative from more fundamental general epistemic principles, such as the principle that one should proportion one's belief to the evidence.[10] And in the case of both *Birds* and *Categorical Imperative*, the evidence is clear—you and your interlocutor are equally likely to be right. This also allows the Sidgwickian to respond to Wedgwood's second argument (234–5) in favor of his view—that it can explain not only cases of epistemic parity, but the wide variety of cases in which we have to respond to the views of others (who may often not be peers).[11]

The third advantage Wedgwood claims for his position is that it can explain why refusal to give up one's moral view in a case such as *Categorical Imperative* may be rational. Wedgwood offers an account of epistemic rationality in terms of general principles concerning conditional beliefs (233). So, to use his example, if he is testing some substance in the laboratory, given his previous mental life, it is rational for him to have a high conditional degree of belief that the liquid he is testing is an acid, once the litmus paper he has inserted into it has turned red. So, in the case of *Categorical Imperative*, you might well, even before you engage in the debate with your colleague, not attach a high conditional probability to the proposition that she is right, on the supposition that she denies the second formulation of the Categorical Imperative. That is, 'the information that I believe *p* may *by itself* give you sufficient reason to think that I am probably less reliable than you are' (236).

The general idea here—that one's assessment of the reliability of a potential epistemic peer should not be independent of the content of that potential peer's view on the question at issue—seems not only correct, but consistent with Sidgwick's principle as I have stated it.[12] If your colleague responds to your assertion of the Categorical Imperative with, say, the principle that one should act so as maximally to promote the doctrines of the Unification Church, it would be absurd not to take this as evidence of one's epistemic superiority to her. But the problem arises in *Categorical Imperative* because you must accept that your colleague's view is as *reasonable* as your own. To assert otherwise seems *unreasonable*, and this provides a response to the final charge Wedgwood makes against Sidgwick's principle—that it is revisionary. Reasonable revision is preferable to unreasonable intransigence.[13]

But must you accept that your colleague's view is indeed as reasonable as your own?[14] I have accepted that, even if before the discussion the evidence of your colleague's epistemic parity was conclusive, if she bases her ethics on the promotion of the Unification Church you are entitled to see yourself as epistemically superior. Why isn't the fact that she denies a principle you see as self-evident, and avers as self-evident a principle you reject, at least *some* evidence of epistemic inferiority—enough evidence to justify you in not suspending judgment?

The reason why mere disagreement is not evidence of epistemic inferiority is that there may be no theory of error available. In *Birds*, had you noticed the grubbiness of your friend's spectacle lenses, you would have had a justification for giving less weight to her interpretation of what you are seeing. Likewise, in the Unification Church case, it would be reasonable for you to assume that your friend has been subjected to some kind of brainwashing technique. But no ethical theorist can plausibly deny that the second formulation of the Categorical Imperative and utilitarianism are equally reasonable. That is why asserting either one cannot be taken, by itself, to be evidence of epistemic inferiority.

But Wedgwood has a further argument in favor of the rationality of moral intransigence in such cases. In a response to an argument for Sidgwick's principle based on work by Allan Gibbard, he points to a difference between my own moral intuitions and those of others (239–41). In *Categorical Imperative*, you can base your belief in the second formulation of the imperative directly on your own moral intuition; but any moral belief you might come to on the basis of your colleague's intuition must be itself based indirectly on beliefs about that intuition:

At least assuming what epistemologists call an 'internalist' view of rationality, the facts that make it rational for one to revise one's beliefs in a certain way must be capable of *directly guiding* one towards revising one's beliefs in that way. But, as I have argued, the fact that someone else has a certain mental state cannot directly guide one in one's revisions of one's beliefs. It is only one's own mental states that can do this. So it is simply out of the question that other people's intuitions should play the same role in rationally guiding my reasoning as my own intuitions. At most, it might be that *my beliefs* about other people's intuitions should play the same role in guiding my reasoning as my own intuitions. But *my intuitions* seem to be such different mental states from *my beliefs about other people's intuitions* that it is implausible to claim that they should play exactly the same role in guiding my reasoning. (240)

There is much to agree with here. One cannot deny Wedgwood's claim that moral intuitions, even if they are themselves beliefs or belief-like states, clearly differ from beliefs about others' intuitions. And for that reason he is right to conclude that these two different items could not plausibly be thought to play the same role in guiding reasoning. As he says, intuitions will play the role of direct guidance, while a belief about others can guide only indirectly. But we might raise the question whether indirectness must be taken to signify epistemic weakness. In our two original cases, you believe that your interlocutor is an epistemic peer, and should therefore conclude, on the basis of the evidence available to you, that, since she is no less likely to be right than yourself, you should suspend judgment. It is true, of course, that if you are asked by a friend for some practical moral advice, you are likely to reason on the basis of the second formulation of the categorical imperative. So in that sense your own moral intuitions will guide you in a way that your colleague's will not. But, again, that reasoning, if properly conducted, should take you only to a judgment that, it *appears* to you that, say, an important promise should be kept, although it is inconvenient to do so.

3. THE CASE OF *R* AND *S*

My earlier paper (2007: 33) included the following case, more thinly described than *Categorical Imperative*:

Consider the situation of an ethical thinker, *R*, who has a normative intuition that *p* which meets all of Audi's requirements

... But now *R* comes across another thinker, *S*, who asserts *not-p*. Immediately, according to the consensus condition,[15] this should impair her confidence in *p* ... [U]nless *S*'s epistemic state is significantly faulty ... *R* may well feel that her trust in *p* has been dented.

Audi's responses to my arguments are tightly constructed. For that reason, rather than summarize his claims, I propose to state them *verbatim* and then provide a commentary and response. About the *R* case, he begins as follows:

In Crisp's example, *R* is supposed to be justified in believing that *S* is in roughly as good an epistemic state as *R*. Should *R*'s confidence diminish? One difficulty with this case is that confidence is a psychological notion whose bearing on justification needs clarification. The strength of our confidence that *p* need not correlate highly with our degree of justification for it. Furthermore, Crisp is thinking of self-evident propositions, which are only one kind I hold to be (often) intuitively knowable. Even when they are known, however, they need not be believed with 'certainty'—an elusive concept I have treated in detail elsewhere (2003, chapter-Chapters 8 and 10). There are also degrees of justification; hence, ample justification for believing a proposition might not be of the high degree appropriate to certainty. (Audi 2007a: 205)

Audi's distinction between psychology and justification here is well taken, and Sidgwick should perhaps have been clearer about it than he was. As we have seen, Sidgwick's principle concerns the question of when a proposition can be said to be of 'the highest degree of certainty.' The ambiguity of 'certain' was present in its Latin root *certus*, which can be used of persons, to mean 'certain of,' or of propositions, to mean 'settled.' I take it that Sidgwick has the second sense primarily in mind, and sees the first as such as to be elucidated by it. In other words, failure by some proposition to satisfy the principle is a failure in objective justification or 'justifiedness,' and the rational response by someone who assents to that proposition and recognizes its failure to meet the condition is lack of a sense of certainty—to the point, indeed, of complete suspension of judgment.

Audi is also right to note that Sidgwick's (and my) focus was on self-evident propositions. As I have already suggested, however, I believe that Sidgwick's principle throws into doubt *any* proposition which fails to meet it. I should also register a certain amount of puzzlement at Audi's suggestion that non-self-evident propositions can be intuitively knowable. I suspect that he may be operating with a non-standard conception of self-evidence here, since on the face of it he seems to have established a definitional connection between knowledge by intuition and self-evidence. Consider for example his claim (2007b: 9) that principles of *prima facie* obligation are self-evident in that: "first, an adequate understanding of them suffices for being *justified* in believing them; second, if we believe them on the *basis* of such an understanding, we know them." Now recall the third requirement Audi places on an intuition: the comprehension requirement—that an intuition must be held on the basis of an adequate understanding of its content. This is not a requirement an intuition must meet if it is to be justified; it is a requirement it must meet if it is to be an intuition in the first place. In other words, a proposition's self-evidence itself consists in the degree to which it is intuitively known.[16]

Finally, I wish to agree with Audi's point that intuitive knowledge does not require certainty in the psychological sense. There are indeed degrees of justification. My claim, however, was that the high degree of *uncertainty* required by proper appreciation of a failure to meet Sidgwick's principle is incompatible both with knowledge and with any plausible claim to it.

4. BIRDS REVISITED

On a case similar to *Birds*, Audi comments as follows:

> From [Crisp's] example concerning disagreement about what kind of bird is before us, it is clear that he takes the notion of an epistemically good 'state' to include things like visual acuity and favorableness of the light. This notion encompasses a huge number of variables. Background beliefs are included, as are inferential capacities, reliability of memory, and conceptual sophistication. He might grant, then, that we are commonly not justified in believing that someone else is in as good an epistemic position as we. (Audi 2007a: 205)

Let me add here another passage:

> What if I believe that (a) the colleague is as rational and as thoughtful as I (in the relevant matter) and (b) has considered the same relevant evidence equally conscientiously? ... Reflection shows ... that it is very hard to be justified in believing (a) or even (b). The breadth, complexity, and quantity of evidence needed about the other person are great, and error in assessing it is difficult to avoid. (Audi 2008a: 489)

For me to have a very well justified belief that some other person is an 'epistemic peer' might indeed require a good deal of evidence about their other beliefs and epistemic capacities in general. Note, however, that Sidgwick's principle does not apply only to cases in which people have such well justified beliefs. All that is required, in a case where I find someone disagreeing with me, is that "I have no more reason to suspect error in the other mind than in my own" (Sidgwick 1907: 342). In the bird cases, then, I was imagining not that each person had any unusually strong evidence about the background beliefs or epistemic capacities of their companion, but merely that each had some such evidence and no reason to think herself in an epistemically stronger position than the other. If one of them knew herself to be an expert on birds, with an excellent memory, and her companion to be a highly forgetful novice, that would be a different matter entirely. My point is that, in typical first-order disputes among moral philosophers, we are in the position of you and your friend in *Birds*.

Audi goes on:

> More important, the fact that it seems very clear to me that, for example, there is a robin before me is some reason to take a person who disagrees *not* to be in as good a position. It might seem that if we could test every epistemically relevant variable, we might instantiate the unfortunate position Crisp describes. But suppose we conscientiously test every variable we consider relevant. Doing so (for the purpose in question) presupposes that we trust our own beliefs enough to make a reasonable comparison of someone else's grounds with our own, now checked out. You must, for instance, ascertain that I discern someone's hurt feelings as clearly as you, if my disagreement is to force you to doubt your judgment that an apology is owed for having hurt them. Now, however, if you finally see, as you list your freshly scrutinized grounds, that I

still cannot be brought to agree that she has been hurt, you may have *better* reason to think you missed some relevant difference between us—a difference favoring you—than to think you should suspend judgment. (Audi 2007a: 205)

If you were an expert ornithologist, even if you did not know your companion to be a novice, you would indeed be justified in thinking that your companion is not in as good a position as you are, even before any disagreement has been voiced. For most people are not experts. And any disagreement would, as Audi says, provide further reason for you to think that your companion is not an epistemic peer. But in a case of disagreement among experts, or among non-experts, as I have suggested above, it is implausible to claim that the fact that p seems very clear to me is in itself a reason to take a person who disagrees with me not to be an epistemic peer. It depends on p and the nature of the disagreement. In *Birds*, p is the proposition: 'this is a redwing'. If your companion claims that this is a song thrush, and you have no other reason to think her in a worse epistemic position, then rather than her disagreement in itself giving you a reason to think her to be in a worse epistemic position, Sidgwick's principle requires you to suspend judgment on whether this is indeed a redwing.

5. SELF-TRUST

Now consider Audi's case in which you think someone deserves an apology for her feelings having been hurt and I don't. Audi is right that your appropriately testing every relevant epistemic variable does presuppose a certain level of trust in your own beliefs. But it does not justify putting any *greater* trust in those beliefs than in mine. What is required is an impartial comparison. If you then discover that I cannot accept even that she has been hurt, this *may* give you a reason to think of me as in a worse epistemic position. But as in the bird scenarios, this depends on the nature of the case. What we want is a case analogous to *Birds*. So imagine that your reason for thinking that she has been hurt is the evidence of her trembling lip as she left the room. I saw that too, and put it down to nervousness in front of an office superior. Here again I cannot see any justification for your thinking that my disagreement with you counts against me epistemically. We agree on the brute facts of the situation, and each of us puts an entirely reasonable interpretation on them. We should suspend judgment until further evidence becomes available.

Audi then says more about self-trust:

> In the very act of conscientiously comparing my epistemic situation with yours, you must, in a certain way, trust *your* judgment along the way if you are thereby to arrive at a conclusion you may justifiedly hold. In particular, you must anchor your judgment that I am in a good epistemic position by presupposing some judgments of yours as to, say, whether I am aware of certain elementary, perceptible facts. You need not *always* favor your judgment over mine when we disagree, but the confidence you have that I am in a good epistemic position must come from relying on *your* epistemic position, and the strength of *that* position will be confirmed by the entire exercise of reconsidering both positions. Dogmatism is undermined; justified conviction need not be. (Audi 2007a: 205–6)

This all seems right to me. Your project of putting my epistemic status to the test without relying at all on (so far untested) beliefs you already hold is literally a non-starter. Nor of course need justified conviction be ruled out in every case (as in the variation in which your companion says the bird is a green woodpecker). But in a case where you decide that I am in a good epistemic position, on the basis of comparing my position with yours, even if you end up thinking that your own epistemic position is also good, it cannot be that the strength of your epistemic position *on the question at issue* will be confirmed by the process of reconsideration of both our positions. If you think that our epistemic positions are equally good, and that both our positions are equally reasonable, then you should suspend judgment.

Audi later (2008a: 490) makes the further point that "we are better positioned to make a critical appraisal of our own evidence and of our responses to it than of anyone else's evidence or responses to that evidence," and goes on:

> [A]s we check and re-check our own grounds for a justified belief that *p* and our responses to them, we tend to increase our justi-fication for believing *p*, at least where we retain that belief (but possibly even if, say from a skeptical disposition, we do not). Thus,

the very exercise of critically seeking to establish the epistemic parity of a disputant may give one a justificatory advantage in the dispute. Perhaps we may conclude that other things being equal, a rational conscientious attempt to establish the epistemic parity of a disputant tends to favor the conscientious inquirer.

Again, this seems hard to deny. But the points apply not only to oneself, but to the other disputant in a disagreement. What we must imagine is that both you and I are 'conscientious enquirers' who appraise our own evidence and responses, and of course that neither of us has reason to believe that the other is any less conscientious or worse *at appraising their own evidence and responses*. Once again, Sidgwick's principle requires suspension of judgment.

6. THE AGREEMENT IN/AGREEMENT ON DISTINCTION

In *The Good in the Right*, Audi drew a distinction between agreement *on* reasons and agreement *in* reasons, which was intended in part to draw the sting from the claim that disagreement has worrying implications for ethical intuitionism. In "Intuitionism, Reflection, and Justification," he says more about this as follows:

> Suppose a Rossian promissory principle is self-evident and that it is correspondingly self-evident that promising to A entails having some reason to A. There is disagreement on both points, but someone who denies that promising entails a reason to A may regularly regard the making of *particular* promises as implying such a reason. Might such a person still accept as true someone's denial of having a reason to A, after having promised to A? Suppose so. We would wonder why. Holding a theory requiring this denial is one possible explanation; another—compatible with this one—is an inadequate understanding of some relevant concept, such as that of *having some reason*. This concept as understood here embodies defeasibility, which is no easy notion to grasp.
>
> These points are among those that make clear how the kind of self-evidence required by (rationalist) ethical intuitionism is compatible with theoretical and other kinds of opposition. But theoretical opposition applies mainly to disagreement *on* reasons and need not be manifested in disagreement in them. (Audi 2007a: 206)

Audi begins by asking us to suppose that a Russian promissory principle is self-evident. Recall Audi's definition of self-evidence mentioned above: a principle is self-evident insofar as an adequate understanding of it suffices for being justified in believing it, and our believing it on the basis of such understanding results in our *knowing* it (*RG* 9). His argument here is that the kind of disagreement we might expect to find about promising does not damage the claim of the Russian principle to self-evidence, since people will generally agree, in particular cases, that someone who has promised to *A* has some reason to *A*, even if they disagree about whether the Russian principle itself is correct.

But the Russian principle is just that —a principle, a theoretical position *on* reasons. It is *that* which the Russian is proposing, not a series of particular judgments about individual cases. And what I want to suggest is that reasonable disagreement about whether the Russian principle is correct or not means that it cannot be said to be self-evident. Note that this is not because I am mistakenly assuming that the self-evident must be obvious. Sidgwick's principle suggests that the conditions for justification and knowledge given by Audi in the definition above are too weak: even if the Russian principle is true, even if I have adequate under-standing of it and believe it on the basis of that understanding, given the level of disagreement by epistemic peers, my belief is not justified, and so of course I do not have knowledge. Indeed I should suspend judgment on it.

To see this more clearly, imagine that there is indeed universal agreement *in* reasons about individual cases of promising. Such agreement will not of course make Russians of everyone. The reasons alleged for promising in each case may differ greatly. The Russians will say that people should keep promises because there is a *prima facie* obligation to do so, while egoists will see it as a self-interested strategy, utilitarians as one of welfare-maximization. So we might (perhaps) be justified in believing (at least) that promise-keeping seems to be something we have a reason to do. But we would not be justified in believing that we have discovered the basis of this reason via an understanding of the very concepts involved. And this means that we are not justified in advocating Russian intuitionism, except to the extent that we admit that it merely *appears* to us to be correct.

7. DELIBERATIVE ROLE

In my original paper, I allowed that we may have some intuitive practical knowledge, but suggested that none of the candidate ethical theories at present available could claim to be self-evident, to be candidates for knowledge, or, in the case of any particular theory, to have any special entitlement to play a significant deliberative role.[17] Audi comments as follows:

> (1) For reasons already offered, the consensus condition is too strong. But suppose it is sufficiently plausible to require suspending judgment on whether Rossian moral principles are self-evident; (2) it does not follow that the principles have no claim to being *known*. Both empirical and certain kinds of *a priori* principles can be known without being self-evident; (3) it also does not follow that the principles have no directly justified role in deliberation, say, that they must be supportable by utilitarian or Kantian considerations. Non-inferential justification for believing them would suffice for the kind of defeasible role my intuitionism requires. (Audi 2007a: 206–7)

Now I have indeed been arguing for the claim—among others— that we should suspend judgment on whether Rossian principles are self-evident. But I claim also that disagreement on these very principles themselves—as opposed to the issue of whether they are self-evident—means that they cannot be known. The force of Sidgwick's principle applies wholesale. Finally, though I accept that non-inferential justification for believing Rossian principles would indeed provide the basis for a defeasible role in deliberation, my suggestion is that this non-inferential justification is unavailable. If I am required by reason to suspend judgment on some principle, it is hard to see how it could play a *directly justified* role in my deliberation, even if its adoption might be instrumental to some goal or other and so indirectly justified.

Audi goes on to consider conflicts of obligations, and in the course of that discussion reverts to the question of the compatibility of Rossian intuitionism with disagreement. In my original paper, I claimed that *if* widespread convergence on some 'comprehensive view' in normative ethics were attained, that view would provide a deliberative role for ethical theory to which as yet it is not entitled. Audi comments:

If a 'comprehensive' view is a master principle view, such as Kant's, widespread convergence on it (on sufficiently good grounds) would entitle it to a practical role. But my efforts in ethical theory have been aimed in part at suggesting that Rossian intuitionism as developed in [*The Good in the Right*] *is* comprehensive in the basic sense of capturing at least the vast majority of our obligations. Its principles may thus serve—and very often do serve—as common ground to be accommodated by competing theories such as Kantian and consequentialist views. They also provide an important *area* of 'convergence.' (Audi 2007a: 207)

Audi may be right that there is some convergence on the Rossian principles (to remind you, the Rossian duties are of seven kinds: fidelity; reparation; gratitude; justice; beneficence; self-improvement; non-injury (Ross 1930: 21; see Audi 2005: 166)). But he is perhaps excessively proprietorial, even by his own lights, in claiming these principles—insofar as there is convergence on them—as the principles of Rossian intuitionism. For if there is convergence, then they are the common property of all those ethical theories which converge on them.

Nevertheless, I think that Audi is right to suggest that there will be a good deal of convergence on these principles, detached from any background theoretical apparatus. (Self-improvement is perhaps an exception, where common-sense morality now—even if it did not in Ross's day—tends to align itself with something like Mill's harm principle, so that a wrongful failure to improve oneself would probably have to be categorized under the heading of non-injury.) But, in a sense, the principles taken in this way are the conclusions of arguments, and philosophy is concerned primarily with premises. And here there will be a huge amount of disagreement. There is a dilemma here for the philosopher who recognizes the implications of disagreement and uncertainty, one lived out by Sidgwick in his later life. On the one hand, pushing a particular theoretical viewpoint seems unjustified, since there is no ground for thinking one's own view superior to several others. On the other, discussing ethics purely in terms of 'middle axioms' seems distinctly unphilosophical, since it requires abstaining from reflection on *why* those axioms are the correct ones (and articulating and elucidating those axioms is almost certainly going to require such reflection anyway).

8. CONCLUSION: ORNITHOLOGY AND ETHICAL THEORY

There is at least one major difference between bird-identification and ethical theory, viz., their methods for resolving differences. In *Birds*, for example, one of the parties to the dispute might produce a camera, the evidence from which can later be used, with the aid of a handbook, to resolve the disagreement to the satisfaction of both parties. The only way for unforced, rational consensus to come about in ethical theory is through long argument and debate. Any such consensus will take many years to achieve. But its prospects are likely to be enhanced, I suggest, through epistemic humility. In that respect, a moral epistemology based on Sidgwick's principle can be seen as constructive rather than destructive.[18]

CONCLUDING PAPER

INTUITIONS, INTUITIONISM, AND MORAL JUDGMENT

Robert Audi, University of Notre Dame

Ethical intuitionism has now taken a place as a major position in contemporary ethical theory. But there is still a widespread impression that the view depends on concepts and theses that are insufficiently clear for the work they must do or, if clear enough to sustain the view, then not plausible. One question here is what constitutes an intuition. Another is how intuitive cognitions differ from inferential ones. There is also a need to address the question of just how ethical intuitionism depends on the answer. This paper addresses all three questions and, in the light of what we find in pursuing them, explores the resources of intuitionist ethical theory for providing an understanding of how moral judgments may be justified.

1. THE NATURE AND VARIETIES OF INTUITIONS

Intuitions are important not only for intuitionist ethical theories but also for philosophy in general. Indeed, even many philosophers who do not speak of intuitions theorize as if they were in part seeking to provide an account of shared intuitions, say intuitions about knowledge or obligation. They are what we might call *intuitivists*. An intuitivist must be responsive to intuitions, but need not be an intuitionist. The term 'intuition' is, in any case, not crucial for understanding intuitionism. The main point is that philosophy, like any theoretical enterprise, requires data, and intuitions are crucial philosophical data. For Rawls among many others, our data include the "considered judgments" that, when suitably placed in reflective equilibrium with principles of justice, confirm the latter.[1] The judgments constituting our data at least roughly fit the characterization of (cognitive) intuitions to be given shortly.

I am taking intuitionism as an ethical theory to be, in outline and in a minimal version, the view that there is at least one moral principle that is non-inferentially and intuitively knowable. Historically, intuitionists have also posited what they consider an irreducible plurality of such principles, and I propose to call this stronger view, on which there is a group of at least several such moral principles (such as we find in W. D. Ross and others) *generic intuitionism.*[2] Conceived more fully, an intuitionist ethics also incorporates a particular set of basic moral principles that directly apply to daily life. A specific intuitionist theory that, like Ross's, achieves this is *an* intuitionism. My intuitionism emphasizes principles expressing obligations of justice and non-injury, of fidelity and veracity, of beneficence and self-improvement, of reparation and gratitude (Ross's list, which I interpret differently at several points), and of liberty and respectfulness—my two additions to Ross's list.[3] More will be said about these ten *Rossian obligations,* as we may call them, when their status has been clarified.

An account of intuitions should clarify at least five related notions. Let me characterize each briefly and then proceed to indicate how some of them figure in ethical intuitionism as I conceive it.

Cognitive intuition. This is the most common kind of intuition considered in ethical literature: it is intuition *that p* (a proposition), say that a student's paper deserves an A or, to take a moral example, that one should not accept a major gift from a salesperson who should be fairly compared with competitors. In the latter case, to be sure, the intuitive proposition could be subsumed under a moral rule; but this need not prevent it from being the object of an intuition, and some who would have it might not accept any such rule—at least antecedently.

Objectual intuition. This is roughly direct apprehension of either (a) a concept, such as that of obligation, or (b) a property or relation, such as the property of being a promise, the property of being unjust, or the relation of entailment. As a kind of knowledge, such intuitions are in a sense *epistemic* and may also be considered cognitive, though not propositional, but I prefer to reserve 'cognitive intuition' for intuitions with propositional objects. In a sense to be explored below, these objectual intuitions constitute intellectual perceptions.

Intuitiveness. This is a property primarily of propositions, but is also predicated of concepts, arguments, and other intellectual phenomena. As predicated of a proposition, it is equivalent to the proposition's being *intuitive*—having the property of evoking (under certain conditions) what might be called *the sense of non-inferential credibility* (this notion may be relativized, e.g. to persons of a certain description or to a certain level of understanding needed for the intuitive sense to be manifested). That sense is roughly equivalent to the sense of a proposition's (non-inferentially) seeming true, and it normally produces an inclination to believe.[4] As predicated of arguments, 'intuitive' means roughly *seeming plausible,* a property an argument may have in virtue of being obviously sound, or quite perceptibly valid and having plausible premises, or something quite similar. As applied to concepts, it means roughly *readily under-standable* in a sense implying that one can imagine instances or at least what they are like. Far more can be said here, but my aim is simply to sketch the basic idea.

Propositional intuition. This is intuition conceived as a proposition taken to be *intuitively known*; say, that capital punishment is wrong, or that what is colored is extended. Hence, unlike cognitive intuitions, propositional intuitions are abstract, non-psychological elements and (on most uses) include only truths.[5] In a wider use, intuitions might be simply propositions that exhibit intuitiveness, as where someone says, "Let's begin our inquiry with a range of intuitions we should take into account."

Apprehensional capacity. This is intuition as a rational capacity—*facultative intuition,* for short—a kind needed for philosophical reflection and manifested in relation to each of the other four cases. It is roughly a non-inferential capacity by whose exercise what is intuitively believed or known is believed or known. Ethical intuition, like logical intuition, is a special case of this capacity (calling it a faculty is simply classificatory as to its scope and implies no implication of modularity of mind or a special kind of intellectual sense). Cognitive and objectual intuition will be my main concern, but the other notions should be kept in mind if only for the clarity we gain by distinguishing them from the former two and connecting them with those when necessary.[6]

There is much to be learned from conceiving facultative intuition as analogous to the 'faculty' of perception and intuitions as analogous to perceptions. Take seeing as a paradigm of perception. Intuitive apprehension is analogous to seeing. First, it has objects, typically, or at least most importantly for our purposes, concepts and properties. (We need not discuss what kinds of objects these are, but I assume they are both abstract and in some way connected with linguistic usage.) Second, in addition to objectual apprehension—apprehension *of*—there is also apprehension *as: aspectual apprehension.* The former, apprehension simpliciter, is *de re* and apparently does not entail cognition, as where a small child apprehends the wrongness of smashing a toy but does not believe that this is wrong or see it *as* wrong. Aspectual apprehension entails at least some degree of understanding of the property the object is apprehended as having, say the wrongness of smashing the toy. Third, given an apprehension, it may also intuitively seem to us *that* (for instance) an act is wrong. Fourth, we may, on the basis of this seeming, believe the act is wrong. Fifth, if this belief is true, then we intuitively see (apprehend) that the act is wrong. Such true doxastic intuition, a case of intuitive belief, would at least normally constitute intuitive knowledge. We thus have, with intellectual perception as with sensory perception, simple ('objectual') perception, aspectual perception, and propositional perception: apprehensions *of* the relevant kind of object, apprehensions of the object *as* something, and apprehensions *that* it is something. Objectual apprehensions have the same kind of veridicality as perceptions of objects; aspectual and propositional apprehensions may or may not embody beliefs, but, when they do, they commonly represent knowledge.

Are there, as the perceptual analogy suggests, apprehensional counterparts of illusion and hallucination? Might someone mistakenly ('illusorily') apprehend the property of redness as coming in precisely discrete shades in concert with its wavelengths? This would be a misapprehension but could still be *of* red, somewhat as visually misperceiving a glass's round rim as elliptical is still seeing that rim. In neither case, moreover, need the illusion produce false belief. An analogue of hallucination is more difficult to delineate. Mere possibilia, such as chimeras, are apprehensible, so—if we assume that hallucinatory perceptions have no object at all—we must focus on something like thinking of a round square.[7] How could one apprehend "round-squarely," even granting that no false belief is implied? Perhaps someone could apprehend each of the elements with a false sense of their unity and perhaps also a sense of properties consequential on or otherwise closely connected with each. One could perhaps speak here of a hypothetical object, analogous to an object that might be posited for hallucinations, but this is not the place to carry the idea further. It is enough that the analogy between intuition and perception is extensive. Let us now explore its application to justification.

2. THE ROLE OF INTUITIONS IN *PRIMA FACIE* JUSTIFICATION

It is widely acknowledged that sensory experience justifies beliefs based on it if anything does. If, for instance, I have a steadfast visual experience as of print before me, then I have *prima facie* justification for believing that there is print there. Is it any less plausible to maintain that when, in the light of understanding a proposition, I have an intuitive sense that it is true (an intuitive seeming), then I have *prima facie* justification for believing it?[8] In many cases of moral propositions, such intuitions are evoked by instances of general propositions that intuitionists consider self-evident (hence *a priori*). An intuition that I should not break a certain promise could, for example, be connected with an *a priori* belief that promise-keeping is *prima facie* obligatory, and thereby with the proposition that promises should not be broken a proposition that, on any plausible understanding of 'should', is entailed. Both beliefs might be partly based on a sense of the fittingness of performing a promise to having made it. This is not to suggest that the general proposition is epistemologically more basic than the instantial one. That is not implied, nor are intuitions inferentially based on premises. The genetic order may indeed be more "inductive,"[9] with moral intuitions commonly serving as a partial basis for holding the principles under which their content is subsumable. The remainder of this section will develop these ideas.

In describing ethical intuitionism, I have treated cognitive intuitions as a kind of belief (e.g. in 2004). One reason for this is that such intuitionists as Moore, Pritchard, Ross, and many later writers (including Rawls) have spoken of intuitions in a way that presupposes that the cognition in question entails, or is a kind of, belief. One way to see that some intuitions are beliefs is to consider how a person who (sincerely) asserts something may in some cases respond when asked for a reason. One answer is "I can't give you an argument; it's just a clear intuition." Similarly, knowledge that an inference is invalid or that a paper deserves an A may be constituted by the kind of intuitive belief sometimes called 'intuition'.

If, however, one begins not with cases in which beliefs are directly in question, but with an analogy to perception and, somewhat controversially, conceives perceptual deliverances as, in the primitive cases, non-belief-entailing, one may arrive at a non-doxastic conception of intuition. Let us consider this analogy.

Suppose we are asked whether p is true. Then, if we are aware that we do not believe p, but it *non-inferentially* seems true—roughly, seems true by virtue of a kind of credibility of its own rather than on the basis of one or more supporting premises—we are likely to say, in careful usage, just that: that it seems true or, in some cases, that it seems intuitive. Indeed, it would in many (though by no means all) contexts be misleading to say that we have an intuition that p but do not believe p. In the intuitional cases of non-inferential credibility, there is a sense of credibility that goes beyond the generic kind of non-inferential seeming true that can also result from a memory impression or other *non*-intuitional source of support, such as a hazy sense-impression that makes it seem to one that a distant shape is a tree. Any cognitive intuition requires *understanding* the content of p and, at least in part on that comprehensional basis, having the impression that it is true. A proposition that is non-inferentially credible on the basis of (e.g.) memory, by contrast, need not seem true in part on the *basis* of its content. Some memories of bare historical facts illustrate this.

The point here, then, is not that there are no non-intuitional sources of non-inferential credibility, such as seeming to remember that p or taking p to have been told to one by someone reliable. It is that, for cognitive intuitions, the intuitive impression of truth is not based on such sources. Granted, there can be justificatory overdetermination, as where memory impressions support a cognitive intuition. But it is probably the "pure" case, where there is no overdetermination, that has been most important in ethics and indeed in understanding the kinds of singular propositions that are justified by thought experiments and are central in supporting philosophical theories.

Suppose, however, that cognitive attitudes are conceived simply as those with truth-valued objects. Then a proposition that is *not* believed but, in the relevant non-doxastic phenomenal way, seems true to us may also be considered an object of intuition. For some philosophers, this non-doxastic notion of an intuitive sense of the truth of a proposition is the primary concept of an intuition.[10] We can accommodate this terminology by dividing cognitive intuitions into those that are doxastic, i.e. a kind of belief, and those that are not doxastic but have the relevant proposition as their content and embody a disposition to believe it based on a non-inferential impression of its truth. I prefer, however, to call the latter *intuitive seemings* rather than intuitions simpliciter, but they may also be called *non-doxastic intuitions*.[11]

This terminology allows us to do justice to the view of intuitions held by most who take seemings to be the primary (or only) cases of cognitive intuitions.[12] More important than which terminology we use is identifying the relation between doxastic intuitions and intuitive seemings. The important point here is that, much as a sensory seeming can be an evidential ground for a perceptual belief, an intuitive seeming that *p* can be an evidential ground for an "intellectual" or other non-perceptual belief that *p*. Intuitionists have typically presupposed this, even when they have conceived intuitions as beliefs. Some have asserted it, sometimes with the idea that just as a perceptual seeming—say, its visually seeming that there is a light way down the corridor—is evidence for the proposition in question, an intuitive seeming that *p* is evidence for *p*.[13] Evidential grounds need not produce overall justification, but they do produce some degree of *prima facie* justification, and in some cases 'justification' will serve us better than 'evidence'.

3. INTUITIVE EVIDENCE AND NON-INFERENTIAL JUSTIFICATION

If the analogy between perceptions and intuitive seemings is sound, we have reason to think that the latter have some evidential weight. But not every proposition that intuitively seems true is true, nor are all the true instances self-evident. Moreover, as is often not realized, some self-evident propositions do not seem true upon initial consideration, even if every self-evident proposition *can* seem true to someone who adequately understands it. The latter point can be clarified in the light of an account of the self-evident by appeal to the understanding of concepts as abstract entities, where this understanding includes an apprehension of their relations.[14] On this account, self-evident propositions are conceived as truths such that (a) in virtue of adequately understanding them one is justified in believing them (which does not entail that all who adequately understand them *do* believe them), and (b) believing them on the basis of adequately understanding them entails knowing them.[15] This is not the place for a full-scale extension of that account, but let me clarify it and then proceed to some points concerning intuitive non-self-evident moral judgments.

Take first the kind of self-evident proposition most readily amenable to explication in terms of the proposed account of the self-evident: analytic propositions. Suppose it is analytic that all vixens are female. If so, then an adequate understanding of the concept of a vixen *contains*, in a certain roughly formal way, that of being female. There are many ways to explicate the relevant kind of conceptual containment.[16] I prefer to do it (as will be apparent) by appeal to abstract entities and their relations, but let us first focus on an account usable even by those who prefer to avoid positing abstract entities.

Consider the phenomenology of conceptualization. Phenomenologically, one way to explicate the containment idea is to say that having a *thought* of a vixen that contains all the elements in the concept—a kind of thought possible in principle for those who adequately understand the concept—also contains the thought of femaleness. To have the former thought entails having the latter, though the point is not as obvious as, say, the thought that someone said that *p* contains the thought that *p* or the thought that if *p*, then *q*, contains the thought that *q*. Even for those who can accept something like this containment aspect of the analytic, it should be clear that moral cases are more difficult to analyze. Take an instance of Rossian principle of "duty" formulated on the assumption that *prima facie* obligations are grounded in certain kinds of facts (I here use 'obligation' for the deontic notion in question): That hitting a person with a cricket bat would cause excruciating pain is a moral reason—roughly, grounds a *prima facie* obligation—not to do it. This does not imply that the *concept* of such hitting is moral, but that the kind of fact in question grounds a moral obligation. It is an obligation-making fact, though not itself a moral fact; it grounds the applicability of, but does not contain, a moral concept. Must the concept of a moral reason for action, then, *contain*, say, the notion of avoidance of causing pain if a Rossian principle of non-injury is genuinely self-evident? Intuitionists need not claim that this containment relation holds, but nothing in the major versions of intuitionism commits them to denying the possibility. They certainly have no need to deny it if, as I suggest, the notion of conceptual containment does not presuppose that only concepts admitting of a full *analysis* may be properly said to contain other concepts.

The non-reductivist containment view that I suggest, then, does not presuppose something that at least *Moorean intuitionism* would imply is impossible: a naturalistic *analysis* of moral (*prima facie*) reasons. It does not presuppose even the weak kind of analysis that would be pluralistic, disjunctive, and non-hierarchical—if we may call that an analysis—a kind on which to be a moral reason is simply to be *either* an obligation of non-injury or an obligation of veracity or an obligation of beneficence ... where the disjunction contains all the basic *prima facie* obligations. The possibility of such an analysis would support a conceptual containment view regarding moral reasons, but a Rossian intuitionism does not presuppose this possibility. It may leave the possibility open for *prima facie* reasons, though almost certainly not for final reasons. To be sure, if we think (as Ross apparently did) that even our most reflectively composed list of basic *prima facie* obligations may be incomplete, we will doubt that we can achieve even a full description, much less an analysis, of the basic constituents of a would-be naturalistic analysis of the notion of a moral reason.

Let us suppose that no naturalistic analysis of *prima facie* obligation is possible. What, then, can be said of the basis of intuitive knowledge of our apparently self-evident moral proposition? Does any containment notion apply here? To see how it might, consider an analogy. Much as we can see that certain items of furniture are in a room without seeing everything therein, we can see that a certain concept is contained in another without seeing all that the former contains. The readiest illustrations are at once phenomenological and conceptual. Suppose we are asked whether there is any moral reason to avoid acts of certain types, such as hitting someone with a cricket bat. In entertaining the thought of moral reasons for action—especially in the context of such a question—it is natural, given time to reflect, to think of *paradigms* of moral reasons, such as reasons to avoid injuring or harming persons, to keep promises, and to avoid lying. This is one way to think of how one might construct a

Rossian list. The first of the three categories of reasons encompasses avoidance of acts of hitting with a cricket bat, even though neither the proposition that this is a moral reason nor the proposition that moral reasons include reasons to avoid such acts is plausibly considered analytic.

We might also begin at the abstract level. Suppose a conceptually sophisticated person is asked what constitutes a moral reason. A natural way to begin is with the uncontroversial idea that a reason gives support to what it is a reason for. A natural second step is to ask what differentiates moral reasons from other kinds. Here nearly anyone familiar with moral discourse (with uses of 'right', 'wrong', 'obligation', 'morally impermissible', and other terms) is likely to think of reasons as supporting some kind of treatment of or inter-actions with others. Morality is at least mainly *social*. What kind of treatment, then? Here divergence is likely to occur—some will think of good treatment, others of respect, still others of specific kinds of treatment, say doing good deeds and avoiding lies. But no one with an understanding of morality and reasons would be likely, if even able, to clarify such notions without pointing to Rossian grounds of obligation. Clarity for such abstractions requires discerning the contours of particularity. This route to understanding does not automatically preclude reaching a plausible analysis—though that seems unlikely—but my point is that any plausible *beginning* will, once elaborated, contain Rossian grounds. Just as any room in a normally occupied domestic residence will contain one or another item of furniture, any concept of a moral reason that corresponds to the inferences crucial for moral reasoning and ethical discourse will contain at least some of the Rossian grounds. But just as there need be no analytically closed list of the contents of a residential room, there need be none for the contents of the concept of a moral reason.

Granted that, in entertaining the thought of moral reasons, one may think of many considerations other than avoiding injuring and harming, this may well come to mind because the category of avoidance of injury and harm obviously and naturally extends to the avoidance of bludgeoning people, which is the case that (in our example) prompts the thought of moral reasons. This is not to imply that reasons such as to avoid injuring persons, to keep promises, and to abstain from lying *must* come to mind in the imagined context of inquiry about moral reasons. But neither must one, upon looking into a room, see everything that is clearly in it. Reflection is not always sufficiently thorough or comprehensive to find what it seeks, and it is sometimes not guided by adequate understanding of the concepts in question.

Taken by themselves, such phenomenological points have limited evidential weight. But they gain support from two complementary points concerning conceptual explanation. One crucial question is how we can explain what *constitutes* a moral reason. A second important (and related) question is whether, for a correct common-sense explanation of why an act is obligatory (or wrong) that cites one or more obligation-making moral reasons and indicates their application to action, there is any need for an inferential justification of taking them to be reasons. Regarding the first question, I do not see how we can properly explain (as opposed to abstractly characterizing) what constitutes a moral reason except by appeal to examples of the kind just given. Concerning the second question, I have argued that certain moral propositions supported by such examples can be justifiedly believed non-inferentially, though they may *also* be justifiedly believed inferentially. The point is that in such cases justified belief is not premise-dependent and so need not be inferential.

4. THE INTUITIVE APPREHENSION OF FITTINGNESS

Suppose that what has been said gives us a basis for explaining the possibility of non-inferential intuitive knowledge of self-evident moral propositions and indeed does so in a way that makes it plausible to claim that there are such propositions.[17] It is quite another thing to explain the possibility of non-inferential intuitive knowledge of singular, *non*-self-evident propositions, such as the moral judgment that, as I encounter a toddler wandering alone on the sidewalk, I have a moral reason to stop to see if the child is lost.

In describing intuitive knowledge, one direction natural for intuitionists is to appeal to fittingness relations (including unfittingness).[18] I take support relations to exhibit a kind of fittingness, and certain relations of incongruity to manifest unfittingness, but here I must be content to clarify these subtle notions mainly with illustrations. In many cases, non-trivial entailment (as opposed to mere strict implication) is a paradigm of fittingness between the entailing and entailed propositions; incompatibility is a paradigm of unfittingness. But entailment is not necessary for the former nor incompatibility for the latter. Surely doing what one promised to do *befits* the promising thereof, whereas lying to a friend *ill*-befits the relation of friendship. By contrast, lying to a would-be assassin to prevent mass murder would not ill-befit the situation, and might be a fittingly deflective act. What explains such points? I suggest that at least part of the explanation is that we apprehend a relation of support between (for instance) the envisaged instance of promising and the envisaged act of doing the promised deed. Suppose this is so. What is required for a person to *respond* to apprehension of a fittingness relation?

At least three cases should be considered. In the most conceptually complex case, the relation perceived in (e.g.) the promising case is *propositionalized*, i.e. formulated or expressed in a proposition, such as the proposition that one should do the promised deed. The proposition may be only thought or perhaps briefly considered. It need not be believed, though believing it would be normal for a child learning the concept in question; nor need we assume that the proposition is linguistically formulated even if it is believed. The second case is less complex: the envisaged property-instances that figure in fittingness relations are *conceptualized* but not propositionalized. This is like seeing something *as* having a property, such as being elliptical, without believing that it has it. As indicated in developing the analogy between intuition and perception, however, discrimination is possible without conceptualization. Much as perceiving a tree provides raw materials for conceiving it as a tree but does not require doing so, apprehending morally important relations provides raw material for, but does not require, conceptualizing them, as we do when we believe that they obtain between one thing and another.

Consider entailment. With that in mind we can see the same levels of responsiveness in relation to fittingness. I begin with the simplest case, which is closest to sensory perception.

Discrimination of properties. Intellectual perception of at least one kind occurs very early in life. A child learning the logic of the syllogism as a way into understanding entailment does not initially believe, of the premises and conclusion of a valid syllogism, *that* the former entail the latter. We illustrate; we draw diagrams; and the child ultimately grasps the entailment relation *in* those cases. This initial grasp is manifested in a discriminative capacity: the ability to distinguish the good syllogisms (the valid ones) from the invalid, for instance to accept the former as "ok" and to reject the latter. Much as perceiving a tree provides raw materials for conceiving it as a tree but does not require doing so, apprehending logical relations like entailment or morally important relations like promissory obligation provides raw material for, but does not require, conceptualizing them as one does when one believes (or even has the thought) that they obtain between one thing and another. We can thus have discrimination without conceptualization.

Conceptualization: from seeing to a kind of seeing *as*. Given discrimination of properties (including relations) viewed as a starting point—or in any event an early point—we can understand how, at some time in the intellectual learning process, the child can conceptualize and perhaps name the entailment relation. Conceptualization requires more than discrimination, including understanding a kind of generality. It is analogous to perceptual seeing *as* but is of course not sensory. The idea is this. We can conceive two property-instances and apprehend a relation (*de re*) between them without believing or even thinking (*de dicto*) something to the effect *that* this relation obtains between them. The properties might be promising to *A* and being obligated to *A*. The relation might be entailment (if the obligation in question is *prima facie*) or a kind of fittingness. One may be *disposed* to think of or indeed believe some such proposition as that if one promises to *A*, then one should *A* or that *A*-ing befits promising to *A*; but that disposition need not be manifested in thinking or believing them, any more than seeing a difference in height between two buildings on the New York skyline entails believing, or even having the thought, that one is taller than the other.

Propositionalization. Given conceptualization, we can have intentionality—thought with an intentional object—whether or not the thought represents believing the proposition in question. When children are in a position to reach this third, propositional stage, they may believe *that* the entailment relation (*following*) holds for the syllogisms in question.[19] Moreover, its holding will often be intuitive for the child; and given the discriminative capacity at the base of the child's conceptualizing the entailment relation, such logical intuitions, though fallible, will commonly be evidential. Now take the relation perceived in (e.g.) the promising case. It is *propositionalized*, i.e. expressed (and sometimes formulated) in a proposition, such as the proposition that one should do the promised deed. The proposition may be only momentarily thought or perhaps briefly considered. It need not be believed, though believing it would be normal for a child learning the concept in question; nor need we assume that the proposition is formulated even if it is believed.

This developmental pattern, with its three stages, illustrates a kind of epistemological particularism in which discrimination of particular relations grounds conceptualization and conceptualization makes possible (though it does not entail) belief formation. The temporal separation between the stages is contingent; there are fast and slow learners. Moreover, even fast learners do not form beliefs of all the propositions for which, given their newly acquired concepts, their experience provides support.

The suggestion, then, is that the fittingness relations between conceptualized property-instances reflect similar relations between the relevant concepts. Where the fittingness is moral, the corresponding relation between the properties in question, say that of being a causing of excruciating pain and that of being an abstention from doing this, is also moral: roughly, obligation-making. The perception of the instances, *given* appropriate discriminative capacities and sufficient conceptual capability, puts us in a position to conceptualize those instances; we can then readily apprehend fittingness relations between them; and on that basis (though not only on that basis) we can come to believe corresponding general moral propositions and, eventually, to understand those adequately for justified belief and knowledge of them.

This picture accords well with a rationalist intuitionism on which basic moral principles are self-evident. But an empiricist account of the relevant kind of non-inferential justification and knowledge can also be given (one on which such knowledge is either empirical or analytic). My preference is a moderately rationalist intuitionism, but my aim here is to extend and defend intuitionism as an overall position more than to show the superiority of a rationalist version.

5. INTUITIONS, INFERENTIAL PROCESSES, AND INFERENTIAL BELIEFS

So far, I have assumed that intuitions are non-inferential. This assumption is natural because (for one thing) they are conceived as direct responses to what is apprehended. The assumption is important because, on the most plausible conceptions of intuitions, they are considered evidentially independent: conceived doxastically, as beliefs, they do not require premises for their (*prima facie*) justification; conceived non-doxastically, as intuitive seemings, they are akin to sensory experiences and do not admit of justification in the first place, though they can confer some measure of it.[20]

Given that doxastic intuitions do admit of justification, why should they be considered non-inferential? One indication—significant though not conclusive—that they are non-inferential is that, if asked (in an informational as opposed to skeptical way) why we believe the relevant proposition (p), the initial tendency, especially if p is not self-evident, is to point to non-propositional grounds-- such as *seeing* that it is true-- on which we believe it or, if p *is* self-evident, to explain what it means or how to see its truth by understanding it. Neither of these responses is a presentation of a premise for p.

To be sure, if we feel challenged by a why-question, we naturally seek to frame an argument. That effort may lead us to adduce premises that were not a basis of the intuition or may indeed have been conceived only as a response to the felt challenge. I suggest that when such a why-question arises, then where our grounds are *non*-propositional and the belief is non-inferential, we do not have the normal tendency that goes with inferential beliefs—to adduce one or more of our premise-beliefs. Granted, a fast thinker may tend to adduce premises on the spot from among propositions not previously believed but quickly conceived as plausible support for p or, if previously believed, not previously a basis of the belief that p. But this facility in supplying rationales manifests a different tendency, though it is easily assimilated to the former.

The role of non-propositional grounds is easily misunderstood. One reason is that *pointing out* a non-propositional ground in explaining or justifying a belief or other cognition—something we commonly do when asked to justify or, sometimes, explain a belief we hold—is itself a *propositional* act. Recall my discovery of a wandering toddler. I immediately lean over and quietly say 'Are you lost?' My sense that the child needs help grounds my judgment that I must inquire. But if someone asks why I spoke to a child who was apparently playing in front of her home, I will readily say that she might have needed help. *Now* I have a belief expressing a premise for my original immediate and intuitive judgment. But such retrospective formation of belief by no means implies that my initial judgment was originally based on believing some such premise. Compare my saying 'I hear it' in answer to 'How do you know that bass note is flat?' My correct response does not imply that I knew (or believed) that proposition (inferentially) on the basis of *believing* that I heard the flatness. My ground is not a belief; it is *hearing* the flatness, which I recognize as I do a familiar kind of dog.

One might now think that *every* ground for a non-inferential moral judgment is articulable as a premise for it and that, since such grounds are 'implicit,' judgments that are *psychologically* non-inferential are nonetheless *epistemically* dependent in an inferential way after all.[21] These claims require several comments.

First, even if every ground can in some way be articulated by *someone,* it does not follow that (a) grounds can do their justificatory work only *in* someone capable of articulating them or (b), in such a person, they cannot do that work without articulation or even conceptualization. The three-stage developmental account given above helps to make this clear. Moreover, even for conceptually mature moral agents, (b) seems false in some cases in which we are just becoming aware of a fittingness relation between a ground and what it supports, as where body language and intonation indicate that one person is intimidating another. Discriminating such relations can be temporally prior to our conceptualizing or formulating them, much as it seems developmentally prior even to the ability to conceptualize or formulate them.

Second, the notion of an "implicit" premise is ambiguous between (at least) (a) one that is believed but not *articulated* and (b) one that the person is *disposed* to believe but does not believe. Intuitionists need not deny that, in at least many cases in which we have non-inferential justification for a moral judgment, we can *find* a premise for it that we are justified in believing. This capacity commonly goes with having an (internally accessible) ground in the first place. But none of these points should lead us to assimilate a disposition to *form* a belief of a premise to an already *existing* dispositional belief thereof.[22]

That (doxastic) intuitions are not premise-dependent does not entail that they are not epistemically dependent at all.[23] Like perceptual beliefs, they are *ground-dependent* (the ground being mainly perceiving, for instance seeing, a morally relevant property or understanding of the relevant concepts and certain of their relations), whereas an inferential cognition is mediated by at least one premise and is in that way indirect: it is doxastically, not just epistemically, ground-dependent. The premise-belief must ultimately trace to a (non-doxastic) ground if it is to be justified (I assume a moderate foundationalist view here). Intuitions are thus viewed as epistemically direct responses to something presented.

Functionally, intuitions, whether doxastic or, by contrast, non-doxastic seemings, commonly save us from needing a premise. They do not, however, make premises impossible or protect us from refutation by premises that cogent critics may adduce for a contrary view. In this way, intuitions are analogous to visual beliefs grounded in seeing, which also provides non-inferential but defeasible justification for those beliefs. But the analogy to seeing must be carefully interpreted: much as a mere glance at an unfamiliar tree may not yield justified visual belief or indeed any belief, a mere thought of a proposition or concept may yield no understanding of it, and reflection on it may be needed to see even what, once it is clearly seen, is intuitive.[24]

I have so far spoken of inferential belief, but not of inference. There is wide agreement that a belief which is premise-dependent is inferential, but there is less agreement on what constitutes *an inference*, in the common sense in which inferences are *made* or *drawn* and making or drawing an inference entails *reasoning*. On my view, an inference is roughly a kind of passage of thought from one or more propositions to another, in part on the basis of a sense of some support relation between the former and the latter.[25] This leaves open whether an inference is valid and whether it is, at the time it occurs, (a) belief-forming—in which case the conclusion belief is at least characteristically based, wholly or in part, on the premise belief(s)—or (b) proceeds from propositions already believed to another that is already believed, or indeed (c), as with disproofs by deductions of absurdities, from propositions only supposed, to another proposition that may be only considered and quickly rejected. The notion of inference is both psychological and, at least on an objective conception of support-relations, epistemic.

The notion of inference is also *phenomenal*: inference is episodic and manifested in consciousness, though there need be no consciousness *of* the inference under any particular description. The point that inference is phenomenal is easily missed because the related notions of *inferential belief* and of inferential (dispositional) judgment are not phenomenal, though they are psychological. A belief that p can be based on a belief that q *without* the person's inferring p from q. I could, for instance, discover q, which is evidence for p, only after *already* believing p (non-inferentially) on testimony. I could then begin to believe p inferentially, on the basis of the (non-testimonial) evidence, q. There need be nothing phenomenal, such as a sense of forming the belief that p, or even my consciously connecting p with q, as where I have a thought of q as supporting p. The kinds of phenomenal elements essential in drawing an inference are not required for a belief to acquire the relevant supporting role: the inferentiality in question is not episodic or even phenomenal; it is a *structural relation* between beliefs. It implies nothing about what occurs in consciousness. We often *make* connections between propositions by drawing inferences; but (by the grace of God or evolution or both) the mind is capable of responding to such connections more spontaneously, without our drawing inferences. Precisely because inferential belief need not arise from inference and because inferentiality need not be phenomenal, showing that intuitions are not inferential is difficult.

6. THE GROUNDS AND EXTENT OF INTUITIVE KNOWLEDGE AND JUSTIFICATION

What kinds of propositions are intuitively knowable is an epistemological question. What kinds are in fact known non-inferentially is not only an epistemological question but also a psychological one and indeed partly relative to the kind of person or social context in question. With at most a few exceptions, anything non-inferentially knowable can, at some time and by some person, be known inferentially; and perhaps anything inferentially knowable at all can be known non-inferentially.[26] Apparent exceptions to the first point arise where there *is* no suitable premise because of, for instance, the strong axiomatic status of the proposition (say that if $2 \times 2 = 4$, then $4 = 2 \times 2$).

Some of the groundwork for an account of intuitive moral justification and knowledge has been laid. We have seen in outline how an adequate understanding of a self-evident proposition can enable one to see its truth by virtue of apprehending conceptual relations and without relying on premises. I have also offered a partial account of intuitive non-inferential justification and knowledge for a related kind of singular moral judgment: the kind involving ascription of obligatoriness to an action or affirming *prima facie* moral reasons for it. We should now consider related kinds of moral judgments, both *prima facie* and final. Let us take these kinds in turn.

An intuitionist, simply as such, has various options for a general epistemology, say rationalist or empiricist; but here I will work from a rationalist perspective, as have Sidgwick, Moore, Ross, Ewing, and other major ethical intuitionists. Let us begin with something that has been in ethical literature at least since Moore: the idea that moral properties are consequential on non-moral ones, in the sense that a thing having moral properties has them in virtue of having certain non-moral properties.[27] An action cannot, then, be brutely obligatory, or brutely wrong. It will be (e.g.) obligatory in virtue of being promised or wrong in virtue of being a lie. Similarly, a just person may be just in virtue of certain intentions and action-tendencies.

Even if we do not take the relevant basis-relations—those expressed by 'in virtue of' here—to be necessary and *a priori*, they imply grounds for justification and knowledge (to simplify matters I'll consider only knowledge). Intuitionists do not deny the possibility (noted earlier) of inferential knowledge by subsumption, say the possibility of knowing that an act is wrong on the basis of knowing that it creates a conflict of interest and that such acts are *prima facie* wrong. This is an important point, since some intuitionists may allow the impression that *only* ethical intuition can justify moral judgment or yield moral knowledge. But it is also important to see how moral justification is possible without subsumption. Consider this. I hear someone promise to mail a letter and then see him slip it into a trash can. Is it not possible for my perception of the presence of the base property, that of being a promise-breaking, to lead to (and ground) my believing, non-inferentially, that the agent is wronging the promisee? Or, suppose I see an elementary school luncheon server give a visibly smaller portion to a black than to a white child. I may immediately and non-inferentially judge that this is unfair. In part because the disproportion is a *prima facie* indication of unfittingness, I "see" the unfairness.[28] Seeing the act in its context provides my ground for the judgment and may precede my making that judgment. Do we have knowledge in such cases?

The beliefs in question seem intuitive, justified, and good candidates for knowledge. The descriptions of the cases do not rule out, however, that some overrider is present. We could then know that the act is *prima facie* unfair but not know that it is unfair all things considered. Suppose we are thinking of *final* (all-things-considered). wrongness or obligation. Must we abandon the claim that these descriptions often yield propositions we can *know*? Certainly skeptics would claim we must. For in my two examples, it is possible that both agents had excuses we did not know of, hence did not violate a final obligation. But surely this possibility may in the context (and in many common contexts) be presupposed to be at best highly unlikely. The intuition may thus be justified. The remaining question is what degree of evidential strength the grounds must have in order to sustain knowledge of a final obligation. Here it is useful to compare the perceptual case. How good a glimpse do we need of a deer grazing in the distance to know that it is a deer? There is no easy answer, but if (with no "Gettier condition") we have a justified true belief based on a ground that is objectively good—though not entailing—evidence, it is plausible to say that we know this.

On my view, we often have such justified non-inferential beliefs ascribing final obligation. Just as a perceptual belief may be produced by a sensory response to the factual conditions in virtue of which it is true, a judgment of final obligation may be produced by a moral response to the descriptive properties of the action in virtue of which it is obligatory. There is a reliable connection in both cases, and both cognitions may constitute knowledge. To be sure, much depends on the ethical sensitivity of the moral judge. But similarly, for everyday observational knowledge much depends on the perceptual acuity of the observer. In ethical matters, intuitive judgments may require moral acuity, and when they do they are a primary realm of the exercise of practical wisdom.

7. INTUITION AND MORAL JUDGMENT

Intuitionism in ethics has often seemed to lack a way to unify the plural standards it endorses. It has also been taken to have at best meager resources for explaining how we should resolve conflicts between *prima facie* obligations. On this resolution problem, W. D. Ross appealed to Aristotelian practical wisdom. He argued that neither Kantian nor utilitarian ethics (the two rival views he considered) offers an adequate alternative.[29] I propose, however, an interpretation of Kant's Humanity Formula of the categorical imperative for which this negative assessment does not unqualifiedly hold. If, as I maintain in contrast to Ross, Moore, and others,[30] many self-evident propositions can be evidenced or even proved by other propositions, the way is open both to support Rossian moral principles by appeal to a more comprehensive principle and to characterize the self-evident in a way that makes it easy to see why self-evident propositions may be not only far from obvious but also subject to rational disagreement.

I understand the Humanity Formula along lines that, though they reflect some important elements in Kant's ethical texts, do not presuppose a specific interpretation of them. In particular, I have sought to show that its negative injunction—which prohibits treating persons merely as means—is explicable in terms of descriptive notions, and its positive injunction, which requires treating persons as ends, is explicable, if not descriptively, then at least without dependence on moral notions.[31] Doing this is important for defending Kantian ethics as well as for providing objective anchors for these notions. If the Humanity Formula is to serve as one of our *basic* guides in making moral judgments, we need a way to understand its requirements that does not depend on prior moral judgments. Otherwise, those judgments would be epistemically prior to it, and in that case it would (in at least some of its applications) lack basic moral force.

Given the detailed development of Kantian intuitionism that I have provided in earlier work, what I will do here is simply clarify the framework sufficiently to indicate how it helps in yielding intuitive resolutions of conflicts of obligation. Suppose I am correct in thinking that treating a person merely as a means is roughly treating the person not just *solely* as a means but (with some qualifications) also with a disposition *not* to be concerned with any *non*-instrumental aspects of the treatment. (This negative disposition is needed to account for the force of 'merely.') An example might be ordering a timid and willing employee to do a risky job, with an intention to let the person struggle alone even if the job becomes highly dangerous. If, as I think plausible, this kind of treatment is *prima facie* wrong—wrong-making, in another terminology—and *prima facie* wrong even if the act-*type*, ordering the job done, is not *prima facie* wrong in the context, then we have a morally relevant factor that can weigh in favor of a Rossian obligation, for instance non-injury.

A different example may help: a conflict between veracity in making a promise and an opportunity for beneficence. Suppose that, in making a promise I do not intend to keep, I would be getting the promisee, who expects to benefit from my keeping my promise, to do a very good thing for a third party. Making such a promise might also manifest the relevant disposition not to be concerned with non-instrumental aspects of the treatment of the promisee, say the person's suffering from the loss of an important opportunity when I break the promise. Let us assume this. The point that in making the insincere promise I would be using the promisee merely instrumentally weighs in favor of not making the promise or, if I do make it, of reversing my course and keeping it after all. It also supports the promissory obligation over the obligation of beneficence (though this does not entail that the support is overriding). The decision whether to keep the promise may still not be easy, though it might be. In any case, the point is that the added moral ground—that making the insincere, manipulative promise would be treating the promisee merely as a means—is helpful and potentially determinative, not that it makes all the conflict cases easy to resolve. That is something no plausible moral view will achieve.

Consider now treating someone as an end, which is mainly a matter of doing—for its own sake—something that is (and is appropriately conceived by the agent as) for the good of the other person. Suppose I have to decide whether to punish a child for bad behavior by keeping the child at home or to make do with a reprimand. Assume that I know this punishment is reasonable but will make the child suffer. Suppose the retributive considerations, together with the good the punishment will do for the child in the long run, are just strong enough to make the decision difficult, given the desirability of avoiding the suffering. Now suppose that I consider not just the two act-types in question, punishing and simply reprimanding—types which some other person could token—but how I would be *treating* the child in each case. It could well be that treating the child as an end requires, not a kind of utilitarian calculation, but tolerating the suffering and carrying out the punishment in the appropriate spirit.

These promissory and retributive examples might give the impression that the notions of merely instrumental and end-regarding treatment simply place two more *prima facie* obligations on a Rossian list and hence are no help either in its unification or in dealing with conflicts of obligations. I have indeed suggested that the non-moral grounds in question—the two kinds of treatment—generate *prima facie* obligations and seem to do so in their own right. Suppose this were all we could say of them: that there are *prima facie* obligations to treat persons as ends and to avoid treating them merely as means. This is significant in itself. The obligations would be morally important by virtue of their *instantial,* as opposed to systematizing, uses. They would not only provide a sense of kinds of acts to be avoided—those that *use* people—and a sense of deeds to be aimed at, such as contributing to the well-being of others; they also figure (as illustrated) in many cases that would otherwise be difficult or impossible to decide in an intuitively satisfactory way.[32] They are, however, more comprehensive than the Rossian obligations. One or the other of them is applicable to all (or virtually all) instances of Rossian obligation. For all of the Rossian obligations, many kinds of fulfillments can be cases of treating someone as an end; and violation of the negative obligations, for instance of non-injury, fidelity, and veracity, are the kinds of actions that tend to manifest or at least approach treatment merely as a means.

These considerations indicate how the notions of avoiding merely instrumental treatment and aiming at end-regarding treatment express broad negative and positive aims proper to the institution of morality—a *telos*, as it were. They characterize, in broad strokes, some of the kinds of evils morality opposes and some of the kinds of goods it honors and promotes. This purposive role that the two notions partly represent is a significant unifying element for the Rossian obligations.

These clarifications of Kantian intuitionism do not provide a formula for dealing with conflicts of obligation, but they do show that the notions of merely instrumental and end-regarding treatment of persons can play positive roles both in providing a comprehensive conceptual framework for conceiving the Rossian obligations and for dealing with certain conflicts between those. I do not claim that every such conflict is better dealt with in the light of those notions, but many are. It is also important to realize that even when conflicting obligations present a difficult case, we may not need to appeal to general principles to apprehend our overall obligation. Again, the analogy to perception is useful: confronted with someone who looks like a man I remember, I may have to look a long time to see that he is. My discriminative faculties may be hard at work and may succeed even if I never draw any inferences, say from the premise that he is too young to be the person I remember or from the premise that, given his unusual diction, he must be that person. Such things might indeed occur to me later; but the supportability of a judgment by a premise by no means implies its antecedent role in arriving at the judgment.

8. REASONS FOR ACTION AND FINAL OBLIGATION

I have been presupposing that a ground of obligation, such as making a promise, is also a reason for action. But not all normative reasons are moral, and I have taken no position on the (normative) strength of moral reasons relative to other kinds.[33] The possibility of conflict between moral and non-moral reasons, such as reasons of pure self-interest, can make more difficult the overall question of what one ought to do (what *to* do, if that question is understood normatively). Non-moral reasons may not only conflict with moral ones but may also support some moral reasons against other moral reasons. Here it is enough to indicate how, on my theory, we should conceive conflicting moral reasons. Much that is said will apply to conflicts between moral and non-moral reasons.

To begin with, I take it that there is no *a priori* hierarchy among the moral reasons represented by the Rossian obligations. Thus, there are apparently no two categories of Rossian obligation, say justice and beneficence, such that *every* obligation in one will outweigh *any* (individual) obligation in the other. An implication of this view—a kind of particularism regarding normative hierarchies—is that a moral reason corresponding to such an obligation is not *a priori* overridden in every case of conflict with a moral reason belonging to a different category of obligation. Note, too, that even on the assumption that a reason of one kind is always overridden in a pairwise conflict with a single reason of some other kind, certain coalitions of reasons on one side might still prevail over any single reason that would always override any one member of the coalition. If, for instance, in conflict cases, any reason of non-injury were to outweigh every reason of gratitude taken by itself, some of the former taken singly might not outweigh every *set* of gratitudinal reasons.

Given these points, might we not formulate some rough generalizations, each rationalizable by, even if not strictly deducible from, the Humanity Formula on my interpretation? Each might be conceived as a kind of *adjunctive principle* that can guide one in dealing with conflicting *prima facie* obligations, whether between two or more of the ten I have posited or within a single category, as where two promises conflict. (I do not take the list of ten as necessarily complete, but it is highly comprehensive and at present I see no clear need to extend it.) These principles are adjuncts to Rossian principles, but do not have the same moral status and need not be self-evident. They might be considered partially adjudicative, in the sense that they have weight in properly determining moral judgment, even if they apply only where there are already conflicting Rossian considerations.

The following are two candidates for partially adjudicative principles that might be plausibly thought to hold when other things are equal in terms of the Rossian obligations.

Treatment of persons. If two options we have are equally well supported by conflicting Rossian obligations, then if one option is favored in terms of our (a) avoiding treating persons merely as a means or (b) treating persons as ends (or both), then that option is preferable, other things equal, with (a) having priority (other things equal) over (b) if (a) supports one option and (b) the other.

The punishment case above illustrates the applicability of this principle. It should be added that although it is not clear that Kant viewed the obligation to avoid merely instrumental treatment as, other things equal, weightier than the obligation to treat persons as ends, this view is independently plausible and provides greater determinacy for my interpretation of the overall moral force of the Humanity Formula. Another principle I take to be supported by (but not only by) the Humanity Formula as I interpret it concerns the political domain (counterparts may be formulated with other realms of conduct):

The principle of secular rationale (roughly, of natural reason): Citizens in a free democracy have a *prima facie* obligation not to advocate or support any law or public policy that restricts human conduct, unless they have, and are willing to offer, adequate secular reason (roughly, natural reason) for this advocacy or support (e.g. for a vote).[34]

Here a secular reason for an action (or a belief) is roughly one whose status as a justifier of action (or belief) does not evidentially depend on (but also does not deny) the existence of God; nor does it depend on theological considerations, or on the pronouncements of a person or institution *as* a religious authority. This notion is epistemic, roughly a matter of evidential grounding, not a matter of the content of the reason. We can imagine a case in which a person's reasons for action include commitments based essentially on religious convictions. Consider a (higher-order) promissory obligation grounded in swearing on the Bible that one will keep a promise to one's priest to support outlawing same-sex unions. The secular rationale principle would call for abstaining from coercion (as opposed to persuasion) in this matter apart from having an adequate reason that does not depend in this way on religion or theology. (If, for instance, the welfare of children could be shown to be adversely affected by such unions, there would be a secular reason.) The secular rationale principle is not clearly entailed by the Humanity Formula as I understand it; but the role that the principle accords to natural reasons is one we would expect them to play on a non-theological understanding of the formula.

It must be granted that even if the adjudicative principles proposed and others like them help in resolving conflicts of Rossian obligations, they themselves may still leave some conflicts unresolved. Indeed, they too can generate difficult cases. Consider treatment of persons. Suppose our only way to stop a drunken man from becoming violent is to manipulate his estranged wife into giving him the sense that she has forgiven his excesses. This would be *prima facie* wrongful instrumental treatment, and it would approach using her merely as a means, but might this *prima facie* wrongful treatment be preferable to risking violence to several innocent bystanders? In cases of this kind, Ross appealed to Aristotelian practical wisdom and to Aristotle's comment that "the decision rests with perception" (1930: 41; *Nicomachean Ethics* 1126b4). Both have intuitive judgments in mind (rather than sensory perceptions), but neither specifies how these are like judgments grounded in sensory perception. Is there sufficient analogy between sensory perception and intuition as intellectual perception to sustain Ross's terminology here?

Consider how one might decide which of two paintings is a copy, or how one can tell Owen from his fraternal twin when we see him in the half-light. The art expert may simply look at both paintings a long time and judge on the basis of the complex visual data. And we may need only a closer look to determine which is Owen and which is John. Might art experts tell us how they do it? Perhaps. And might there even be a true generalization linking observable properties of the original painting to its author's work? Certainly. Arguably, if there are, as there surely must be, observable indications that ground ordinary perceptual knowledge, then, in principle, there *must* be a generalization, however complex, linking them to authorship. Think of the distinctive brush strokes of van Gogh, easily recognizable but difficult to describe in a way that distinguishes them from those a forgery might display. And if I can (visually) tell Owen from John, must there not be observable features, perhaps a multitude of them, by which I do it? The answer seems positive, but it does not follow that our singular judgments are tacitly *subsumptive* or otherwise inferential. On the contrary, it is in part because our intuitive singular judgments are trusted and confirmed that we can arrive at the relevant generalizations in the first place.

The visual perceptions just described are themselves intuitive and apparently rest on a sensory seeming. There is no reason to consider intellectual perception of the kind represented by certain intuitions to be different on this score. My sense that I should not break the promise is a response to the apprehension of the case before me. In the case of the wandering toddler, I may have a moral perception that *embodies* the intuitive sense of what I should do. This sense, which is a kind of moral seeming, yields a judgment that embodies belief and that, leaving skepticism aside, can constitute knowledge. The intuitions appear, moreover, both *prima facie* justificatory for the beliefs they support and epistemically prior to knowledge of the generalizations that connect the intuitively discerned elements to the moral attributions these elements ground, say, on the one hand, the disoriented look of the toddler amid the threatening circumstances of the street and, on the other, the attribution of a prima obligation to check on the child.

These points are entirely compatible with taking the capacity of intuitions to yield true beliefs to depend on such connections between properties. These are the kinds of connections that, as illustrated by cases like that of the promise and the wandering toddler, the generalizations express. It would indeed be surprising if a discriminative grasp of the connections underlying singular moral truths were not epistemically prior to our knowledge of those connections. There is, then, much to be said for the analogy between sensory and intellectual perception and for the capacity of both to yield justification and knowledge.

***

The status of ethical intuitionism depends largely on the power of our rational capacities to perceive truth by certain kinds of non-inferential discernment of properties and propositions. This discernment may or may not be produced by or even accompanied by reflection. On rationalist versions of intuitionism, even general moral principles may be directly (non-inferentially) known—though neither indefeasibly nor, invariably, in a way that is wholly unmediated by reflection.[35] Reflection may be necessary even to see the truth of a self-evident proposition: being self-evident does not entail being obvious, unprovable, or beyond rational dispute. As I have developed intuitionism, the required apprehensional power of reason to ground non-inferential knowledge, and non-inferentially justified belief, of general moral principles is essentially like the power needed for knowledge of the *a priori* in general; and its power regarding the grounding of singular judgments is highly analogous to the epistemic power by which we acquire perceptual knowledge. In both cases there are evidential grounds, but these need not provide support only in inferential ways. In extending the comprehensive intuitionism constructed in earlier work, this essay shows how my account of intuitions accommodates intuitive seemings and the related phenomenon or apprehending fittingness relations. I have connected both of these notions with doxastic intuitions on the model of the relation between perceptual seemings and the beliefs they justify. I have also clarified the notion of self-evidence, the way in which it makes non-inferential general knowledge possible, and how such knowledge, as well as adjunctive principles it warrants, can guide intuitions in resolving conflicts of obligation. In the light of the accounts of self-evidence and intuitive justification sketched here, ethical intuitionism can be seen as a plausible framework for understanding justification in ethics.[36]

ENDNOTES

INTRODUCTION

1 Mark Timmons, John Greco, and Alfred R. Mele, eds., *Rationality and the Good: Critical Essays on the Ethics and Epistemology of Robert Audi* (Oxford: Oxford University Press, 2007).

2 See esp. Henry Sigdwick, *The Methods of Ethics,* seventh edition (London: Macmillan 1907); and G. E. Moore, *Principia Ethics* (Cambridge: Cambridge University Press, 1903).

3 Ross said, e.g., "A statement is certain, i.e. is an expression of knowledge, only in one or the other of two cases: when it is either self-evident, or a valid conclusion from self-evident premises ... we are never certain that any possible act ... is right nor certain that it is wrong." See *The Right and the Good* (Oxford: Oxford University Press, 1930: 30–1). There is a shift here from the epistemic to the psychological use of 'certain'; the first is crucial for the question of moral knowledge, and on my view, neither is a necessary condition for knowledge and some propositions expressing final obligation are knowable.

4 Roger Crisp has written in detail on this problem, generally supporting Sidgwick's cautious skepticism (which differs from Ross's) and in my paper at the end of this volume and elsewhere I have responded with a non-skeptical defense.

5 There is even a way for my view to be adapted to noncognitivism, as I noted in *The Good in the Right: A Theory of Intuition and Intrinsic Value* (Princeton: Princeton University Press, 2004: 151). But noncognitivism is not, to be sure, a natural option for an intuitionist.

6 See Ross 1930: 29–30. He said, e.g., that "In our confidence that these propositions [the principles of *prima facie* duty] are true there is involved that same trust in our reason that is involved in our confidence in mathematics ... we are dealing with propositions that cannot be proved but that just as certainly need no proof" (30). On the previous page he had called these propositions "self-evident *just as* a mathematical axiom, or the validity of a form of inference, is evident" (italics added). If the 'just as' were warranted, we would be unlikely to find any plausible way to explain apparently rational disbelief of at least some of these propositions. As to how they may be rationally doubted, I have given a detailed explanation in "Intuition, Inference, and Rational Disagreement in Ethics," *Ethical Theory and Moral Practice* 11 (2008a: 475–92).

7 How this foundational though defeasible role is possible is indicated in my paper that concludes this volume.

8 My (1999) contains a more detailed account of self-evidence than (2004), and some extensions of both treatments are made in my (Audi forthcoming). I should add that we might also speak of *full* understanding to avoid the suggestion that adequacy implies sufficiency only for some specific purpose. Neither term is ideal, but 'full' may suggest maximality, which is also inappropriate.

9 See Brad Hooker's *Ideal Code, Real World* (Oxford University Press: 2000) for an indication of how a rule-consequentialism may be squared with giving special status to common-sense intuitive moral principles.

10 My theory of value and a sketch of my theory of reasons for action as related to intrinsic value are provided in Chapter 4 of *The Good in the Right: A Theory of Intuition and Intrinsic Value.*

11 "Moral Perception and Moral Knowledge," *Proceedings of the Aristotelian Society*, lxxxiv (2010b: 79–97).

12 Ross's translation of *Nicomachean Ethics* 1109 b23. See Ross (1930: 42).

CHAPTER ONE

1 See notes 9, 10, and 14 below; as well as my *Moral Skepticisms* (New York: Oxford University Press, 2006: Chapter 9, 184–219). The version that I give here is most closely related to "How to

Apply Generalities: A Reply to Tolhurst and Shafer-Landau" in *Moral Psychology*, Volume 2: *The Cognitive Science of Morality*, ed. W. Sinnott-Armstrong (Cambridge: MIT Press, 2008: 97–105).

2   I will have in mind the sophisticated version of moral intuitionism developed by Robert Audi in, among other places, *The Good in the Right: A Theory of Intuition and Intrinsic Value* (Princeton: Princeton University Press, 2004). However, my argument will also apply to many other recent moral intuitionists as well.

3   The inference need not be present. Suppose I base a belief on an inference and later forget the inferential basis but still hold the belief. If I believe it at the later time only because of the inference at the earlier time, then this later belief is not immediate or an intuition, because it is based on a past inference. Another tricky case is testimony, but I am inclined to think of a testimony-based belief as based on an inference from a belief that someone said it, which explains why testimony-based beliefs also do not count as intuitions. Luckily, nothing in my argument hinges on whether such tricky cases are classified as immediate or as intuitions.

4   For more detail on the relevant way of being justified, see my *Moral Skepticisms*, Section 4.2, 63–72.

5   This notion of commitment to an inferential structure replaces the notion of ability to infer in my previous formulations. My notion is close to what Audi calls "an appropriate accessible path leading (perhaps by natural inferential steps) from justificatory materials accessible to us to an occurrent justification for the proposition" (*The Good in the Right*, 50–1; see also 'Structural Justification' in *The Structure of Justification*, Cambridge: Cambridge University Press, 1993).

6   *The Good in the Right*, 48–9. This is not all of Audi's definition.

7   *Moral Skepticisms* (New York: Oxford University Press, 2006: Chapter 10, 220–51).

8   Some moral anti-realists might object to talking about truth and falsity of moral beliefs, but they can substitute 'acceptable' for 'true' and 'unacceptable' for 'false' as long as they admit that some combinations of moral judgments are not acceptable or are unacceptable. In any case, my target here is moral intuitionism, and almost all moral intuitionists (including Audi) are moral realists.

9   For details on disagreement, see my "Moral Relativity and Intuitionism," *Philosophical Issues, Volume 12: Realism and Relativism* (2002: 305–28).

10   For details on partiality (as well as other factors), see my "Moral Intuitionism Meets Empirical Psychology," *Metaethics After Moore*, ed. T. Horgan and M. Timmons (New York: Oxford University Press, 2006: 339–65).

11   Thalia Wheatley and Jonathan Haidt, "Hypnotic Disgust Makes Moral Judgments More Severe," *Psychological Science* 16 (2005: 780–4).

12   S. Schnall, J. Haidt, G. Clore, and A. Jordan, "Disgust as embodied moral judgment," *Personality and Social Psychology Bulletin* 34 (2008: 1096–109).

13   I do not deny that emotion sometimes aids moral belief, such as when it results from conditioning from certain experiences, so I need not disagree with John Allman and Jim Woodward, "What are Moral Intuitions and Why Should We Care about Them? A Neurobiological Perspective" in *Philosophical Issues, 18, Interdisciplinary Core Philosophy* (2008: 164–85).

14   For details on order and wording effects, see my "Framing Moral Intuitions" in *Moral Psychology*, Volume 2: *The Cognitive Science of Morality*, ed. W. Sinnott-Armstrong (Cambridge: MIT Press, 2008: 47–76).

15   See Thomas Nadelhoffer and Adam Feltz, "The Actor–Observer Bias and Moral Intuitions: Adding Fuel to Sinnott-Armstrong's Fire," *Neuroethics* 1 (2008: 133–44).

16   See Joris Lammers and Diederik A. Stapel, "How Power Influences Moral Thinking," *Journal of Personality and Social Psychology* 97, 2 (2009: 279–89).

17   See William D. S. Kilgore, Desiree B. Kilgore, Lisa M. Day, Christopher Li, Gary H. Kamimori, and Thomas J. Balkin, "The Effects of 53 Hours of Sleep Deprivation on Moral Judgment," *Sleep*, vol. 30, no. 3 (2007), 345–52; and Olav Kjellevold Olsen, Stale Pallesen, and Jarle Eid, "The Impact of Partial Sleep Deprivation on Moral Reasoning in Military Officers," *Sleep* vol. 33, no. 8 (2010), 1086–90.

18   The qualification 'much' indicates that your impression might make it reasonable for you to change your probability assessment slightly. However, a slight change is not enough to overcome the large chance of error that creates the basic problem for moral

intuitionism. So I will not worry about whether the neophyte's impression makes it reasonable to increase the probability assessment slightly.

19 I will not focus on externalism here, because Audi is an internalist about justified belief and, presumably, reasonableness.

20 To call something reasonable is not yet to call its denial unreasonable, since incompatible alternatives might each be reasonable. Hence, it might be better to substitute a slightly weaker principle: If it is unreasonable for a person to deny a large probability that a certain belief is false, then that person is not epistemically justified in holding that belief. To reduce negations, I will work with the stronger principle, but my argument would not be affected substantially if I substituted this weaker principle.

21 Russ Shafer-Landau, "Defending Ethical Intuitionism" in *Moral Psychology*, Volume 2: *The Cognitive Science of Morality*, 83.

22 See W. D. Ross, *Foundations of Ethics* (Oxford: Clarendon Press, 1939: 168–70).

23 Audi might respond that conclusions of reflection need not be conclusions of inference. However, this distinction requires a more precise account of inference than has been provided. See my "Reflections on Reflection in Audi's Moral Intuitionism," in *Rationality and the Good,* edited by Mark Timmons, John Greco, and Alfred R. Mele (New York: Oxford University Press, 2007: 19–30); and Audi's reply on 202–4. In any case, reflection involves beliefs that commit the believer to a justificatory inferential structure even if the believer does not base his 'conclusion of reflection' on any actual inference.

24 Thanks to Robert Audi for helpful discussion and comments on a draft as well as for stimulating me and so many others who work on these issues.

CHAPTER TWO

1 My thanks to Robert Audi for suggesting this title, as well as for several enlightening discussions.

2 Neither desire nor felt obligation have as part of their content a determinate answer as to what will occur or be done; both, therefore may be considered open as to what actually will occur.

Felt obligation is however closed in this sense: that it presents the action in question as (*prima facie*) the only one that is permitted. This is not a matter of the action in question being straightforwardly good; it may belong to a set of alternatives all of which are in the end bad. Still less is it a matter of the action being the best alternative available; we are in general not obligated to do what is best. Rather, felt obligation involves a sense of deontic necessity, a sense that the action in question would occur in any permissible future beginning from the way things now stand. This, I take it, implies that what is obligatory is not *reducible* to what is good. It might still develop, however, that what is obligatory is coextensive with what is good or best in some way.

3 Cognitive intuitionists would of course deny that our faculties of cognitive perception are attuned only to the naturalistic dimension of things. I shall have more to say about this in the next section.

4 This claim will remind some readers of Mill's argument in *Utilitarianism* that just as the only proof capable of being given that things are visible and audible is that people actually see and hear them, so the only proof that things are desirable is that people desire them. J. S. Mill, *Utilitarianism*, Chapter 4, para. 3. This argument has been justly criticized on the basis that 'visible' and 'audible' mean only *capable* of being seen and heard, whereas desirable in this context has to mean *deserving* of being desired, or good. The fact that the analogy fails does not show, however, that the conclusion is false. Indeed, the very idea that, in the sense intended, 'desirable' things must be *worthy* of being desired may be taken as indicative that when we desire things we *do* in fact value them—i.e. that correctly or not, the things we desire present themselves to us in the very experience of desiring them as desirable in the evaluative sense. The question is just whether this feature of desire may be taken as disclosing to us anything objectively real. Mill's belief, however poorly argued, is that it does, and that is the thesis of conative intuitionism also.

5 Unless of course one were color blind—in which case, for most of us at least, it would be the other way around.

6 For a development of cognitive intuitionism that reflects these points see Robert Audi, *The Good in the Right: A Theory*

of Intuition and Intrinsic Value (Princeton, NJ: Princeton University Press, 2004) especially Chapter 2.

7   See my "The Will and the Good," in S. Nannini and C. Lumer, eds. *Deliberation, Intentionality, and Autonomy: The Action-Theoretic Basis of Practical Philosophy* (Aldershot, England: Ashgate, 2007: 119–33).

8   This is a controversial claim, in that there is a widespread view, sometimes called motivational internalism, that at least some judgments of this kind imply or include motivation to act. For discussions of motivational internalism see Audi, "Moral Judgment and Reasons for Action," in his *Moral Knowledge and Ethical Character* (New York: Oxford University Press, 1997a), Chapter 10; and Sigrun Svavarsdóttir, "Moral Cognition and Motivation," *The Philosophical Review* 108 (1999: 161–219).

9   For more on what it is to act for a reason and its role in practical rationality see my 2007.

10 For this sort of objection see Robert Audi, "Intuition, Reflection, and Justification," in *Rationality and the Good*, eds. M. Timmons, J. Greco, and A. R. Mele (New York: Oxford University Press, 2007a: 201–21, 208–10).

11 The exact nature of the representations that pertains to various mental states and events, and the language in which to convey them, is a complicated subject. Beyond the few remarks that follow above, it is too much to go into here.

12 Cf. Maurice Mandelbaum, *The Phenomenology of Moral Experience* (Baltimore, MD: Johns Hopkins Press, 1969: 60).

13 Perhaps the best known argument of this kind is given by J. L. Mackie in discussing what he calls the queerness of morality. *Ethics: Inventing Right and Wrong* (Harmondsworth: Penguin Books, 1977: 38).

14 This paper was presented at the Brackenridge Symposium on the Ethical and Epistemic Dimensions of Robert Audi's Intuitionism, University of Texas at San Antonio, 2009. I am grateful for the comments received on that occasion.

CHAPTER THREE

1   Walter Sinnott-Armstrong, "Reflections on Reflection in Robert Audi's Moral Intuitionism," in *Rationality and the Good: Critical Essays on the Ethics and Epistemology of Robert Audi,*

eds. Mark Timmons, John Greco, and Alfred R. Mele (Oxford: Oxford University Press, 2007: 19).

2   Charles S. Peirce famously attacks Cartesian, or 'paper doubt' in a number of places, including "Some Consequences of Four Incapacities," *The Collected Papers of Charles Sanders Peirce*, eds. Charles Hartshorne and Paul Weiss (Cambridge: Harvard University Press, 1931–1935: esp. 5, 264–8) and "How to Make Our Ideas Clear," (5, 388–410).

3   Mary Midgley, "Trying Out One's New Sword," in *Heart and Mind* (St. Martin's: 1981), rpnt. John Arthur and Steven Scalet, eds, *Morality and Moral Controversies*, 8th edition (Upper Saddle River, NJ: Pearson/Prentice Hall, 2009: 35).

4   G. E. Moore, "A Defence of Common Sense," in *Philosophical Papers* (New York: Macmillan, 1966: 32–59). See also his "Proof of an External World," ibid. 126–48.

5   Similar things can be said, *mutatis mutandis,* about being justified in believing that *p.*

6   William P. Alston, "Realism and the Tasks of Epistemology," *Realism/Antirealism and Epistemology*, ed. Christopher B. Kulp (Lanham, MD: Rowman & Littlefield, 1997: 57). Actually, Alston thinks that, properly speaking, the T-schema is not a definition of truth: "First ... it does not give us a contextual definition of 'true.' Second, it is not a statement at all, much less an unqualifiedly general statement as to the conditions under which a proposition is true. It is merely a scheme for statements," ibid. Instead, he settles on the following version—a principle *about* the T-schema: "Any instance of [the T-schema] is necessarily true by virtue of the meaning of, *inter alia,* 'true'" ibid. (my insertion).

7   Alston, "Realism and the Tasks of Epistemology," op. cit. 58. See 58ff for elaboration. But contrast Richard Rorty's view on this conception of truth qualifying as realist: see his "Realism, Antirealism, and Pragmatism: Comments on Alston, Chisholm, Davidson, Harman, and Searle," in Christopher B. Kulp, ed. *Realism/Antirealism and Epistemology* (Lanham, MD: Rowman & Littlefield, 1997: 159).

8   What follows is developed in much greater detail in John Searle, *The Construction of Social Reality*, Chapter 9 (New York: Free Press, 1995: 199–228).

9   Ibid. 219; italics mine.

10   Ibid.

11   Ibid.

12   Ibid., my insertion. I shall return to the issue of 'facts' and 'states of affairs' below.

13 John Searle, op. cit. 220; quotation in my insertion from ibid. 206.

14   I return to this issue below.

15   See Ramon M. Lemos, *Metaphysical Investigations* (London and Toronto: Associated University Presses, 1988); and also his "Bearers of Value," *Philosophy and Phenomenological Research*, Vol. LI, No. 4 (December, 1991: 873–89). Lemos's work has a substantial influence on what I say throughout this section of the paper.

16   Sentence-tokens of this ilk may not, however, be strictly adequate to express a determinate proposition. For example, one would need to include a temporal, and probably also a spatial indexical. I pass over these matters as peripheral to our present concerns.

17   Lemos, "Bearers of Value," op. cit. 873. I will refine this notion a bit momentarily, in a way that differs somewhat from Lemos.

18   See ibid. 874–6, for elaboration.

19   Sense 1 and Sense 2 of the term 'fact' are obviously closely connected. In Sense 1, 'fact' refers in any given instance to the *state of affairs* that obtains; in Sense 2, 'fact' refers in any given instance to the *obtaining* of the state of affairs.

20   Sense 4, for example, is not commonly used in philosophical parlance. And some uses of the term are more philosophically problematic than others. For example, even though the term 'fact' is certainly *used* in the third sense, in some cases without relevant confusion, I think Searle is right that we shouldn't simply identify the two, at least not in any wholesale way.

21   Ibid. 876.

22   Indeed, even my elaboration to follow is little more than a sketch.

23   See page 59 above; this is Lemos's wording, op. cit.

24   Cf. Roderick M. Chisholm, *The First Person*, 9 (Minneapolis: University of Minnesota Press, 1981). I owe the notion of applying a type/token distinction to the analysis of the concept of a state of affairs to Robert Audi.

25   "*May be* attributable" as opposed to "*is* attributable," since I leave it open whether these attributions are overridable. Thus, it may be that the benefactor's generosity is not morally good if it

comes at the cost of inflicting great hardship on those to whom he has a pre-existing obligation.

26 I am not trying here to give a full analysis of the necessary and sufficient conditions for the truth of propositions of the form '*S* is enslaved by *X*.' Perhaps, indeed probably, a person could be enslaved at time *t* but not be physically restrained at *t* from doing what she occurrently, and rightfully wills. Perhaps such a case of enslavement is better described as 'mental' or 'emotional' than physical. But all this is really beside the point at issue; for all I seek to do here is provide a briefly-described example of enslavement properly understood as *centrally possessing a physical component*.

27 See Russ Shafer-Landau, *Moral Realism: A Defence* (Oxford: Oxford University Press, 2003) 72ff for worthwhile discussion of the relevance of a naturalist (physicalist) theory of mind to moral metaphysics. I am largely in agreement with Shafer-Landau. I should note that this is not to imply that *only* minded beings can instance moral properties. Non-persons can too, but the latter can only instance a subset of the former. My point here, however, has to do with the moral properties unique to minded beings.

28 For example, if person $A \neq$ person B, but A and B share all non-relational physical properties, then, controlling for differences in relevant non-physical properties, if any—perhaps attitudinal properties, for example—if A were to do x to Z at t, and if B were to do x to Z at t, then A's doing x to Z at t is right (wrong) *iff* B's doing x to Z at t is right (wrong). The point is that changes in physical properties—if they are the *right* physical properties—make a difference to moral properties, but that wouldn't be the case unless the two were somehow related.

29 See Jaegwon Kim, "Concepts of Supervenience," rpnt. in *Supervenience and Mind: Selected Philosophical Essays*, eds. Jaegwon Kim and Ernest Sosa 53–78 (Cambridge: Cambridge University Press, 1993–). Cf. Brink, *Moral Realism and the Foundations of Ethics* (Cambridge, 1988: 160–1). This could be generalized to any type of base and supervening properties.

30 Audi, *The Good in the Right,* 33–5: this is not a direct quote.

31 Regarding being 'evident,' this is in the spirit of Roderick Chisholm. See, for example, his *Theory of Knowledge,* 2nd edition (Englewood Cliffs, NJ: 1977, Chapter 2) . See also ibid 135: "D1. 5: *h is evident* for S = Df (i) *h* is beyond reasonable

doubt for S and (ii) for every i, if accepting i is more reasonable for S than accepting h, then i is certain for S." I do not mean to endorse the second clause.

32 This is Robert Audi's wording, communicated to me in private correspondence.

33 This isn't to imply that this or any other intuition need be instantaneous upon contemplation of the relevant issue. An intuition may be the result of prolonged thought. The issue here is its non-inferentiality.

34 Pragmatists like Dewey and Rorty, for example, fall into this camp.

35 Of course the criteria relevant to testing one type of theory may be quite different from that appropriate to testing another type. Contrast testing theories in chemistry with testing theories in mathematics.

36 I know, for example, that my wife should not be shot to death while writing a letter to me; that my mother should not be shot to death while writing a letter to me; that my wife should not be *burned* to death while writing to me, or while talking to me on the telephone; etc., etc. etc. These examples could be multiplied *ad nauseum.*

37 See e.g. Shelly Kegan, "Thinking About Cases," in *Moral Knowledge*, eds. Ellen Frankel Paul, Fred Miller, and Jeffrey Paul (Cambridge: Cambridge University Press, 2001: 44–63).

38 I of course regard some intuitions as foundational *knowledge.*

39 My thanks to James Felt, Jill Hernandez, Philip J. Ivanhoe, Mane Hajdin, and especially Robert Audi for helpful comments on previous versions of this paper.

CHAPTER FOUR

1 Audi, *The Good in the Right*, (2004: 2).

* Many thanks to Robert Audi for his encouragement and advice throughout the process of writing this paper. Stavroula Glezakos, George Graham, John Heil, Michaelis Michael, Timm Triplett, and Julian Young helped greatly by providing extensive written comments, in some cases on more than one draft. John Heil's 2006 National Endowment for the Humanities Summer Seminar on Mind and Metaphysics provided the occasion and incentive for my beginning to think about the issues of this paper, so many thanks to the NEH for that support. Finally, I would like to express my appreciation for helpful comments from my colleagues Emily Austin, Adrian Bardon, Christian Miller, and Patrick Toner.

2 Ibid.

3 Markie, "The Mystery of Direct Perceptual Justification," (2005).

4 Audi, *Epistemology*, (2003: 29–30).

5 Lyons, *Perception and Basic Beliefs*, (2009).

6 Audi, "Moral Perception and Moral Knowledge," (2010b: 81).

7 Audi, *Epistemology*, (2003: 29–30).

8 Audi, "Justification, Truth, and Reliability," (1988: 19–20); See also Audi, "Justifying Grounds, Justified Beliefs, and Rational Acceptance," (2007d: 222).

9 Pryor, "The Skeptic and the Dogmatist," (2000: 536).

10 I follow Audi in using 'as of' non-committally "to cover both veridical and non-veridical experiences." Audi, "Justifying Grounds, Justified Beliefs, and Rational Acceptance," (2007d: 223).

11 Harman, "The Intrinsic Quality of Experience," (1990: 39). See also Tye, "Visual Qualia and Visual Content" (1992); Dretske, *Naturalizing the Mind* (1995), and others for similar claims.

12 BonJour writes: " … it seems to me important to ask just what the significance of these characterizations of experience in physical-object terms really is and what it is about the experience that makes them seem so obviously appropriate." "Are Perceptual Beliefs Properly Foundational?"(2007: 88).

13 Ibid. 86–7.

14 Audi, "Justification, Truth, and Reliability," (1988: 17–18).

15 BonJour, "Are Perceptual Beliefs Properly Foundational?" (2007: 92).

16 See e.g. Markie, "Epistemically Appropriate Perceptual Belief," (2006: 118). Thanks also to John Heil for reminding me of this point. Here I engage—harmlessly, I hope—in the conceit that colors are genuine properties.

17 Davidson, "A Coherence Theory of Truth and Knowledge," (2008: 127).

18 BonJour and Sosa, *Epistemic Justification*, (2003: 164).

19 Audi, "Justifying Grounds, Justified Beliefs, and Rational Acceptance," (2007d: 223)."My claim was that we cannot know *a priori* that there is an *objective* likelihood of truth, one entailing that in at least the majority of relevantly similar possible worlds the proposition in question is true."

20 BonJour, "Are Perceptual Beliefs Properly Foundational?"(2007: 88).

21 BonJour and Sosa, *Epistemic Justification*, (2003: 164).

22 Ibid. 164–5.

23 Sellars' presentation is difficult and has no settled canonical interpretation. My version is at best 'Sellarsian' and is certainly not the result of scholarly exegesis on my part. I base it on the following formulation by Audi in *The Architecture of Reason*, 17: "if experiences are non-conceptual, they do not stand in need of justification but have none to give; and if they are conceptual (e.g. entailing belief) they may provide justification but also stand in need of it and hence cannot play a foundational role. This argument may be buttressed by the idea that only propositions stand in logical relations to the propositional objects of beliefs, and non-conceptual experiences can at best stand in causal relations to the beliefs in question." For Sellars' original statement, see his "Empiricism and the philosophy of mind," reprinted in Sellars, *Science, Perception and Reality*, (1963: 127–96, esp. 131–2).

24 Audi, *The Architecture of Reason*, (2001: 17)

25 Huemer, *Skepticism and the Veil of Perception*, (2001: 97).

26 Audi, *The Architecture of Reason*, (2001: 17).

27 Ibid.

28 Ibid.

29 Audi, "Moral Perception and Moral Knowledge," (2010b: 87).

30 Audi, "Justifying Grounds, Justified Beliefs, and Rational Acceptance," (2007d: 223).

31 BonJour, "Are Perceptual Beliefs Properly Foundational?" (2007: 88).

32 Alston, "Back to the Theory of Appearing," (1999: 194).

CHAPTER FIVE

1 An ancestor of this paper has been presented at the *Brackenridge Philosophy Symposium on Robert Audi* at the University of Texas at San Antonio in 2009. I am grateful to the participants of this symposium, especially to Roger Crisp, Jill Hernandez, and Mark Timmons. My deepest thanks to Robert Audi, for his criticisms, patience, and unfailing support.

2 For some, the perceptual model has a limited application, Robert Audi, "Moral Perception and Moral Knowledge," *Proceedings of the Aristotelian Society Supplementary Volume* 84 (2010b:

79–97). Cf. also Justin P. McBrayer "Limited Defense of Moral Perception," *Philosophical Studies,* forthcoming. For others, moral knowledge can be explained solely in terms of seeing, see Richard Norman, "Making Sense of Moral Realism," *Philosophical Investigation* 20 (1997: 117–35, 122). M. Watkins, and K. Jolley, "Pollyanna Realism: Moral Perception and Moral Properties," *Australasian Journal of Philosophy,* 80 (2002: 75–85).

3   Audi, "Moral Perception and Moral Knowledge," (2010b: 87).

4   Dancy, "Moral Perception," *Aristotelian Society Supplementary Volume* (2010: 99–117), 105. Resultance (or consequentiality) is an ontic relation, but Dancy indicates that it is associated with a specific epistemic relation.

5   The appeal to moral experience is considered the main argument for realism, see Jonathan Dancy, "Two conceptions of Moral Realism," *Proceedings of the Aristotelian Society* 60 (1986: 167–87), 171. Cf. also Michael Smith, "Objectivity and Moral Realism: On the Significance of the Phenomenology of Moral Experience," in Michael Smith (ed.), *Ethics and the A Priori* (Cambridge: Cambridge University Press, 2004); Terence Horgan, and Mark Timmons "What Does Phenomenology Tell Us About Moral Objectivity?," in Ellen Frankel Paul, Fred D. Miller, and Jeffrey Paul (eds.), *Objectivism, Subjectivism, and Relativism* (Cambridge: Cambridge University Press, 2008: 267–300); Don Loeb, "The Argument from Moral Experience," *Ethical Theory and Moral Practice* 10 (2007: 469–84). Carla Bagnoli, "Objectivity and the Misrepresentation of Moral Experience," ms.

6   In his view, "values are the children of our sentiments in the sense that the full explanation of what we do when we moralize cites only the natural properties of things and natural reactions to them. But they are not the children of our sentiments in the sense that were our sentiments to vanish, moral truths would alter as well. The way in which we gild or stain the world with the colors borrowed from internal sentiment gives our creation its own life, and its own dependence on facts," Blackburn, *Spreading the Word* (Oxford: Oxford University Press, 1984: 219).

7   John, McDowell, "Values as Secondary Qualities," 1985.

8   Iris Murdoch, "Vision and Choice in Morality," *Proceedings of the Aristotelian Society,* 30 (1956: 32–58), *The Sovereignty of Good (*London: Routledge, 1971). Diamond, Cora "We are

Perpetually Moralists: Iris Murdoch, Fact and Value," in Maria Antonaccio and W. Schweiker (eds.) *Iris Murdoch and the Search for Human Goodness* (Chicago: University of Chicago Press, 1996: 79–109); Putnam, Hilary, *Reason, Truth, and History* (Cambridge: Cambridge University Press, 1981: 32–3, 157).

9   McDowell, "Values as Secondary Qualities" (1985: 142).

10   Audi, "Moral Perception and Moral Knowledge," 90.

11   It should be noted that moral perception does not have to be of something wrong or obligatory *on balance*, though these cases are the best examples.

12   Murdoch, "Vision and Choice in Morality," *Proceedings of the Aristotelian Society,* 30 (1956: 32–58), *The Sovereignty of Good* *(*London: Routledge, 1971).

13   I offer an unconventional analysis of this case in Carla Bagnoli, "The Exploration of Moral Life," to appear in *Iris Murdoch, Philosopher*, ed. by J. Broackes (Oxford: Oxford University Press, 2011: 193–221).

14   This trend in Kantian ethics is to be traced back to Kant, *DV*, Ak 6: 379–382. Barbara Herman, *Moral Literacy* (Cambridge, MA: Harvard University Press, 2008).

15   Cf. Sarah McGrath, "Moral Knowledge by Perception," *Philosophical Perspectives* 18 (2004: 209–28), 221.

16   On moral perception as detection of patterns, see Timothy Chappell, "Moral Perception," *Philosophy* 83, (2008: 421–37), 425.

17   David McNaughton, *Moral Vision* (Oxford: Basil Blackwell, 1988), 57.

18   McGrath, "Moral Knowledge by Perception," 221.

19   Andrews Cullison, "Moral Perception," *European Journal of Philosophy*. On a recent discussion of these objections, see David Copp, "Four Epistemological Challenges to Ethical Naturalism: Naturalized Epistemology and the First-Person Perspective," *Canadian Journal of Philosophy*, 26 (2000: 31–74).

20   Audi, "Moral Perception and Moral Knowledge," 90.

21   These general beliefs may be of self-evident propositions, but they may not.

22   Audi, *The Good in the Right*, 40–54.

23   Ibid. 32–9, 40–54.

24   Ibid. 45.

25   The point is that not all moral knowledge is inferential, Audi, "Moral Perception and Moral Knowledge," 91. This is not to

say that all non-inferential moral knowledge of perceptible moral facts is perceptual, since we know from testimony and memory (Audi, "Moral Perception and Moral Knowledge," 90). On this equivalence with judgment, Audi agrees with Jonathan Dancy: "though we can discern reasons across the board, our ability to do it is not sensory; it is not sensibility that issues in the recognition of reasons (though sensibility may be required along the way); it is rather our capacity to judge ... We might, I suppose, conceive judgment in general as a *response* to recognized reasons," Dancy, *Ethics Without Principles* (Oxford: Clarendon Press, 2004): 144.

26 See, for instance, Murdoch; see also Lawrence Blum, "Moral Perception and Particularity," *Ethics,* 101 (1991: 701–25).

27 See, for instance, Blackburn's, McDowell's, and Murdoch's models, mentioned in section §1.

28 Blum, Lawrence, "Moral Perception and Particularity."

29 According to Audi, this example should be characterized as a case of 'intellective perception,' a category that covers even, e.g. logical insights.

30 Audi, "Moral Perception and Moral Knowledge," 88–9.

31 Ibid. 90.

32 Ibid. 92.

33 Ibid. 93. Moral properties are non-natural but anchored in natural properties.

34 G. E. Moore, "The Concept of Intrinsic Value", 'The Conception of Intrinsic Value' in *Philosophical Studies* (K. Paul, Trench, Trubner & Co, London, 1922).

35 Notice that Moore's compound test does not imply that the attribution of goodness involves no description, as non-cognitivism has it. On the contrary, Moore's test emphasizes the relevance of descriptive features for the evaluation, avoiding the naturalist reduction. The description of an object and the attribution of goodness necessarily co-vary but are not identifiable.

36 J. L. Mackie, *Ethics: Inventing Right and Wrong* (London: Penguin, 1977): 41.

37 Cf. Nicholas Sturgeon, "Harman on Moral Explanations of Natural Facts," *The Southern Journal of Philosophy,* 24 (1986: 69–78).

38 Audi, "Moral Perception and Moral Knowledge," 95.

39 Dancy, "Moral Perception," *Aristotelian Society Supplementary Volume* (2010: 99–117), 105. On the claim that one can perceive

moral properties without perceiving their bases, and possible analogies with chicken sexers, see also Cullison, "Moral Perception."

40 Audi, "Moral Perception and Moral Knowledge," 90.

41 Let's say that there is a federal law governing milk production, which accords precise *quota* to different countries. This law has some perverse results: in countries exceeding quotas milk is wasted and must be destroyed to keep the trade fair. Local trades are in trouble and local producers are on strike. Meanwhile, on the market there is milk with chemicals and additives. The buyer wonders whether it is morally wrong to violate the law and buy healthy milk from local producers.

42 "A intuition must be regarded as rational judgment, though not one based on argument, even if capable of confirmation by it, and not as a mere feeling ... The best and most reliable intuition comes from reasoning and not before," A. C. Ewing, *Ethics* (London: Macmillan, 1953: 123). Even though not to be regarded as a definite inference from premises, intuitions may be "determined by our whole previous slowly developed view of ethical conduct and ideas," 124. Ewing adds that his view "must not be in any way regarded as a protest against the use of reasoning in ethics," 124.

43 J. O. Urmson, "A Defense of Intuitionism", *Proceedings of the Aristotelian Society*, 1979; Bernard Williams, "What Does Intuitionism Imply?," *Making Sense of Humanity* (Cambridge: Cambridge University Press, 1995: 153–92).

44 Dancy, *Moral Reasons* (Oxford: Blackwell, 1993) 64. Cf. Smith, Benedict, *The Space of Moral Reasons*, Palgrave-Macmillan (2010) 60.

45 Audi, *The Good in the Right* (Princeton, NJ: Princeton University Press, 2004); Audi, "A Kantian Intuitionism," *Mind* 110 (2001: 601–35). Cf. Bagnoli, "The Appeal of Kantian Intuitionism," *European Journal of Philosophy*, 17/1 (2009: 152–8).

46 Kant, *Groundwork*, 4: 397–8.

47 Kantian constructivism is often associated with an objectionable form of proceduralism, where moral truths are whatever the decision procedure issues, given the relevant facts. Constructivists have always warned against considering the categorical imperative simply as a decision procedure. They have always insisted that we should take it as a device of self-representation, which indirectly selects ends for our will, see John Rawls, *Lectures on Moral Philosophy* (Cambridge,

Mass.: Harvard University Press, 2000: 212–14, 240–52). On the difference between rule-bound practices and principled justification, see Barbara Herman, *The Practice of Moral Judgments* (Cambridge, MA: Harvard University Press, 1983). See also Onora O'Neill, *Constructions of Reason*, (Cambridge University Press, 1989).

48 For a recent study of these features of judgment in Kantian moral epistemology, see Stephen Engstrom, *The Form of Practical Knowledge*, Harvard University Press, 2009. Cf. Bagnoli, "Morality as Practical Cognition," *Analytic Philosophy*, forthcoming; Engstrom, "Bringing Practical Knowledge into View: Response to Bagnoli, Hill, and Reath", *Analytic Philosophy,* forthcoming.

49 Audi, *Moral Knowledge and Ethical Character*, Oxford University Press, 1997a: 198).

50 Audi, *Moral Knowledge and Ethical Character*, 201.

51 Kant, *Groundwork for the Metaphysics of Morals*, 4: 440. (All references to Kant's work refer to *Kants gesammelte Schriften, Königlich Preußische Akademie der Wissenschaften*, de Gruyter, Berlin, 1902).

52 Audi, *Moral Knowledge and Ethical Character*, 195.

53 Ibid. 196.

54 Ibid. 197.

55 Ibid. 205.

56 Ibid. 205.

57 By contrast, aesthetics judgments involve the capacity to feel pleasure and displeasure, and thus belong to receptivity.

58 Kant, *Critique of Pure Reason*, A 69/B 94, A 348/B 406.

59 Kant, *Groundwork*, 4: 412.

60 Kant, *Critique of Pure Reason*, B xxvi, B 145, A 104–5. Cf. Engstrom, *The Form of Practical Knowledge*, 101–6.

61 Cf. O'Neill, "Vindicating Reason," in *The Cambridge Companion to Kant*, ed. Paul Guyer (Cambridge: Cambridge University Press, 1992: 280–308); O'Neill, "Self-Legislation, Autonomy and the Form of Law," 13–26; T. E. Hill, "The Kantian Conception of Autonomy," in *Dignity and Practical Reason* (Ithaca, New York: Cornell University Press, 1992: 76–96); J. B. Schneewind, *The Invention of Autonomy* (Cambridge: Cambridge University Press, 1998).

62 Korsgaard, *The Constitution of Agency* (Oxford: Oxford University Press, 2008) 3. See also Korsgaard, *Self-Constitution*

(Oxford: Oxford University Press, 2009). I take Korsgaard as an example of Kantian ethics because her recent work focuses on reflexivity and self-consciousness. Of course, these claims allow for differing interpretations. However, the basic tenet that the appeal to universality is strictly connected to reflexivity and self-consciousness is, beyond doubts, Kant's own claim, and widely discussed in recent Kantian scholarship, see Engstrom, *The Form of Practical Knowledge.*

63 Kant, *Groundwork*, 4: 412. Cf. Engstrom, *Form of Practical Knowledge*, 125–7.

64 On practical inferentialism, see Candace Vogler, "Anscombe on Practical Inference," in E. Millgram (ed.), *Varieties of Practical Reasoning*, Cambridge: MIT Press, 2001), Vogler, *Reasonably Vicious* (Cambridge: Harvard University Press, 2002); Michael Thompson, *Life and Action* (Cambridge: Harvard University Press, 2008). In this paper I take practical inferentialism about practical reason to commit to a calculative view of action. By contrast, I take Kantian constitutivism to commit to the authorship view of action. See also Elijah Millgram, "Practical Reason and the Structure of Actions," *Stanford Encyclopedia of Philosophy*, March 2009, http://plato.stanford.edu/entries/practical-reason-action/

65 Korsgaard, *The Constitution of Agency*, 213.

66 Engstrom, *The Form of Practical Knowledge*, 98–101.

67 Engstrom, *The Form of Practical Knowledge.*

68 Audi, *The Good in the Right*, 87.

69 Ibid. 88.

70 Ibid. fn14 219.

71 Smith, *The Space of Moral Reasons*, 66, see also Chapters 3, 6.

72 Ibid. 66, see also Chapter 3.

73 Dancy, *Ethics Without Principles*, 142.

74 Ibid. 144, also 148.

75 Korsgaard, *The Constitution of Agency*, 206.

76 Korsgaard, *The Constitution of Agency*, 206.

77 This is an objection to Dancy's view, which holds that perception is not mere reception and yet it not principled. It is not an objection against Audi, though.

78 Blum, "Moral Perception and Particularity," 702.

79 Cf. Engstrom, *The Form of Practical Knowledge*. I am grateful to Audi for prompting this objection.

CHAPTER SIX

1 I was incredibly fortunate to have had the chance to study with Robert Audi while I was doing my graduate work at the University of Nebraska. I learned a great deal from him and want to thank for him for the support and encouragement he has given me over the years. This includes comments he provided on this paper. Thanks also to Matthew Bedke for his comments.

2 The justification we have for non-inferentially justified beliefs can be defeasible and provided by experience or intuition even if these are fallible guides to the truth. The sort of foundationalist view I have in mind is modeled on the moderate foundationalist view defended in Audi (1993).

3 See Audi (2004: 34) and Sinnott-Armstrong (2007: 19).

4 See Huemer (2005; 2006).

5 The responses I offer should cover a range of views, such as views that think of the justification of moral judgment as involving a grasp of self-evident propositions. For a discussion of such views, see Audi (1999). Bedke (2008) objects to his account on the grounds that it is too restrictive since it covers only true propositions. This objection assumes that the justification of a moral belief doesn't turn on whether it's true. I don't think we should assume that this is true. If someone acts on a mistaken moral belief (e.g. the mistaken belief that it's permissible to Φ when it's actually impermissible to Φ), the best this person could hope for is an excuse. If the action is excusable at best, why think that the belief that rationalizes the action is justified and not just excusably held? For arguments that the normative standing of a belief is constitutively linked to the actions the belief rationalizes, see Gibbons (2010) and Littlejohn (Forthcoming B).

6 Bedke (2008) suggests that there is a potential difference between intuitive seemings and perceptual seemings. In the second case, he suggests that it's part of the content of the representational state that things seem or appear certain ways. While I agree that these states represent appearances or looks, I think we'll give experiences the wrong contents and wrong veridicality conditions if we say that when we have the sort of experience we have when we see our hands the experience's representational content

is that it seems there are hands there. Such an experience would be veridical in cases of illusion and hallucination.

7   See Audi (2010b) and McGrath (2004) for discussion of the perceptualist view. The perceptualist view isn't a competitor to the intuitionist view. Someone could consistently maintain that experientially grounded moral judgments and moral judgments based on intuition constitute non-inferential moral knowledge.

8   There is one potential difference between these views worth mentioning. Moral properties don't figure in the representational content of our perceptual experiences, but they do figure in the representational content of the intuitions that intuitionists say provide reasons for our moral judgments. Does this difference matter? I don't think this difference puts the perceptualist approach at any serious disadvantage. On the one hand, the scope of perceptual knowledge is not limited to knowledge of those properties that figure in the content of our perceptual experiences. See Millar (2000) for discussion and defense of the view that the scope of non-inferential perceptual knowledge is not exhausted by knowledge that some perceptible object has the properties experience attributes to it. If there's something wrong with the perceptualist approach to moral knowledge, it cannot *just* be that the contents of our moral judgments and perceptual experiences don't perfectly match. Even if you don't accept this point, it seems to be a contingent fact about our psychological makeup that moral properties aren't among the properties represented by perceptual experience. So, even if you thought that the scope of non-inferential moral knowledge is limited to knowledge that the properties attributed by some experience obtain, you wouldn't be committed to the skeptical view that it's impossible to have non-inferential moral knowledge based on experience.

9   Sinnott-Armstrong, Young and Cushman (2010: 247).

10   Sinnott-Armstrong (2008a). The classic example is one in which subjects are told that 600 patients are in danger of being killed by an outbreak of an unusual Asian disease. One group of subjects is given the choice between pursuing a program that will save 200 and a program that has a one-third probability of saving all as well as a two-thirds probability of saving none. Another group is given the choice between pursuing a program where 400 will die and then given the same second options.

There's a strong preference for the first option over the second in the first set of choices and a strong preference for the second option over the first in the second set of choices. See Tversky and Kahneman (1981) for discussion. For further empirical attacks on intuition, see Nadelhoffer and Feltz (2008). To my knowledge, Horowitz (1998) was the first to suggest that framing effects undermine intuition-based arguments in ethics. For a response, see van Roojen (1999).

11 Cohen (1984: 281).

12 On this point, I'm conceding more than might be warranted by the currently available evidence. The evidence I've seen suggests that our verdictive moral judgments *can* be influenced by various factors that don't seem to bear on whether those verdicts are correct. To establish that all of our intuitive moral judgments are unreliable, we would need to know how often these factors actually influence our judgments. The reliability of a belief-forming method is measured in terms of the ratio of true to false beliefs that method produces in specified circumstances and I don't think the case has been made that the distorting factors are regular features of the circumstances in which we make judgments about what ought to be done all things considered. The skeptic's pessimism is unwarranted if there's not also evidence that shows that these distorting factors affect intuitive judgments concerning general principles and particular reasons.

13 Audi suggested that Sinnott-Armstrong might say in response that evidence of the unreliability of intuition is widely available and that everyone should take account of it even if they don't. This evidence might not come from studies of framing effects, but from evidence of widespread moral disagreement. I'd say two things in response. First, it's certainly possible for there to have been individuals very similar to us who don't have this evidence in their possession. So, I don't think observations having to do with disagreement can support anything quite as strong as ST1 or ST2. Second, it's not clear to me that the evidence concerning disagreement supports the weaker claim that we don't have moral knowledge or justified moral judgment. If we ought to give our opinions and the opinions of our peers equal weight when we have similar reasons, perhaps disagreement could support a weakened skeptical argument.

For a defense of the equal weight view, see Feldman (2006). If we ought to reject that view, it's harder to see how the skeptical argument from disagreement is supposed to go. For critical discussion of the equal weight view, see Kelly (2010) and Weatherson (ms).

14 Sinnott-Armstrong (2006: 79–80).

15 Audi (2011: 351) and Pryor (2000: 522).

16 Sinnott-Armstrong (2006: 192).

17 For an interesting series of arguments against the orthodox view that distinguishes knowledge from justified belief, see Sutton (2007).

18 See Williamson (2000) for a defense.

19 See Conee and Feldman (2008).

20 See Williamson (2007) for discussion.

21 Bedke (2009: 196).

22 Ibid. 197. Emphasis is mine.

23 For a discussion of chicken sexers, reliabilism, and moral judgment, see Star (2008). His paper is a helpful corrective that counters much of what I think of as misplaced skeptical concerns about moral judgment.

24 See Bird (2007) for a discussion on this point. He thinks that the concept of justification is one that marks off that which conforms to the norms governing belief or fails to do so for reasons that are (in some sense) beyond the subject's control. While I think there's a sense in which a person can be justified in violating a norm, I don't think the belief that violates a norm without sufficient reason to override the norm is properly regarded as justified. For a helpful discussion of the distinction between personal and doxastic justification, see Lowy (1978).

25 Adler (2002) suggests that we can use Moore's Paradox as a guide to uncovering the norms that govern belief.

26 For discussion, see Engel (1992) and Pritchard (2005).

27 For arguments for the truth-requirement, see Williamson (2000). For arguments against, see Comesaña and Kantin (2010). Audi (2007c: 148) argues for a middle-ground approach on which truth isn't required for reasons someone has but is required for reasons there are. For reasons discussed here, I think this approach doesn't handle the linguistic data quite as well as a view that takes the reasons there are and the reasons we have to be facts. For further discussion, see Littlejohn (ms).

28 See Unger (1975) for discussion.

29 For a helpful discussion of tests for entailment, see Stanley (2008).

30 I develop these arguments in greater detail in Littlejohn (Forthcoming A).

31 There are arguments from McDowell (1998) that might cause trouble for this combination of views insofar as those arguments purport to show that we can avoid skepticism if we say adopt a view on which our mental states and experiences are 'broad enough' to encompass external facts. I'll bracket these arguments for now. I address them in Littlejohn (ms).

32 See Reichenbach (1949) for discussion.

33 Reichenbach 1949 quoted from Enoch and Schechter (2008).

34 Enoch and Schechter (2008: 556).

35 A point stressed by Sutton (2007). For further defense, see Nelson (2010).

36 This approach to rationality is discussed and defended in Foley (2001) and Wedgwood (2002).

37 Williamson (2000) argues that the knowledge norm is the fundamental norm of belief. See also Adler (2002) and Sutton (2007). In Littlejohn (2010; Forthcoming B), I argue that the fundamental norm of belief is the truth norm, the norm that enjoins us not to believe false propositions.

CHAPTER SEVEN

1 I didn't study much epistemology in graduate school, though I wrote a dissertation on testimony and soon found myself teaching epistemology courses and seminars. Robert Audi's collection of papers in epistemology was a godsend. And more than any of the others, 'Justification, Truth and Reliability' made a huge impact on my understanding of the central issues in epistemology, especially the theory of justification. I had the further good fortune early in my career to get to know Robert personally. I continue to benefit from his advice, encouragement, and philosophical good sense.

2 Sellars is rightly accused of denying representational capacities to animals in "Empiricism and the Philosophy of Mind." Sellars (1981) later cautioned against denying animals genuinely perceptual representational systems. Animals, he claimed,

possessed 'propositional' representations but lacked 'logical' representations. Propositional representations refer and predicate, while logical representations require the capacity to draw the whole suite of logical inferences, and so require concepts for logical concepts, variables and quantifiers. As I am using the terms, a representation with non-propositional structure refers and predicates but does not require the whole logical suite, but a representation with propositional structure requires at least some logical inferential capacities, though not necessarily all. An animal might be able to perform disjunctive syllogism, for example, without being able to represent generality. Logical capacities are possibly diverse, and needn't come as a complete package. So a Sellarsian 'propositional' representation can have a non-propositional structure, and representations with propositional structure requires logical concepts and capacities, but not necessarily the whole suite; propositional representations needn't be fully 'logical' representations.

3   Warranted *reasons* are propositional contributions to warrant. When we reason from one belief or set of beliefs to another (from premises to conclusion), our propositionally structured beliefs comprise our *reasons*. Reasons are, or play the role of, arguments. The premises, when warranted, contribute to the warrant for the conclusion.

Reasoning transitions from premises to conclusion. When we reason well we conform in our reasoning to various rules or forms of good inference: so conforming contributes to the warrant for the conclusion; not just any old transition will do.

We do not always represent the rules of good inference or that fact that our reasoning is good in a good amount of our reasoning—especially unreflective, uncritical reasoning. We are not always aware, or do not always appreciate, that we are making a good inference. We don't have as a premise within the argument the recognition that our reasons and reasoning conforms to a good inference rule. Nor do we have a recognition or awareness outside of the argument that our reasons and reasoning conforms to a good inference rule. Critical reasoning differs. In critical reasoning—especially reflective reasoning—we are usually aware that our reasons and reasoning are good. 'Inferential internalism' may be true of critical reasoning (Leite 2008).

So in ordinary, unreflective, uncritical reasoning we are also entitled to rely on transitions from premises to conclusion. We are entitled to rely on forms or patterns of good inference. The premises and the entitlement to rely on the transition from premises to conclusion contribute to the overall warrant for the conclusion. The warrant for beliefs through inference is a mix of both warranted reasons and entitlements, while the warrant for perceptual beliefs is paradigmatically just from entitlements.

I failed to notice some of these distinctions when I wrote "Testimonial Entitlement and the Function of Comprehension" (Graham 2010b). In that paper I claimed that comprehension-based beliefs enjoy entitlements for a function of comprehension-with-filtering is to reliably induce true beliefs. I failed to note that comprehension-states—our representations of the assertive speech acts of others—have propositional structure. I now see that our warrant for comprehension-based beliefs is mixed: it involves reasons and entitlements. What matters to a broadly anti-reductionist point of view regarding testimony is that not all of our warrants for testimony reside solely in reductive first-hand arguments for the reliability of our interlocutors.

CHAPTER EIGHT

1   See Crisp (2007: 33); see also e.g. Christensen's restaurant bill case (2007: 193), Elga's horse-race case (2007: 486), or McGrath's train case (2008: 91–2).
2   I take the name for the principle from Wedgwood (2010: 224). Cf. Elga's *equal weight view* (Elga 2007: 484).
3   See e.g. Kelly (2005).
4   See Fumerton (2010: 97).
5   See Audi (2005: 90).
6   The case is somewhat artificial, of course, but avoids disanalogies that would arise through introducing several interlocutors, knowledge of widespread past and present disagreement, 'hypothetical' disagreement, 'rigging' (Killoren 2010), and so on. See Christensen (2009: 765). Nor shall I discuss in depth whether the skeptical implications of Sidgwick's principle extend beyond ethics (on this question, see e.g. Thune 2010: 369–70).

7　Audi (2008a: 489) suggests that we can reject particularism because of its 'unsound reasoning.' If particularists were, say, failing to respect *modus ponens*, I would agree with him. But it seems to me that once again we may have a disagreement over what is really self-evident. The problem with particularism as I see it is that—especially if one takes the history of philosophy into account—it is a view denied by *nearly everyone*. Even Jonathan Dancy appears now to reject some of its major tenets (such as a denial of any invariance in reasons).

8　Note that in a sense general principles are more specific than specific principles, since they apply to one particular type of mental state: beliefs.

9　Wedgwood's version of Sidgwick's principle is (224): "If you have a belief about a (first-order) question, and then acquire the (higher-order) information that another thinker disagrees with you about that question, you are rationally required to suspend judgment about that (first-order) question, unless you have *independent* grounds for thinking that the other thinker is less reliable about that question than you are yourself."

10　I am not claiming that it could easily be derived from the kind of Bayesian conditionalization favored by Wedgwood. But the construction one puts on such conditionalization is itself going to be influenced by one's attitude to Sidgwick's principle, which, as I am suggesting, may be derivable from certain widely held, general epistemic principles.

11　An alternative would be to tweak the principle itself, allowing the level of credence required to reflect the believed epistemic status of one's interlocutor.

12　There is no reference to independence in the statement of the principle in the *Methods*. Wedgwood cites a passage from a posthumously published paper by Sidgwick (2000: 168). Of a disagreement of the kind we are discussing, Sidgwick says: "The natural man will often decide unhesitatingly that the error is on the other side. But it is manifest that a philosophic mind cannot do this, unless it can prove independently that the conflicting intuitor has an inferior faculty of envisioning truth in general or this kind of truth." Sidgwick goes on to refer to the statement of the principle in the *Methods*. I take Sidgwick to be claiming not that the proof of inferiority has to be entirely independent of the content of the conflicting intuition itself, but that it has to be independent of the *mere* fact of disagreement itself.

13 See Kornblith (2010: 52).

14 I owe the following line of argument to Daniel Star.

15 This was my name for the version of Sidgwick's principle I used in that paper.

16 Ben Sherman has pointed out to me that there may be other constructions to put on the comprehension requirement. So it could be, for example, that I believe that p on the basis of my understanding that p when my understanding of p causes me to believe that p, or when my understanding of p is a necessary condition for my having justification for believing that p (and the understanding of p alone need not suffice for there being any justification for believing p.) These readings seem to me available but less natural than mine.

17 Since I allow that philosophical deliberation can continue through the sharing of appearances, I accept that ethical theories can play a deliberative role in that sense.

18 For discussion and comments on previous drafts, I am most grateful to Robert Audi, Ben Sherman, Daniel Star, Ralph Wedgwood, and attendees at the 2009 Brackenridge Philosophy Symposium convened by Jill Graper Hernandez at the University of Texas, San Antonio. The paper was completed during my tenure of the Findlay Visiting Professorship in the Department of Philosophy, Boston University. I would like to thank the department for its intellectual, social, and practical support.

CONCLUSION

1 Rawls (1971) says that "any ethical theory is bound to depend on intuition to some degree at many points" (40), and that "there is nothing irrational in the appeal to intuitions to settle questions of priority" (41). His later discussion of "considered judgments" and their role in reflective equilibrium (47–8) indicates nothing inconsistent with taking those to be a kind of intuition. They are certainly not represented as premise-dependent. Cf. Tim Mulgen's view that "One primary purpose of a moral theory is to unify and make sense of our considered judgments or intuitions ... A *decisive* intuition represents a judgment any acceptable moral theory must accommodate" (2006: 2).

2   This characterization can probably include all major intuitionists if we distinguish irreducibility from underivability. Sidgwick, e.g., may have regarded the kinds of principles I call Rossian as derivable (even if not rigorously deducible) from his overall utilitarian formula; but derivability does not entail reducibility, and I do not think he considered them reducible to formulas expressible wholly in utilitarian terms. Indeed, in a general characterization of intuitionism he calls it "the view of ethics which regards as the practically ultimate end of moral actions their conformity to certain rules or dictates of Duty" (1907: 96), using the plural. Moreover, his own view affirms more than one ethical axiom; see e.g. 1907: 382. I leave aside the question whether strong particularists should count as intuitionists if they countenance non-inferential knowledge of singular but not general moral propositions. If they do not countenance such knowledge of *some* ethical generalities, I prefer to speak of their being *particularistic intuitivists*. For distinctions among various forms of ethical particularism and criticism of some, see my 2006a.

3   Chapter 5 of my (2004) introduces and clarified these last two principles and proposes some improvements in Ross's interpretation of the others.

4   One might think intuitions are constituted by "a subclass of inclinations to believe," as argued by Erlenbaugh and Molyneux (2009). It seems to me that an entailment here is the most that can be claimed, at least on the plausible assumption that we are speaking of (occurrent) phenomenal states and may take inclinations to believe as dispositional in nature.

5   Moore said of propositions about the good, for instance, that "when I call such propositions 'Intuitions' I mean merely to assert that they are incapable of proof." See (1903: 36). See Sellars (1968) for his use of 'intuiteds' for intuited propositions (this category is wider than Moore's in that he intended to use 'intuition' as he here characterizes it for propositions that do not meet Moore's strict standard for intuitions.

6   Most of these notions are discussed in my (2004), e.g. 32–9, 48, and 208 note 37. But it contains little explicit treatment of intuitive seemings.

7   For detailed discussion of the ontological and other aspects of hallucination (as well as an account of the *a priori* that supports intuitionism), see Chapters 1, 2, 5, and 6 of my 2010a.

8   This principle is stronger than phenomenal conservatism as formulated by Huemer (2005: 99)—a principle one might also call *phenomenal liberalism* given how permissive it is. I have defended principles like this one in several parts of (2004) and will suggest some indications of their plausibility below.

9   Indeed, in (2004) I noted how intuitive induction could help to explain how we come to understand, and thereby to believe, self-evident moral propositions such as those Ross formulated (e.g. 62–3). I also allowed that property intuitions—apprehensions of properties—might be more basic than propositional intuitions (208, n. 37), and, as will be apparent below, this may help to explain how we gain the concepts whose apprehension is crucial for intuitive justification and knowledge for singular as well as general propositions.

10   See e.g. Bealer (1998), Sosa (1998), and Huemer (2005). Sosa's notion may allow that both beliefs and seemings can count as intuitions (see e.g. 258–9); but for Huemer intuitions are a distinct type of propositional attitude, evidenced when someone admits that *p* is intuitive (e.g. seems to be true), but denies believing it. Cf. Sinnott-Armstrong's definition of 'moral intuition' as "a strong immediate moral belief" (2009: 47).

11   Intuitive seemings might include such property (*de re*) intuitions as occur when something seems to have a property where there is no proposition in question. This might occur where one person is seen as more sincere than another, though one has not conceptualized the difference in any particular way, say as providing an advantage in leadership.

12   Tolhurst (1998).

13   See e.g. Huemer (2005: 102), who calls "an intuition that *p* a state of its seeming to one that *p*".

14   For a brief account of how the relevant understanding underlies justification and knowledge, see my 2008b.

15   My (1999) contains a more detailed account of self-evidence than (2004), and some extensions of both treatments are made in my (forthcoming). I should add that we might also speak of *full* understanding to avoid the suggestion that adequacy implies sufficiency only for some specific purpose. Neither term is ideal, but 'full' may suggest maximality, which is also inappropriate.

16   There has been much controversy over whether the notion of the analytic is adequately clear for purposes of philosophical

analysis. In Chapter 4 of (forthcoming) I defend the view (e.g. against objections by Quine) that the notion is adequately clear for such modest use as I make of it here.

17 It is worth emphasizing that my account of self-evidence does not carry the burden of building in necessity as a further condition, though it leaves room to argue for the necessity of self-evident propositions. This is explained in my (1999) and further in my (2008b).

18 See e.g. Broad (1930: 220–2) and Ross (1930), where at least Chapter 2 seems to employ the notion implicitly and Ross (1939: esp. 79–85) where fittingness is discussed at length in relation to Broad's view; and Ewing (1953: 119).

19 The idea that we can have a *de re* grasp of relations and can take the relata (e.g. propositions) to stand in them without believing the proposition that they so stand—where this *de dicto* belief requires conceptualizing the relation—is illustrated and applied in my (1986a).

20 I have made no commitment to cognitive intuitions necessarily being justified, though I believe they at least very commonly are justified.

21 Sellars (1975) probably thought this.

22 The distinction between dispositional beliefs (the non-occurrent kind stored in memory and not in consciousness at the time in question) and dispositions to believe is explicated and defended in my (1994).

23 The non-inferential justification in question here is not "self-justification"—a notion that is misleading. Ground-dependence in fact entails the existence of something *other* than the cognition that justifies it.

24 The point that what is intuitively known may be knowable only through reflection though still known non-inferentially is defended and developed in my response to Sinnott-Armstrong (2007) in my (2007a). Cf. the misleading idea, common among twentieth-century intuitionists (as noted in *The Good in the Right*), that we 'just see' the truth of self-evident and many other kinds of intuitive true propositions.

25 The notion of inference and related notions, such as inferential belief, are explicated in my (1986b), and especially in Chapters 4 and 8 of (2006b). I should add that I assume that a *belief* that the premises support the conclusion may be taken to be a special

(perhaps phenomenally thin) case of the sense of support in question. Unfortunately, my (2004) did not refer to (1986b) or other works in which I have explicated the notion of justified belief and did not reproduce the account. It is understandable, then, that Shafer-Landau (2007) finds such an account needed.

26 I ignore one arguable exception: first-person propositions that only the believer can genuinely understand. As to the clear cases of propositional knowledge, in (1995) I explain why memory beliefs should be considered non-inferential, and in (1997b) I make a case for treating testimony-based beliefs as also non-inferential (though they have an *operational dependence,* as opposed to a premise-dependence, on perception). Kappel (2002) seems unaware of such cases when he says, "For Audi, intuitively known propositions are simply non-inferentially known propositions" (292).

27 Consequentiality entails supervenience but is stronger. Supervenience is not a determination relation having explanatory power. The consequentiality relations central for the Rossian principles are apparently also, as mere supervenience relations need not be, both *a priori* and necessary.

28 This is a case of moral perception, in a sense explicated in my 2010b.

29 See Ross (1930: esp. 18–20). It is noteworthy that Ross evaluated Kantian resources on the assumption that they must accord with Kant's view that "there are certain duties of perfect obligation, such as those of fulfilling promises ... which admit of no exception whatever in favor of duties of imperfect obligation, such as that of relieving distress" (18). Whatever the status of Kant's apparent endorsement of this implausible position, no such view is required by a plausible interpretation of the categorical imperative framework, as will be shown in this paper.

30 See Chapters 1 and 2 of my 2004 for references to Pritchard, Moore, and Ross's claims that the self-evident is unprovable and for a detailed account of self-evidence that indicates why this requirement is mistaken. Consider a simple case: If p entails q and q entails r but r is false, then p is false. This is self-evident but readily provable.

31 I developed Kantian intuitionism in (2001b) and further in (2004), especially Chapter 3. Particularly in the latter I appealed to the notion of dignity as adding a dimension to the framework;

but, contrary to the suggestion of Gert (2006), I did not depend on the notion for the clarity or defense of the overall view; and I sought to clarify the notion independently, e.g. on 99, 157–8, and 176–7. For a detailed discussion of Kant's conception of duty and of the proper treatment of persons see Stratton-Lake (2000), esp. Chapters 2–4.

32 I leave open whether it is self-evident that the two kinds of treatment ground *prima facie* obligations; they can play the indicated role even it this is not self-evident.

33 A theory of reasons and of the possible kinds of relations that hold between moral and non-moral reasons is provided in my (2001a), e.g. Chapters 5 and 6. To be sure, the notion of a *moral* reason is not sharp. For extensive discussion of the relative weights of practical reasons and, in particular Sidgwick's problem of the dualism of practical reason, see Crisp (2006), especially Chapter 5.

34 This formulation is drawn from Audi 2000: 86, though I published essentially the same version much earlier in (1989).

35 It may be thought that non-cognitivism avoids the problem of determining the scope of reason in ethical matters, as suggested by e.g. Kappel (2002: 411). But any plausible non-cognitivist view must account for what constitutes a relevant (and indeed a good) reason for holding a non-cognitive pro or con moral judgment. How we might know or justifiedly believe such an account seems to me a problem in moral epistemology much akin to the kind I have been dealing with here.

36 This essay has benefited from comments by many philosophers and from discussion with various audiences. I would particularly like to thank Jens Timmermann for comments when an earlier version was presented at the University of St. Andrews and Robert Cowan for detailed comments when it was presented at the University of Glasgow. Many of the contributors to this volume have also been of great help to me in thinking the problems through on one occasion or another. I much regret that space does not permit responding to points they raise bearing on my position; but this essay may at least provide an indication of how I might respond, and the future will surely hold many more opportunities for discussions that advance understanding of the issues.

REFERENCES

Adler, J. (2002) *Belief's Own Ethics.* Cambridge, MA: The MIT Press.
Alston, William P. (1993) "Epistemic Desiderata." *Philosophy and Phenomenological Research* 53: 527–51.
—(1999) "Back to the Theory of Appearing." *Noûs* 33: 181–203.
—(2001) "Doing Epistemology Without Justification." *Philosophical Topics* 29, 1–18.
Audi, Robert (1986a) "Acting for Reasons." *Philosophical Review* 95(4): 75–205.
—(1986b) "Belief, Reason, and Inference." *Philosophical Topics* 14(1): 27–65.
—(1987) *Belief, Justification, and Knowledge.* Belmont, CA: Wadsworth.
—1988) "Justification, Truth, and Reliability." *Philosophy and Phenomenological Research* 49(1) (September): 1–29. Reprinted in R. Audi, *The Structure of Justification.* Cambridge and New York: Cambridge University Press, 1993.
—(1989) "The Separation of Church and State and the Obligation of Citizenship," *Philosophy & Public Affairs* 18(3), 259–296.
—(1993) *The Structure of Justification.* Cambridge and New York: Cambridge University Press.
—(1994) "Dispositional Beliefs and Dispositions to Believe." *Noûs* 28(4): 419–34.
—(1995) "Memorial Justification." *Philosophical Topics* 23(1): 31–45.
—(1997a) *Moral Knowledge and Ethical Character.* New York: Oxford University Press.
—(1997b) "The Place of Testimony in the Fabric of Knowledge and Justification." *American Philosophical Quarterly* 34(4): 404–22.
—(1999) "Self-Evidence." *Philosophical Perspectives* 13: 205–28.
—(2000) *Religious Commitment and Secular Reason.* Cambridge and New York: Cambridge University Press.
—(2001) *The Architecture of Reason: The Structure and Substance of Rationality.* New York: Oxford University Press.
—(2003) *Epistemology: A Contemporary Introduction to the Theory of Knowledge.* Second Edition. London: Routledge.

REFERENCES

—(2004) *The Good in the Right: A Theory of Intuition and Intrinsic Value.* Princeton, NJ: Princeton University Press (hardback).

—(2005) *The Good in the Right: A Theory of Intuition and Intrinsic Value.* Princeton, NJ: Princeton University Press (paperback).

—(2006a) "Ethical Generality and Moral Judgment," in Dreier 2006, 285–304.

—(2006b) *Practical Reasoning and Ethical Decision.* London: Routledge.

—(2007a) "Intuition, Reflection, and Justification," in Timmons, Greco, and Mele, 201–21.

—(2007b) "Rationality and the Good," in Timmons, Greco, and Mele, 3–16.

—(2007c) "The Grounds and Structure of Reasons for Action," in C. Lumer and S. Nannini (eds.) *Intentionality, Deliberation, and Autonomy: The Action-Theoretic Basis of Practical Philosophy.* Burlington, VT: Ashgate Publishing, 135–56.

—(2007d) "Justifying Grounds, Justified Beliefs, and Rational Acceptance," in Timmons, Greco, and Mele, 222–47.

—(2008a) "Intuition, Inference, and Rational Disagreement in Ethics." *Ethical Theory and Moral Practice* 11: 475–92.

—(2008b) "Skepticism About the *A priori*," in Greco 2008, 149–75.

—(2010a) *Epistemology: A Contemporary Introduction to the Theory of Knowledge.* New York: Routledge (hardback).

—(2010b) "Moral Perception and Moral Knowledge." *Proceedings of the Aristotelian Society* 84: 79–97.

—(2011) *Epistemology: A Contemporary Introduction to the Theory of Knowledge.* Third Edition. New York: Routledge (paperback).

—(forthcoming 2011) *Rationality and Religious Commitment.* Oxford University Press.

Bealer, George (1998) "Intuition and the Autonomy of Philosophy," in M. DePaul and W. Ramsey, 201–39.

Bedke, M. (2008) "Ethical Intuitions: What They Are, What They Are Not, and How They Justify." *American Philosophical Quarterly* 45: 253–70.

—(2009) "Intuitive Non-Naturalism Meets Cosmic Coincidence." *Pacific Philosophical Quarterly* 90: 188–209.

Bird, A. (2007) "Justified Judging." *Philosophy and Phenomenological Research* 74: 81–110.

BonJour, Laurence (2001) "The Indispensability of Internalism." *Philosophical Topics* 29: 47–65.

—(2007) "Are Perceptual Beliefs Properly Foundational?" in Timmons, Greco, and Mele, 85–99.

—(2010) *Epistemology: Classic Problems and Contemporary Responses*, Second Edition. Lanham, MD: Rowman & Littlefield.

BonJour, Laurence, and Sosa, Ernest (2003) *Epistemic Justification: Internalism vs. Externalism, Foundations vs. Virtues.* Great debates in philosophy. Malden, MA: Blackwell.

Broad, C. D. (1930) *Five Types of Ethical Theory.* London: Routledge & Kegan Paul.

Burge, Tyler (1993) "Content Preservation." *The Philosophical Review* 102(4): 457–88.

REFERENCES

—(1996) "Our Entitlement to Self–Knowledge." *Proceedings of the Aristotelian Society* 96: 91–116.

—(2003) "Perceptual Entitlement." *Philosophy and Phenomenological Research* 67(3): 503–48.

—(2009) "Five Theses on De Re States and Attitudes," in J. Almog and P. Leonardi (eds.) *The Philosophy of David Kaplan*. Oxford: Oxford University Press, 246–306.

—(2010) *Origins of Objectivity*. Oxford: Oxford University Press.

Call, J. (2006) "Descartes' Two Errors: Reason and Reflection in the Great Apes," in S. Hurley and M. Nudds (eds.) *Rational Animals?* Oxford: Oxford University Press, 219–34.

Castaneda, Hector-Neri (ed.) (1975) *Action Knowledge, and Reality: Essays in Honor of Wilfrid Sellars*. Indianapolis: Bobbs-Merrill.

Christensen, D. (2007) "Epistemology of Disagreement: The Good News," *Philosophical Review* 116: 187–217.

—(2009) "Disagreement as Evidence: The Epistemology of Controversy." *Philosophy Compass* 4/5: 756–67.

Cohen, S. (1984) "Justification and Truth." *Philosophical Studies* 46: 279–95.

Comesaña, J. and Kantin, H. (2010) "Is Evidence Knowledge?" *Philosophy and Phenomenological Research* 80: 447–54.

Conee, E. and Feldman, R. (2008) "Evidence," in Q. Smith (ed.) *Epistemology: New Essays*. New York: Oxford University Press, 83–105.

Crisp, Roger (2006) *Reasons and the Good*. Oxford: Oxford University Press.

—(2007) "Intuitionism and Disagreement," in Timmons, Greco, and Mele, 31–9.

Davidson, Donald (2008) "A Coherence Theory of Truth and Knowledge," in Ernest Sosa, Jaegwon Kim, Jeremy Fantl, and Matthew McGrath (eds.) *Epistemology: an Anthology*. Second Edition, Malden, MA: Blackwell Publishing, 122–33.

DePaul, Michael, and Ramsey, William (eds.) (1998) *Rethinking Intuition*. Lanham, MD: Rowman & Littlefield.

Dreier, James (ed.) (2006) *Contemporary Debates in Moral Theory*. Malden, MA: Blackwell Publishing Ltd.

Dretske, F. (1981) *Knowledge and the Flow of Information*. Cambridge, MA: The MIT Press.

—(1986) "Misrepresentation," in R. Bogdan (ed.) *Belief: Form, Content, and Function*. Oxford: Oxford University Press.

—(1995) Naturalizing the Mind. Cambridge, MA: The MIT Press.

Elga, A. (2007) "Reflection and Disagreement." *Noûs* 41: 478–502.

Engel, M. (1992) "Is Epistemic Luck Compatible with Knowledge?" *Southern Journal of Philosophy* 30: 59–75.

Enoch, D. and Schechter, J. (2008) "How Are Basic Belief-Forming Methods Justified?" *Philosophy and Phenomenological Research* 76: 547–79.

Erlenbaugh, Joshua, and Molyneux, Bernard (2009) "Intuitions as Inclinations to Believe." *Philosophical Studies* 145: 89–109.

Ewing, A. C. (1953) *Ethics*. New York: The Free Press.

REFERENCES

Feldman, R. (2006) "Epistemological Puzzles About Disagreement," in S. Hetherington (ed.) *Epistemology Futures*. New York: Oxford University Press, 216–26.

—(2008) "Moderate Deontologism in Epistemology." *Synthese* 161: 339–55.

Feldman, T. and Warfield, R. (eds.) (2010) *Disagreement*. Oxford: Oxford University Press.

Foley, Richard (2001) "The Foundational Role of Epistemology in a General Theory of Rationality," in A. Fairweather and L. Zagzebski (eds.) *Virtue Epistemology: Essays on Epistemic Virtue and Responsibility*. New York: Oxford University Press.

Fumerton, R. (2010) "You Can't Trust a Philosopher," in Feldman and Warfield, 91–110.

Gert, Joshua (2006) "Review: Robert Audi's *The Good in the Right.*" *Mind* 115(457): 121–25.

Gettier, E. (1963) "Is Justified True Belief Knowledge?" *Analysis* 23: 121–3.

Gibbons, J. (2010) "Things that Make Things Reasonable." *Philosophy and Phenomenological Research* 81: 335–61.

Godfrey-Smith, P. (1996) "Indication and Adaptation." *Synthese* 92(2): 283–312.

Graham, P. J. (2010a) "Perceptual Entitlement and Basic Beliefs." *Philosophical Studies* 153: 467–75.

—(2010b) "Testimonial Entitlement and the Function of Comprehension," in A. Haddock, A. Millar, and D. Pritchard (eds.) *Social Epistemology.* Oxford: Oxford University Press, 148–93.

—(2011a), Epistemic Entitlement. *Noûs*, 45: no. doi: 10.1111/j.1468-0068.2010.00815.x

—(2011b) "Natural Selection and Intelligent Design: Two Sources of Purpose and Plan." Oxford Studies in the Philosophy of Religion 3.

—(in preparation-a) "Intelligent Design Reliabilism."

—(in preparation-b) "Perceptual Entitlement and Natural Norms."

Graham, P. J. and Petersen, Nikolaj Jang (2011c) *Essays on Entitlement.*

Greco, John (ed.) (2008) *Handbook of Skepticism.* Oxford: Oxford University Press.

Harman, Gilbert (1990) "The Intrinsic Quality of Experience," in James Tomberlin (ed.) *Action Theory and the Philosophy of Mind*, 4: 31–52. *Philosophical Perspectives*. Atascadero: Ridgeview.

Hatfield, G. (1998) "The Cognitive Faculties," in D. Garber and M. Ayers (eds.) *The Cambridge History of Seventeenth-Century Philosophy.* Cambridge: Cambridge University Press.

Horowitz, T. (1998) "Philosophical Intuitions and Psychological Theory." *Ethics* 108: 367–85.

Huemer, Michael (2001) *Skepticism and the Veil of Perception.* Lanham, MD: Rowman & Littlefield.

—(2005) *Ethical Intuitionism.* Basingstoke & New York: Palgrave-Macmillan.

—(2006) "Phenomenal Conservatism and the Internalist Intuition." *American Philosophical Quarterly* 43: 147–58.

Hurley, S. and Nudds, M. (eds.) (2006) *Rational Animals?* Oxford: Oxford University Press.

Kappel, Klemens (2002) "Challenges to Audi's Intuitionism." *Ethical Theory and Moral Practice* 5: 391–413.

Kelly, T. (2005) "The Epistemic Significance of Disagreement," in J. Hawthorne and T. Gendler (eds.) *Oxford Studies in Epistemology* 1: 167–96.

—(2010) "Peer Disagreement and Higher-Order Evidence," in R. Feldman and T. Warfield (eds.) *Disagreement*. New York: Oxford University Press, 111–75.

Killoren, D. (2010) "Moral Intuitions, Reliability, and Disagreement." *Journal of Ethics and Social Philosophy* 4: www.jesp.org

Kornblith, H. (2010) "Belief in the Face of Controversy," in Feldman and Warfield, 29–52.

Leite, A. (2004) "On Justifying and Being Justified." *Philosophical Issues* 14: 219–53.

—(2008) "Believing One's Reasons are Good." *Synthese* 161: 419–41.

Littlejohn, C. (2010) "Moore's Paradox and Epistemic Norms." *Australasian Journal of Philosophy* 88: 79–100.

—(ms) Disjoining Disjunctivism.

—(Forthcoming A) "Evidence and Knowledge." *Erkenntnis*.

—(Forthcoming B) "Reasons and Belief's Justification," in A. Reisner and A. Steglich-Petersen (eds.) *Reasons for Belief*. Cambridge: Cambridge University Press.

Lowy, C. (1978) "Gettier's Notion of Justification." *Mind* 87: 105–8.

Lyons, Jack C. (2009) *Perception and Basic Beliefs: Zombies, Modules, and the Problem of the External World*. Oxford: Oxford University Press.

Markie, Peter J. (2005) "The Mystery of Direct Perceptual Justification." *Philosophical Studies* 126(3) (December): 347–73.

—(2006) "Epistemically Appropriate Perceptual Belief." *Noûs* 40(1): 118–42.

McCann, Hugh J. (2007) "The Will and the Good," in S. Nannini and C. Lumer (eds.) *Deliberation, Intentionality, and Autonomy: The Action-Theoretic Basis of Practical Philosophy*. Aldershot, England: Ashgate, 119–33.

McDowell, John (1998) "Criteria, Defeasibility, and Knowledge," in his *Meaning, Knowledge, and Reality*. Cambridge, MA: Harvard University Press.

McGrath, S. (2004) "Moral Knowledge by Perception." *Philosophical Perspectives* 18: 209–29.

—(2008) "Moral Disagreement and Moral Expertise," in R. Shafer-Landau (ed.) *Oxford Studies in Metaethics* 3: 87–107.

Millar, A. (2000) "The Scope of Perceptual Knowledge." *Philosophy* 75: 73–88.

Millikan, R. (1984) *Language, Thought, and Other Biological Categories*. Cambridge, MA: The MIT Press.

Moore, G. E. (1903) *Principia Ethica*. Cambridge: Cambridge University Press.

Mulgan, Tim (2006) *Future People*. Oxford: Clarendon Press.

REFERENCES

Nadelhoffer, T. and Feltz, A. (2008) "The Actor–Observer Bias and Moral Intuitions: Adding Fuel to Sinnott-Armstrong's Fire." *Neuroethics* 1: 133–44.

Nelson, M. (2010) "We Have No Positive Epistemic Duties." *Mind* 119: 83–102.

Plantinga, A. (1993), Warrant and Proper Function. New York: Oxford University Press.

Pollock, J. (1999) "Procedural Epistemology," in E. Sosa and J. Greco, *The Blackwell Companion to Epistemology*. Oxford: Blackwell Publishers.

Pollock, J. and Cruz, J. (1999) *Contemporary Theories of Knowledge*, Second Edition. Lanham, MD: Rowman & Littlefield.

Premack, D. and Premack, A. J. (1994) "Levels of Causal Understanding in Chimpanzees and Children." *Cognition* 50: 347–62.

Pritchard, D. (2005) *Epistemic Luck*. New York: Oxford University Press.

Pryor, James (2000) "The Skeptic and the Dogmatist." *Noûs* 34(4): 517–49.

Pust, Joel (2001) "Against Explanationist Skepticism Regarding Philosophical Intuitions." *Philosophical Studies* 106: 227–58.

Rawls, John (1971) *A Theory of Justice*. Cambridge, MA: Harvard University Press.

Reichenbach, H. (1949) *The Theory of Probability*. Berkeley: University of California Press.

Rescorla, M. (2009) " 'Chrysippus' Dog as a Case Study in Non-Linguistic Cognition," in R. Lurz (ed.) *The Philosophy of Animal Minds*. Cambridge: Cambridge University Press.

Ross, W. D. (1930) *The Right and the Good*. Oxford. Oxford University Press.

—(1939) *Foundations of Ethics*. Oxford. Clarendon Press.

Sellars, Wilfrid (1956) "Empiricism and the Philosophy of Mind," in H. Feigl and M. Scriven (eds.) *The Foundations of Science and the Concepts of Psychoanalysis, Minnesota Studies in the Philosophy of Science, Vol. I.* Minneapolis, MN: University of Minnesota Press; reprinted in Sellars (1963). Reissued in 1991 by Ridgeview Publishing Co., Atascadero, CA, 127–96.

—(1963) *Science, Perception and Reality*. International Library of Philosophy and Scientific Method. London: Routledge & Kegan Paul Ltd; and New York: Humanities Press.

—(1968) *Science and Metaphysics*, London: Routledge & Kegan Paul.

—(1975) "The Structure of Knowledge," in Castaneda (1975).

—(1981) "Mental Events," *Philosophical Studies* 39: 325–345.

Shafer-Landau, Russ (2003) *Moral Realism: A Defence*. New York: Oxford University Press.

—(2007) "Audi's Intuitionism." *Philosophy and Phenomenological Research* 74(1): 250–61.

Sidgwick, H. (1907) *The Methods of Ethics*. Seventh Edition. London: Macmillan; Chicago: University of Chicago Press, 1962.

—(2000) "Further on the Criteria of Truth and Error," reprinted in M. G. Singer (ed.) *Essays on Ethics and Method*, 166–70. Oxford: Clarendon Press.

Sinnott-Armstrong, W. (2006) *Moral Skepticisms*. New York: Oxford University Press.

—(2007) "Reflections on Reflection in Robert Audi's Moral Intuitionism," in Timmons, Greco, and Mele.

—(2008a) "Framing Moral Intuitions," in his (2008b), 47–76.

—(ed.) (2008b) *Moral Psychology Volume 2: The Cognitive Science of Morality: Intuition and Diversity*. Cambridge, MA: The MIT Press.

Sinnott-Armstrong, W., Young, L., and Cushman, F. (2010) "Moral Intuitions," in J. Doris (ed.) *The Moral Psychology Handbook*. New York: Oxford University Press.

Sosa, Ernest (1998) "Minimal Intuitionism," in DePaul and Ramsey, 257–69.

Stanley, J. (2008) "Knowledge and Certainty." *Philosophical Issues* 18: 33–55.

Star, D. (2008) "Moral Knowledge, Epistemic Externalism, and Intuitionism." *Ratio* 21: 329–43.

Sutton, J. (2007) *Without Justification*. Cambridge, MA: The MIT Press.

Thune, M. (2010) "'Partial Defeaters' and the Epistemology of Disagreement." *Philosophical Quarterly* 60: 357–72.

Timmons, Mark, Greco, John, and Mele, Alfred R. (eds.) (2007) *Rationality and the Good: Critical Essays on the Ethics and Epistemology of Robert Audi*. Oxford: Oxford University Press.

Tolhurst, William (1998) "Seemings." *American Philosophical Quarterly* 35: 293–302.

Tversky, A., and Kahneman, D. (1981) "The Framing of Decisions and the Psychology of Choice." *Science* 21: 453–8.

Tye, Michael (1992) "Visual Qualia and Visual Content," in Tim Crane (ed.) *The Contents of Experience*. Cambridge: Cambridge University Press.

Unger, P. (1968) "An Analysis of Factual Knowledge." *The Journal of Philosophy* 65(6): 157–70.

—(1975) *Ignorance*. New York: Oxford University Press.

van Roojen, M. (1999) "Reflective Moral Equilibrium and Psychological Theory." *Ethics* 109: 846–57.

Walsh, V. and Kulikowski, J. (eds.) (1998) *Perceptual Constancy*. Cambridge: Cambridge University Press.

Watson, J., Gergeley, G., Csanyi, V., Topal, J., Gacsi, M., and Sarkozi, Z. (2001) "Distinguishing Logic From Association in the Solution of an Invisible Displacement Task by Children (*Homo sapiens*) and Dogs (*Canis familiaris*): Using Negation of Disjunction." *Journal of Comparative Psychology* 115: 219–26.

Weatherson, B. (ms) "Disagreements, Philosophical and Otherwise."

Wedgwood, R. (2002) "Internalism Explained." *Philosophy and Phenomenological Research* 65: 349–69.

—(2010) "The Moral Evil Demons," in Feldman and Warfield, 216–46.

Williamson, T. (2000) *Knowledge and its Limits*. New York: Oxford University Press.

—(2007) *The Philosophy of Philosophy*. Malden, MA: Blackwell.

Wright, L. (1973) "Functions." *The Philosophical Review* 82: 139–68.

INDEX